The Northern Pime[ría]

1691-1767

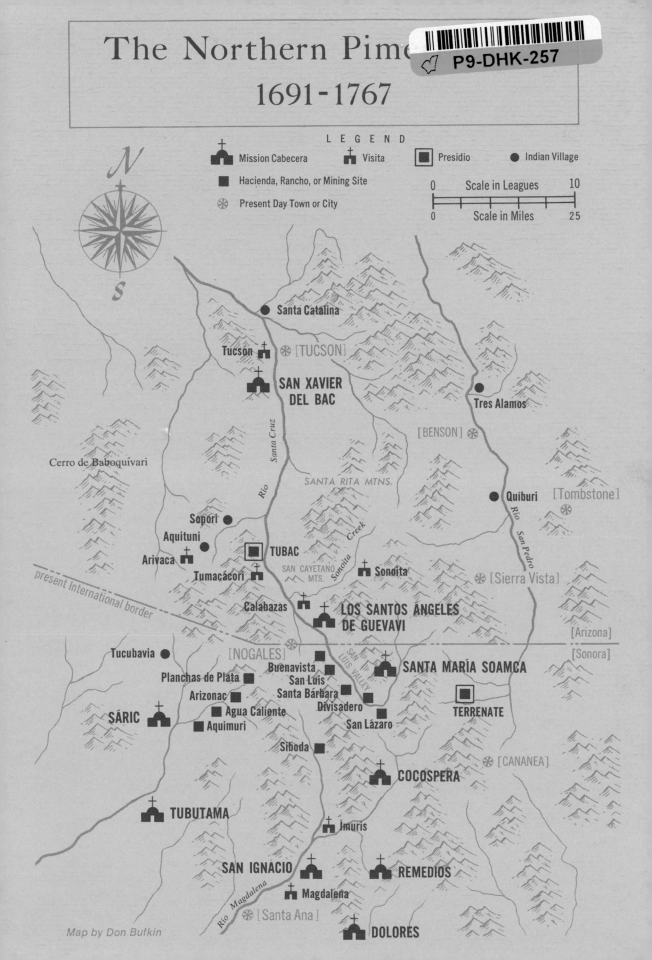

LEGEND

✚ Mission Cabecera   ⛪ Visita   ▣ Presidio   ● Indian Village

■ Hacienda, Rancho, or Mining Site

✳ Present Day Town or City

Scale in Leagues   0 — 10

Scale in Miles   0 — 25

N / S

● Santa Catalina

Tucson ✳ [TUCSON]

✚ SAN XAVIER DEL BAC

● Tres Alamos

[BENSON] ✳

Cerro de Baboquívari

Santa Cruz

Río

SANTA RITA MTS.

● Quíburi   [Tombstone] ✳

Río San Pedro

● Sopori

Aquituni ■

Arivaca ⛪

Tumacácori ⛪

▣ TUBAC

SAN CAYETANO MTS.

Creek

Sonoita

⛪ Sonoita

[Sierra Vista] ✳

present International border

Calabazas ✚

✚ LOS SANTOS ÁNGELES DE GUEVAVI

[Arizona]

[Sonora]

● Tucubavia

[NOGALES] ✳

SAN LUIS VALLEY

Buenavista ■

Planchas de Plata ■

San Luis

Arizonac ■

Santa Bárbara

Divisadero ■

✚ SANTA MARÍA SOAMCA

SÁRIC ⛪

Agua Caliente ■

Aquimuri ■

San Lázaro ■

▣ TERRENATE

Siboda ■

[CANANEA] ✳

✚ COCOSPERA

TUBUTAMA ✚

⛪ Imuris

SAN IGNACIO ✚

✚ REMEDIOS

⛪ Magdalena

Río Magdalena

✳ [Santa Ana]

✚ DOLORES

Map by Don Bufkin

MISSION OF SORROWS
Jesuit Guevavi and the Pimas, 1691-1767

Guevavi in ruin, 1889

THE UNIVERSITY OF ARIZONA PRESS
Tucson, Arizona

John L. Kessell

Foreword by Ernest J. Burrus, S. J.

MISSION OF SORROWS
Jesuit Guevavi and the Pimas, 1691-1767

About the Author . . .

JOHN L. KESSELL is a co-author of *Father Kino in Arizona,* and a contributor to the *New Mexico Historical Review, Arizona and the West, The Kiva,* and the *Journal of Arizona History.* A visiting assistant professor of history at the University of New Mexico in 1969–70, he holds the Ph.D. degree from that institution. He is a graduate of Fresno State College, and took his M.A. degree at the University of California, Berkeley. It was while serving as historian at Tumacacori National Monument, Arizona, that he recognized the need for a history of Mission Guevavi. Kessell has traveled extensively in Mexico, and during 1968–69 spent six months in Spain.

THE UNIVERSITY OF ARIZONA PRESS

S.B.N. 8165-0192-0
L.C. No. 79-101098

For Marianne
who never failed to smile when
she might have pouted

Foreword

THE MISSION OF GUEVAVI was not established nor administered in isolation; it formed part of a vast enterprise begun before the close of the sixteenth century and extending over the greater portion of colonial Mexico.

King Philip II of Spain, who authorized the coming of the first Jesuits to Mexico in 1572, stated specifically that they were to devote their efforts to the conversion of the Indians. Yet nearly two decades were to pass before any Black Robes could turn their attention to missions among the unconverted natives of New Spain.

Previous training and inclination fitted them better for the classroom than for the wilds of the missions. Schools on the secondary and college levels were needed in the larger centers such as Mexico City, Puebla, and Guadalajara. True, the first university in the New World had been founded in the Capital of Mexico nineteen years before their arrival, but inadequate preparatory schools kept the number of students attending it to a mere handful. In the smaller cities such as Pátzcuaro, Valladolid (Morelia), and San Luis Potosí, schools were needed even more badly. Through nearly two centuries, the Jesuits educated the greater portion of the lay and ecclesiastical leaders of the most advanced nation in the New World.

Hence, they consoled themselves that they were obeying in spirit the royal decree which authorized their presence in Mexico, inasmuch as their educational network redounded to the good of the natives through the formation of upright and enlightened Spanish and *criollo* leaders. Then, too, schools specifically for the converted Indians were established

[vii]

in Mexico City, Tepotzotlán, and Puebla. Wherever local prejudice or governmental interference did not exclude Indian children, the Jesuits gladly admitted them into their schools. After the establishment of missions for unconverted natives, the missionaries' brightest hopes for a better future were in the small schools conducted in every center (*cabecera*), where the Indian children learned to read, write, count, and sing (*leer, escribir, contar y cantar*).

Before taking up the work of missions among the heathen natives, the Black Robes had also built churches in the same cities where they conducted schools. They proved to be centers of spiritual betterment in behalf of the four groups which made up Mexican colonial "society" — the privileged Spaniards, the ambitious Creoles, the poor Indians, and the enslaved Negroes.

From 1590 until Charles III's decree of expulsion in 1767, the Jesuit missionaries carried the light of the Gospel and European culture northwestward through Sinaloa, Durango, Chihuahua, Sonora, and other regions into northern Lower California and southern Arizona.

The multiple activity of the Black Robes as educators, parish priests, and missionaries has not remained unrecorded. Even in colonial times competent historians — mainly of the Order itself — such as Pérez de Ribas, Venegas, Ortega, Baltasar, Clavigero, and the most scholarly and scientific of all the Jesuit colonial writers, Francisco Javier Alegre, delved deep into sources or recorded their own experiences to make known the apostolate of the Jesuits. Distinguished scholars of a later time — Bolton, Shiels, Dunne, Jacobsen, Bannon, Pradeau, to name but a few — have, through their research and writing, contributed greatly to our knowledge and understanding of the role of the Jesuits in New Spain.

With this brief sketch as background, I should like to present to readers John Kessell's documented and fascinating account. The extraordinary significance of the book derives primarily from its uniqueness as the first and only study in depth of a single missionary center, that of Los Santos Ángeles de Guevavi, in southern Arizona, on the Santa Cruz River. The story of Guevavi does not represent constant progress, much less an uninterrupted series of triumphant victories over ignorance and poverty. The difficulties to be overcome were staggeringly discouraging, as the reader soon learns: indifferent or hostile natives, unjust and oppressive colonists, marauding savages.

To tell this story the author has drawn upon a large number of key publications and has consulted to obvious advantage the most important pertinent manuscript sources. Above all, he has subjected his abundant data to an exceptionally penetrating analysis.

Not a few readers will already know many of the Guevavi missionaries, especially Kino, Campos, Velarde, Segesser, Stiger, Keller and Pfefferkorn. Of these, some were nonresidents: "Fathers Kino and Campos, and perhaps Father Velarde, passed through Guevavi occasionally, preaching, baptizing, and encouraging its natives to visit them at their missions farther south. Fathers Stiger and Keller of neighboring San Xavier and Soamca looked in on the people of Guevavi when the mission was without a Padre of its own" (Appendix I: The Jesuits of Guevavi).

We are also introduced to other less well-known Guevavi missionaries: Grazhoffer, Rapicani, Torres Perea, Peña, Garrucho, Pauer, and Ximeno, the details of whose portraits are filled in for the first time.

In this important study, Mr. Kessell has the leisure and space to furnish us with abundant biographical data on Guevavi's missionaries, and he details their activity and methods of dealing with the natives, all of which would not be feasible in a book treating a broader theme. *Mission of Sorrows: Jesuit Guevavi and the Pimas, 1691–1767,* written in a clear and refreshing style, is objective history; its author presents his facts calmly and dispassionately, allowing them to speak for themselves. Readers will be grateful to one who has already published several scholarly studies and who now offers them an important contribution to the history of the Spanish Borderlands.

ERNEST J. BURRUS, S.J.

Preface

IN ANTICIPATION, A LIVELY CROWD had begun to gather around the corral where the bullfights would soon begin. Solemn Mass and the procession were over now. They were laughing and gossiping — ranchers and settlers, prospectors and soldiers, dozens of them, relatives and compadres — dressed in their gaudy best and come from leagues around at Father Joseph Garrucho's invitation to join in the patronal feast. In honor of the day he had suspended work on the new church, and Don Joachín de Cásares, master builder from Arizpe, was enjoying himself with the others.

Even the mission Indians looked less sullen this day. Some of them joined in capriciously. They never seemed to tire of pageantry and pranks and noise and chocolate. Over in front of his adobe house their Padre appeared to be admonishing a couple of uninvited natives from another village. Two less-experienced missionaries, his guests, looked on. But this was no day for dissension, rather for eating, for drinking aguardiente, for singing romances and shooting off black powder. It was a day of joyful, hectic relaxation. It was the Day of San Miguel at the mission of Guevavi, September 29, 1751. It was a day to remember, long ago completely forgotten.

For seventy-six and a half years, on and off, the cluster of brush-and-earth and adobe houses that was Guevavi served as a focal point of missionary endeavor, of intense give and take between resolute, black-robed Jesuits and the not-always-receptive Pima Indians they sought to convert on New Spain's far northwestern frontier. It was a dynamic if less than impressive outpost of two empires, the Jesuits' missionary empire and the larger, coexistent Spanish colonial empire.

To the Indians the village became a concentration camp — no matter how benevolent its purpose — where they learned new and sometimes useful ways and on occasion earned a foreign salvation. For three quarters of a century the often-painful business of replacing one culture with another, which lay at the heart of the Spanish mission system, went on at Guevavi, today a crumbling ruin ten miles northeast of Nogales, Arizona. Three quarters of a century — yet all but the initial years, the years of Father Kino, forgotten.

Few would argue that Kino, the hard-driving pioneer whose brethren in the 1960s introduced his cause for canonization, deserves less than the attention he has received. Father Kino was unquestionably the foremost apostle to the Pimas. But by placing the emphasis on him alone, on his powerful performance in Act One, we have tended to distort the whole drama. We are apt, for example, to cite the Pimas' notable readiness to accept what the missionaries had to offer, basing our judgment almost totally on the career of a charismatic bringer of gifts and novel good tidings. That the natives of Guevavi allegedly murdered their next missionary comes as something of a surprise. Perhaps then, if we must limit ourselves, a study of one mission — Guevavi in this case — from the first to the final act, from Kino to Ximeno, will give us a clearer picture of what went on in Pimería Alta during the Jesuit occupation.

Because of its extremely precarious advanced position on the northern frontier, the mission of Guevavi was not entirely representative of the establishments farther south. It was farther from the seats of Church and State control. Because the area around it was not so attractive to other frontiersmen, Guevavi was less affected by, though by no means exempt from, the bitter competition for resources between missionary and colonist. It was closer to the Apaches, and farther from help.

For much of the time that a Black Robe resided at Guevavi he did double duty, administering distant and difficult San Xavier del Bac as well. Theoretically then, his responsibility, and hopefully his influence, spread out over all the converted and all the heathen souls scattered across some nine or ten thousand square miles: from the headwaters of Sonoita Creek west into the vast, desert Papaguería, and from the big bend of the Santa Cruz north to the Gila. As if that were not enough, he ministered, not always cheerfully, to Spanish cattlemen and mestizo farmers and miners at Arivaca, Sopori, Tubac, and along the San Luis Valley. And when soldiers came to live at Tubac, he found himself acting as interim chaplain to the garrison and more than once as godfather to the captain's children.

Though much of the Guevavi story may justly be termed local history, I have tried to acknowledge those men and events that refused to be contained on the local scene. One unusually outspoken Jesuit, for example, escaped more serious censure because he happened to be the son of a Swedish queen's favorite. A young lieutenant who passed through Guevavi in the train of a Spanish *marqués,* three decades later posed for Goya. England and Spain went to war over freedom of the seas and the Padre bound for Guevavi found himself a castaway on the shores of Cuba. And because the "enlightened" faction prevailed at the Court of Madrid, one of Guevavi's Jesuits died on a death march across Mexico.

I have chosen not to modernize Spanish names; they appear in the text as they do in the documents. Father Garrucho always signed himself "Joseph," not José; Father Segesser, "Phelipe," not Felipe; and Guevavi's last Jesuit, "Ximeno," instead of Jimeno. The signatures of all of Guevavi's Padres, with the exception of Father Grazhoffer whose signature has not been located, are reproduced herein. It is interesting to note that most of the Jesuits who served at Guevavi wrote *IHS* or *JHS,* the monogram for Jesus, before or after their names to distinguish themselves as members of the Society of Jesus. Only Alexander Rapicani used the now-standard S.J., for Societatis Jesu, after his signature.

A majority of the material I have drawn upon is to be found in the original or on microfilm at the University of California's superb Bancroft Library, whose chief librarian, Dr. John Barr Tompkins, and staff were more than helpful. I am also indebted to the National Park Service, particularly to Superintendent Irving McNeil, Jr., of Tumacacori National Monument, and to Mr. Robert M. Utley, Chief Historian, Office of Archeology and Historic Preservation, for their continued interest and assistance. Father Norman M. Whalen of Benson, Arizona, kindly loaned me his microfilm of documents in the Mexican Biblioteca Nacional. Father John A. Donohue, s.j., of Loyola University in Los Angeles, and others patiently answered my pleas for additional information.

When finally I put the manuscript in draft form, several obliging persons read it through and offered salutary comment. Among them were: Father Ernest J. Burrus, s.j., of the Jesuit Historical Institute in Rome, who also generously took time out from a globe-circling schedule to write the Foreword; the genial Mrs. Judy England of the Rock Corral Ranch, Tumacacori, Arizona; and the distinguished Dr. Alberto F. Pradeau of Los Angeles. Dr. Donald C. Cutter of the University of New Mexico also offered criticism and then permitted me to revise the manuscript in his seminar in the History of the Southwest. Dr. William J. Robinson, who supervised recent archaeological excavations at Guevavi in 1965 and 1966, provided the floor plan of the mission complex. Both the Arizona Pioneers' Historical Society and the Roman Catholic Diocese of Tucson provided illustrations. And Kit Scheifele of the University of Arizona Press, with deft touch and great patience, shepherded me and the book through to press.

Finally, to Dr. Bernard L. Fontana of the Arizona State Museum, to Dr. Odie B. Faulk of Oklahoma State University, and to Father Kieran McCarty, o.f.m., Superior and historian at Mission San Xavier del Bac, special thanks for their always good-humored reassurance, without which I surely would not have got the job done.

JOHN L. KESSELL

Contents

Abbreviations

AGI   Archivo General de Indias, Sevilla, Spain
    Guad.   Audiencia de Guadalajara
AGN   Archivo General de la Nación, México, D.F.
AHH   Archivo Histórico de Hacienda, México, D.F.
    Temp.   Temporalidades
APHS   Arizona Pioneers' Historical Society, Tucson
ArizHR   *Arizona Historical Review*
AW   *Arizona and the West*
BL   Bancroft Library, University of California, Berkeley
BNMex   Biblioteca Nacional, México, D.F.
BRP   Bolton Research Papers, BL.
Civ. Col.   Selected documents relating to Pimería Alta, mainly 1767–1800, from the Fr. Marcellino da Civezza Collection, Pontificio Ateneo Antoniano, Roma; microfilm 305, UAL.
CPA   "Colección de Pimería Alta," baptismal, marriage, and burial books from the missions of Pimería Alta, collected by Alphonse L. Pinart, BL.
JAH   *Journal of Arizona History*
MA   *Mid-America*
M-M   Mexican Manuscripts, BL.
NMHR   *New Mexico Historical Review*
UAL   University of Arizona Library
WBS   W. B. Stephens Collection, Latin American Collection, University of Texas Library, Austin.

MISSION OF SORROWS
Jesuit Guevavi and the Pimas, 1691-1767

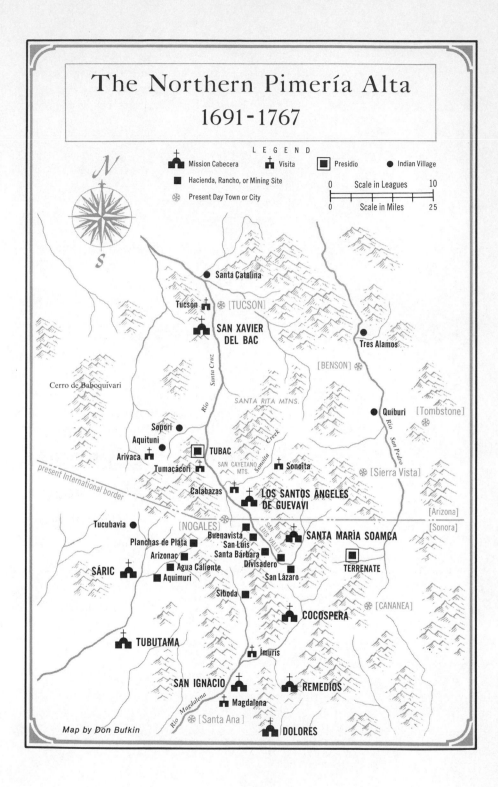

The Northern Pimería Alta
1691-1767

L E G E N D

✚ Mission Cabecera   ✚ Visita   ■ Presidio   ● Indian Village

■ Hacienda, Rancho, or Mining Site

✺ Present Day Town or City

Scale in Leagues   0 ————— 10

Scale in Miles   0 ————— 25

N / S

● Santa Catalina

Tucsón ✚   ✺ [TUCSON]

SAN XAVIER DEL BAC

● Tres Alamos

[BENSON] ✺

Cerro de Baboquívari

Río Santa Cruz

SANTA RITA MTNS.

● Quíburi   [Tombstone]

Río San Pedro

● Sopori

Aquituni ✚

Arivaca ✚

■ TUBAC

Tumacácori ✚

SAN CAYETANO MTS.

Sonoita Creek

✚ Sonoita

✺ [Sierra Vista]

Calabazas ✚

LOS SANTOS ÁNGELES DE GUEVAVI

[Arizona]

Tucubavia ●

[NOGALES] ✺

[Sonora]

Buenavista ✚

San Luis ■

Planchas de Plata ■

Santa Bárbara ■

Arizonac ■

Agua Caliente ■

Aquimuri ■

SAN LUIS VALLEY

Divísadero ■

San Lázaro ✚

SANTA MARÍA SOAMCA

■ TERRENATE

✺ [CANANEA]

SÁRIC ✚

Siboda ■

COCOSPERA ✚

TUBUTAMA ✚

✚ Ímuris

SAN IGNACIO ✚

✚ **REMEDIOS**

Magdalena ✚

Río Magdalena

✺ [Santa Ana]

✚ **DOLORES**

present international border

Map by Don Bufkin

I.

Before Guevaví

MILITANT FRIAR AND SPANISH SOLDIER were very close. For centuries they had fought the infidel side by side. They had won great battles, perhaps none more glorious, none more gratifying, than that which culminated in the reconquest of Granada in 1492. That very year, as if ordained, a whole new world began to open up, a vastly enlarged arena in which the alliance of cross and sword might be tested anew. There, the staggering feats of Cortés, the undreamed-of wealth of Peru, together with tens of thousands of native converts, dramatically convinced comrades in habit and suit of mail that their collaboration was blessed by God Himself.

And yet the alliance by its very success was doomed to dissolution. Only so long as it was sustained by conquest, by the victory not yet won, did the indomitable union endure. Once heathen resistance was struck down, once the heat of conquest had cooled and the daily business of imperial consolidation began, when the chaplain became a missionary and the soldier turned colonist, the holy alliance of cross and sword fell apart. Only then were the divergent purposes for which they had fought laid bare. The victors fell to quarreling over the spoils.

Foremost among the spoils were the native peoples. What was to be their lot in the new order — salvation or exploitation? Was the missionary or the colonist to prevail in the Indies? Only the Spanish

Crown, owner of this new world and arbiter of its destiny, could resolve the quarrel.

The Crown, however, had committed itself to both courses at once, to salvation *and* exploitation, and thus could offer no simple solution. As the price for secular control of the Church in the Indies, Ferdinand and Isabella had given the Papacy their word that the kings of Spain henceforth would provide for the Christianization of all those new-found lands. Apparently they considered this religious commitment not incompatible with the prevailing concept of mercantilism which obliged rulers to exploit their colonies for all they were worth.

Plainly then, the natives of America had to be made over both spiritually and physically; they must become not only orthodox but productive as well. Just how this two-fold transformation was to be accomplished, a transformation seemingly based upon the naive supposition that you could save a man's soul while you were breaking his back, became the burning issue of the day.

While the Crown vacillated, the missionary took matters into his own hands. By gathering all the Indians he could into protected, self-sufficient, mission towns he tried to shield them from cruel exploitation and from the corrupting example of European civilization, even to discouraging their use of the Spanish language. In central Mexico, where the natives were largely sedentary, where the trauma of conquest had rendered them docile, pockets of mission Indians lived isolated in hundreds of these planned communities presided over by paternalistic friars. On New Spain's northern frontier, however, isolation was impractical.

On the frontier, potential mission Indians were neither so sedentary nor so docile. There, moreover, the conquest dragged on; final victory was never won. There, implacable bands of shrieking "wild men," upon whose fate — extinction or slavery — everyone but them agreed, forced missionary and colonist to renew their alliance. But because life on the frontier involved not only the unifying element of conquest, or common defense, but also divisive competition for available resources, the alliance was brittle. Just beneath the surface, the conflict between missionary and colonist over Indian lands and labor remained constant, welling up time and again in bitter, mutually destructive discord.

That the frontier mission differed from the established mission community of central Mexico seems obvious. The former was a "mission of penetration"; the latter a "mission of occupation," to borrow the terms of Professor Ricard.[1] As a tribute to the former, Bolton wrote his famous essay, "The Mission as a Frontier Institution in the Spanish-American Colonies."[2] Unlike the mission of occupation, a deliberately isolated enclave surrounded by dense settlement, the frontier mission was thrust forth in advance of military conquest or as an adjunct to it. It became, in short, an "outpost of empire."

As Spain in the New World turned increasingly "aggressive for defensive reasons,"[3] as she sought to beat off the circling pack of foreign predators, she came to rely more and more on the frontier missionary as an aggressive defender. When the pearl fisher failed to effect permanent occupation of Baja California, the missionary accomplished it. When LaSalle pointed a French dagger at the mineral heartland of New Spain, the missionary was dispatched to blunt it. On the frontier, Crown and missionary had discovered an opportune coincidence of interests.

As an aggressive defender of empire the missionary took on a variety of roles — explorer, diarist, map maker, royal Indian agent, recruiter and, on occasion, leader of native auxiliaries against the enemies of the realm. His mission, if only an adobe hut, was positive evidence of Spanish possession; his neophytes, potentially useful imperial subjects.

Rarely did the missionary fail to point out the material benefits of his services when competing for a share of royal subsidies or parrying the charges of hostile colonists. He was a realist. And though he often appeared overly concerned with worldly matters, nothing, to his way of thinking, could have been further from the truth. His primary purpose was to save native souls; that did not change. If, however, he could combine imperial expansion with spiritual expansion, so much the better. To serve God, the missionary had learned, he had first to serve the Spanish Crown.

---

[1] Robert Ricard, *The Spiritual Conquest of Mexico: An Essay on the Apostolate and the Evangelizing Methods of the Mendicant Orders in New Spain, 1523–1572,* trans. Lesley Byrd Simpson (Berkeley: University of California Press, 1966), pp. 77–78.

[2] Herbert E. Bolton, "The Mission as a Frontier Institution in the Spanish-American Colonies," *American Historical Review,* Vol. XXIII (1917), pp. 42–61; reprinted in John Francis Bannon, s.j., ed., *Bolton and the Spanish Borderlands* (Norman: University of Oklahoma Press, 1964), pp. 187–211.

[3] Charles E. Chapman, *Colonial Hispanic America: A History* (New York: Macmillan, 1933), p. 92.

Where the Indians lived in fixed villages, the pueblos of New Mexico for example, the missionary simply moved in and built his church. More often, however, he had to gather up and concentrate semi-nomadic peoples in mission villages of his designation, to "reduce" them systematically. The resultant concentrations ranged in size from the extensive Jesuit reductions of Paraguay and the Franciscan establishments of Alta California at their height, with thousand of neophytes, to Guevavi where the Padres struggled to maintain a population of a hundred or two.

The natives did not always oppose reduction, at least not initially. There were inducements — simple curiosity, glass beads or tobacco, a particularly persuasive Padre, livestock and new crops and a full stomach, security from former enemies, the impressive ceremonialism, or the lance of a Spanish soldier at one's back.

Once "under the bells," the Indian faced a whole new way of life based upon a discipline that by his former standards seemed unusually strict. If he did not die of measles or smallpox, if he did not rebel, he found himself attending classes in doctrine and coming to recognize at least the outward signs of the Faith. He learned, often from a hispanicized Indian recruited farther south, to form adobes in the Spanish way and to dress a beam with adz and whipsaw. In the fields of the mission farm he tried using plow and sickle. Several of his number, who may or may not have been headmen before, accepted batons with silver knobs and ribbons, symbolic of a new and closely supervised executive authority in the village.

Everything about the mission involved discipline and learning. The whole point of this authoritarian and paternalistic regime within the mission was education, temporal as well as spiritual. From it the Indian was supposed to emerge a loyal and Christian, if lowly and exploitable, member of Spanish colonial society. Too often, however, after years of dependence, he was ill-prepared to emerge at all.

To the august Council of the Indies sitting in Spain, it seemed reasonable to set a ten-year limit on the missionizing process. After that period of time, the home government decided, the Indian should take his place in society and pay tribute. Mission lands previously held in common and in trust should then be divided among the neophytes, whose mission training unfortunately had taught them next to nothing about private ownership. After ten years, by the process known as secularization, the mission church should become a parish church as secular priest replaced missionary. By design then, the frontier mission was a transient institution, meant to move on, ever expanding the empire. On paper the ten-year plan looked neat and progressive; in the field it proved virtually unworkable.

If the Indians happened to be intractable or inattentive; if the supply of missionaries or parish priests to replace them was short or royal subsidies inadequate; if the physical environment or the mission's neighbors, Spaniards or Indians, were harsh — then missionization dragged on. A combination of all these adverse conditions forced the extension of the mission period at Jesuit Guevavi and its successor, Franciscan Tumacácori, to ten times ten years and then some.

The frontier missionary may have considered his role as aggressive defender of empire an unavoidable obligation, but he took to heart the aggressive defense of his neophytes. Father Kino arrived in Pimería Alta bearing a governmental decree exempting native converts from labor in the mines and on haciendas for a period of twenty years after baptism. Miner, *hacendado,* soldier, itinerant merchant, and shiftless vagabond — each in his way constituted a threat to the missionary's control over his Indians. Yet frequently the missionary found himself forced to cooperate with these disruptive elements.

Putting aside his misgivings, he requested that soldiers be assigned to guard duty in the mission, to protect it from raiding hostiles or from its own unruly neophytes. To raise funds, in excess of the royal stipend, for building a fine church and furnishing it to the greater glory of God, or for clothing his natives in a civilized fashion, he sold meat and grain to the frontier garrison, hides to the mines, or livestock to a would-be hacendado. In the absence of a secular priest he administered the sacraments to all elements of the population. On occasion he won a round with the locals by withholding mission produce or his services as a priest.

Relations between the missionary and the local non-mission population, by no means always strained, were likely to be worse in areas where missions had been long established and where neighboring Spanish communities were expanding. Pressure to secularize a mission, based on the ten-year law, thus releasing coveted lands and labor, was often exerted on a Padre who for one reason or another was not ready to give up his vested interest in the Indians. As long as his mission served as an effective buffer against nomad or foreigner, as long as the Crown had no one else to do his job, the frontier missionary went right on presiding over and defending his wards.

That it was a black-robed Jesuit who came first among the Pima Indians of Guevavi was no accident. For a hundred years the keenly disciplined members of that order had extended their operations northward along both slopes of the Sierra Madre Occidental from river valley to river valley, from barranca to barranca, until they had built a missionary empire in northwestern New Spain as large as the Iberian Peninsula.

The Jesuits had come late to New Spain, relatively speaking. Even before Ignacio de Loyola got papal approval for his Compañía de Jesús, Franciscans, Dominicans, and Augustinians had begun to lay out their Mexican spheres of interest. The first Jesuit missionaries to the New World landed on the coast of Brazil in 1549, just nine years after the order's formal recognition. In 1566 other Jesuits arrived to engage in a courageous but ill-conceived apostolate along the coast of La Florida. Then, in 1572, a select fifteen reached New Spain. Far from impeding the zealous young order's subsequent success, the Black Robes' late entrance worked marvelously in their favor.

The Jesuits were meant to excel. Chosen on the basis of mental and physical fitness, good appearance and family background, and, above all, suitability for a life of rigorous discipline, complete obedience, and unswerving devotion, trained long and honed on the *Spiritual Exercises* to a fervent edge, full members of the Society of Jesus emerged as superbly confident soldiers of God. They were different from the three major mendicant orders already ensconced in New Spain. As a religious body they were better trained than the friars. They were eminently adaptable and qualified to serve as priests, teachers, or missionaries. Moreover, the Jesuits arrived with conquering momentum, which, unlike many of the friars who settled down to enjoy the fruits of earlier prodigious labors, they managed to maintain. The Black Robes, too, could be overweening, inflexible, and hard on those who did not measure up. As a result, they made enemies easily, even among the clergy.

A further difference between the Jesuits and the other orders, one that worked against them later on, resulted from their supra-national cohesion and their direct allegiance to the Papacy. The Society of Jesus did not feel particularly beholden to the kings of Spain as patrons of the Spanish Church, but rather to the Church militant international.

Once in New Spain the Jesuits devoted most of their first two decades to stiffening the moral and mental fiber of *criollo* society.[4] Not till 1591, while continuing to found *colegios* in the cities, did some of them enter the great heathendom that would become in the seventeenth century their northwest missionary empire.

The seventeenth century in New Spain has been characterized as a century of depression. The first great silver boom had ended and the economy contracted and turned inward upon itself. The white ruling class swelled in numbers while the native population upon which it depended for food and labor continued to shrink at an alarming rate. The troublesome, shiftless mixed-blood element became a drag on a rigid colonial society unprepared and unwilling to assimilate it. The high and mighty — though frequently money-poor — owners of great estates, who added to and entailed their holdings for the sake of prestige rather than production, epitomized the static, feudal-like economy.

The seventeenth century was also one of relative mediocrity, unfolding sluggishly between centuries of great conquest and great reawakening. Under the sad later Hapsburgs the heavy imperial bureaucracy proliferated, spawning countless petty officials who owed their places not to talent but to outright purchase, bribery, or nepotism. So long as the Crown kept surrendering former royal prerogatives in hopes of making ends meet, New Spain lay in the sun undisturbed by reform.

The Church bureaucracy too, suffering from overextension and moral laxity, reflected society's general dissipation. Doubtless there flowed beneath the stagnant surface of this "Baroque age" unperceived currents of great portent, which even welled up now and again in a *tumulto*, but to the eye of a progressive, Mexico seemed to slumber.

That the dynamic, hard-hitting, progressive Society of Jesus succeeded in static seventeenth-century New Spain should come as no surprise. The Jesuits' zealous efficiency was in sharp contrast to the apathy around them; their classrooms, their great estates, and their missions prospered, enclaves of intense activity in a languid environ-

---

[4] See Jerome V. Jacobsen, s.j., *Educational Foundations of the Jesuits in Sixteenth-Century New Spain* (Berkeley: University of California Press, 1938).

ment.[5] Heavily endowed as teachers and spiritual guides to the colonial aristocracy, the Black Robes put their wealth to work in a hundred ways, and as a result waxed more influential than their small numbers would indicate. When, under the reforming influence of the eighteenth-century Bourbons, New Spain woke up, the Jesuits were a power to reckon with.

Because Charles III stood for secularism in the interest of reform and for the subjection of all the clergy to his centralized state, neither of which aim the orthodox, ultramontane Jesuits could tolerate, there was bound to be a clash. The Society of Jesus, intellectual backbone of the conservative faction, had to go.

Despite charges that their missions monopolized land and labor and stifled the economy in some areas, the Crown had no quarrel with the Jesuit frontier missionary. As aggressive defender of empire he had served exceptionally well. Had he not been tied by such intense loyalty to every other Jesuit, Charles might have excepted the frontier missionary when he banished the order in 1767. But there was no divorcing a Jesuit from his brethren. So they all went, victims of changing times and international affairs.

To explain the expulsion in terms of local events is impossible.[6] The king did not cast the Jesuits out of all his domains or even out of Pimería Alta because the Pimas had rebelled back in 1751. (Had the king expelled missionaries for causing native rebellions, he soon would have had no missionaries at all. Rebellions were an unfortunate by-product of the process.) Nor was the German or Italian nationality of a Jesuit missionary enough in itself to cause banishment or even suspicion; Charles was at the very time hiring German mining engineers and Italian army officers, though presumably they had no ties to an organized body international. No matter how loudly the Society's individual enemies on the local level applauded the expulsion or took pleasure from

---

[5] The Jesuits' "understanding of economics, their business sense, and their efficient exploitation of landed property struck a relatively new and discordant note in the Indies, where so many hidalgos and cattle barons were disdainful of economics." François Chevalier, *Land and Society in Colonial Mexico: The Great Hacienda,* trans. Alvin Eustis, ed. Lesley Byrd Simpson (Berkeley: University of California Press, 1966), p. 250.

[6] For some idea of how complex the explanations can get and how widely historical interpretation varies, see Magnus Mörner, ed., *The Expulsion of the Jesuits from Latin America* (New York: Knopf, 1965).

their alleged parts in it, the fact remained: the Jesuits had simply outlived their usefulness to the absolutist king of Spain. In the day of Charles III, the Black Robes still represented the thinking of Philip II.

Even before the death of Philip in 1598, the Jesuits had laid the foundations of their northwest missionary empire.[7] A century later it had reached Pimería Alta, homeland of the Upper Pima Indians. There, however, the monumental offensive, mounted a thousand miles to the south, finally stalled, though not for lack of Jesuit zeal.

A series of dynastic and colonial wars far beyond the missionaries' control sapped the Spanish treasury. Black Robes laboring in Pimería Alta in the eighteenth century found it increasingly difficult to win support for the maintenance and expansion of their apostolate. Further advance in that quarter of the empire, the authorities were keenly aware, implied a conquest of the formidable, highly mobile Apaches, a conquest the Spanish Crown was ill-prepared to undertake. Had the French built a fort on the Colorado River, somewhere money would have been raised for defensive expansion. To the missionary it seemed unjust that purely political considerations should take precedence over the needy, ever-beckoning heathen peoples *más allá.*

A hot, dry land of desert valleys and scattered mountain ranges, Pimería Alta became the capstone on the northwest missionary empire. Today the area is split by the international border between Sonora of

---

[7] Because the building of the northwest missionary empire of the Jesuits was so dramatic and so successful, and because most of the accounts of it were written by the Black Robes themselves, the story we get is understandably one of almost unrelieved praise for the missionary. See W. Eugene Shiels, s.j., *Gonzalo de Tapia (1561–1594), Founder of the First Permanent Jesuit Mission in North America* (New York: United States Catholic Historical Society, 1934); four works by Peter Masten Dunne, s.j., *Pioneer Black Robes on the West Coast* (Berkeley: University of California Press, 1940), *Pioneer Jesuits in Northern Mexico* (Berkeley: University of California Press, 1944), *Early Jesuit Missions in Tarahumara* (Berkeley: University of California Press, 1948), and *Black Robes in Lower California* (Berkeley: University of California Press, 1952); and Bannon, *The Mission Frontier in Sonora, 1620–1687* (New York: United States Catholic Historical Society, 1955). There is some indication that the story had another side, that what was best for the Jesuits was not always best for the rest of northwestern New Spain, but historians have extolled the missions so much that it is difficult to see. A recent study which points the way by emphasizing the other side is Luis Navarro García, *Sonora y Sinaloa en el siglo XVII* (Sevilla: Escuela de Estudios Hispano-Americanos, 1967). See also James Rodney Hastings, "People of Reason and Others: The Colonization of Sonora to 1767," *Arizona and the West (AW)*, Vol. III (1961), pp. 321–40.

Mexico and Arizona of the United States. On Spanish maps it appeared north of Sonora, west of New Mexico, and contained by a shifting enemy territory labeled simply Apachería. Pimería Alta was, more specifically, an area of some fifty thousand square miles stretching north from the Altar and Magdalena River valleys to the banks of the Gila, and from the San Pedro River Valley west to the Gulf of California and almost to the Colorado River. Even when thus defined, it was larger than the Kingdom of Portugal, though far less hospitable.

The summer heat, which withered the zeal of more than one European Jesuit, could build up to a hundred and ten or fifteen degrees Fahrenheit. The winters were mild yet invigorating. The few dependable rivers, hardly more than streams, meandered along the margins of the Pimería, their courses well marked by a comparatively luxuriant and wholly dependent following of cottonwood and willow trees. The chaparral vegetation back from the rivers declined in the driest expanses to little more than scattered creosote bushes and barrel cactuses. On the lower slopes of parched sierras grew stands of erect saguaro cactus, and almost everywhere the scrubby mesquite.

It rained in the summer, from July through August, when great heavy clouds built up over the mountains and the arroyos from time to time ran full of churning, muddy water. The higher humidity and swarms of insects made the summer rainy season the most uncomfortable. Rain was sporadic in the winter and almost absent in the spring. On the average, six out of seven days in Pimería Alta were clear and dry, and it was never certain that it would rain on the seventh.

No Spaniard who had heard tales of the lordly Aztecs would have thought any of the roughly thirty thousand Upper Pima Indians very advanced. They were hunters and gatherers who farmed when location or season permitted. They shared a common language and to a marked degree a common culture, but they were in no sense united as a single tribe. To certain groups of them therefore, the Spaniards gave distinguishing names. Along the San Pedro lived the "haughty" Sobaípuris. As a group they enjoyed a certain bargaining power with the Spaniards, so long as they fended off the attacks of hostile nomads from the north and east. The Pima proper dwelled on the banks of the other regularly flowing rivers. Toward their more-or-less permanent villages, or rancherías, the missionary directed his major effort.

Out on the inhospitable desert to the west, where a harsh environment imposed certain limitations on the basic Piman culture, lived a group called by the Spaniards Pápagos,[8] or Bean People. Less sedentary than their river relatives, they migrated seasonally between farming and hunting grounds. During the summer a Pápago family lived near its fields at the mouth of an arroyo. Close by, its members dug a waterhole, or *charco* in Spanish. After the first rains had softened the ground, they planted what beans and maize they could, then waited for the arroyo to channel several more good floodings down over the crops, which even in the best years provided no more than a quarter of their diet. Once the harvest was in and the rainwater in the charco had dried up, the family moved to a winter hunting ranchería near a permanent spring in the mountains.

Periodically the Pápagos came in to trade with or work for the relatively better-off river Pimas. These temporary refugees from the desert were later to provide the missionary with a convenient reserve: as the river Pimas died off a mission could be kept alive by inducing the visitors to stay. The Pápagos' tendency to flee back to their desert homes from time to time, however, caused the Padres to characterize them as fickle and irresponsible, as prone to wander as gypsies.

A representative river Pima ranchería consisted of a number of related families living in a loose cluster of dome-shaped brush-and-earth houses. Storage huts of the same shape, open ramadas, outside cooking areas, tiny isolation huts for women during the mysterious times of menstruation and childbirth, as well as a single large ceremonial or council house completed the picture. In nearby irrigated fields the Pimas grew maize, squash, and beans, usually planting twice each year between first and last frosts. They relied, too, on game — deer, rabbits, rodents, dove, quail — and on wild foods — mesquite beans, cactus fruit, mescal — which made up as much as 60 percent of their total food supply.

They grew, wove, and wore cotton; made pottery, willow baskets,

---

[8] Today the name Pápago applies not only to the desert dwellers on the vast Pápago reservation centered at Sells, Arizona, but also to the remnant river Pima population mixed with Pápagos on the San Xavier reservation immediately southwest of Tucson. The name Pima is now restricted exclusively to the more northerly Gila River Pimas, whom the Spaniards never reached with permanent missions.

and reed mats; used both stone and wooden tools; dressed in breechclout or skirt of deer skin or cotton, wore their hair long, and adorned themselves with shells, turquoise, and paints made from clay. They enjoyed kickball, foot races, and numerous games of skill and chance — often competing as villages, one against the other — and they delighted in gambling on the outcome.

A hereditary ceremonial leader and giver of wise counsel presided over the ranchería as sort of a patriarch. By moral suasion, not force, he made his influence felt. In his care was placed the village fetish, which brought the rains. A messenger and a village crier assisted this headman. In the realms of war, the hunt, and games other designated leaders took the initiative. Yet the real governing power in the ranchería resided in a council of elders, the "ripe men" of experience and maturity.

Almost nightly the council met, and its members while smoking ceremonial cigarettes engaged in lengthy dialogues for the purpose of determining a mutually acceptable course of action. The mission government, in which decisions were imposed from the top and enforced by threat of corporal punishment, was to contrast painfully with the Pimas' traditional way of governing themselves.

The Pimas fought when they had to, but not, like the Yumas to the west, simply for the glory of it. They used bow and stone-tipped arrow or shield and club. For obvious reasons their word for enemy came to be synonymous with Apache. War, the Pimas believed, could be the source of useful power, but it was nothing to trifle with. He who had slain an enemy and taken a scalp, for example, was forced to undergo sixteen days of isolation and purification. Having thus tamed his new power the warrior returned a "ripe" man, and his scalp trophy if properly cared for helped protect him and his family and bring rain.

To explain their being the Piman peoples told a creation story. They believed that Itoi, or Elder Brother, had led them up out of the underworld, that he had taught them all they knew, and that he continued to watch over them. Some of them would think of Elder Brother when the missionary was describing Jesus Christ. They also venerated eagle feathers and a variety of other sacred objects. They thought animals had special powers and the ability to control certain diseases. In a dream it was possible for a Pima to establish a rapport with an animal and learn something of its powers. The experience of taking an enemy scalp, of capturing an eagle, or of journeying for salt to the Gulf of California, these also imbued the individual with special powers.

For every season or occasion the Pimas had magical recitations and songs. They performed corn dances, puberty dances, deer dances, and scalp dances. Their ceremonial duty to get gloriously saturated with cactus liquor at the summer rain festival; their reliance on medicine men, or shamans, whom the Spaniards called *hechiceros;* their sanctioning of periodic orgies, plural wives, and divorce by simple consent; and their tolerance of homosexuals and transvestites — all these were to become sources of cultural conflict when the missionary arrived.

Yet because they did not carve great stone idols or construct secret subterranean kivas, certain of the Padres concluded, incorrectly, that the Pimas had no religion at all. This imagined void the missionary sought to fill with the saving knowledge of his Christian Faith, without which, he truly believed, the Pimas were damned.[9]

---

[9] A handy popular treatment of the Piman peoples is Ruth M. Underhill, *The Papago Indians of Arizona and Their Relatives the Pima* (Lawrence, Kansas: Haskell Institute, 1941). Of the same author's numerous scholarly publications her *Social Organization of the Papago Indians* (New York: Columbia University Press, 1939) is the most inclusive. See also Edward F. Castetter and Willis H. Bell, *Pima and Papago Indian Agriculture* (Albuquerque: University of New Mexico Press, 1942).

2.

Christianity on Their Terms
The Tutelage of Father Kino and After, 1691-1731

HE WAS BENT OVER setting up a portable altar when he first heard
the shouting. Eagerly he jumped up. The soldiers were scurrying for
their weapons. Now he could see them. A band of naked Waicuris,
feathers in their hair and painted for war, approached yelling and
brandishing their bows and arrows. He and the other missionary, who
had worked before among heathens, grabbed up some biscuits and glass
beads, and walked cautiously toward them. One false move, one over-
anxious soldier or savage could have meant death or at least an inaus-
picious beginning.

The Indians refused to take the gifts from the missionaries' hands;
instead they motioned them to put their offerings on the ground. Standing back, the two European Jesuits studied these godless creatures with
compassion. One by one the natives examined what had been given
them. They began to loosen up. Before the afternoon was over they had
reciprocated with "roasted mescal heads, which were very good, little
nets very well made, and feathers of birds which they wore on their
heads." But more significant, the two Padres had shown to the unknow-
ing Indians an image which would change their lives, a small likeness of
a thin man on a cross. Thus, on the parched and rocky shore of Baja

[17]

California in the spring of 1683, began the remarkable missionary apostolate of Eusebio Francisco Kino.[1]

He stood about five feet, six inches, somewhat taller than average for his day, and was solidly built. His countenance was impressive: a broad nose and deepset eyes beneath a strikingly pronounced brow.[2] His skin tended toward dark, or *moreno;* his hair was black and wavy.[3]

Christened Eusebius Chinus on the day he was born, August 10, 1645, Kino, as he came to spell his name in the New World, had grown up in his native village of Segno near Trent in the Italian Tyrol where the Chini belonged to the minor nobility. At age eighteen, as he lay suffering from a "mortal illness," the lad Eusebius had vowed to become a missionary. To prepare himself he entered the Society of Jesus at Landsberg, Bavaria, on November 20, 1665. Because he fervently desired to labor in the exotic Orient, young Kino probably paid little heed to the king of Spain's recent concession to the Society. In an effort to alleviate the critical manpower shortage which threatened to destroy the Jesuits' northwest missionary empire in Mexico, Philip IV had decreed that a certain number of non-Spanish Jesuits be allowed to serve in his Indies.[4] The door was now open.

Persuasive, talented, and ambitious, Kino had excelled in his studies, particularly in mathematics and science. Ever loyal to his vow, however, he had turned down an enticing offer to teach those subjects at the University of Ingolstadt in Bavaria. Repeatedly he petitioned for appointment as a foreign missionary. Finally in 1678, a year after his ordination, he was on his way, but headed west, not east. Two appointments had

---

[1] Bolton, *Rim of Christendom: A Biography of Eusebio Francisco Kino, Pacific Coast Pioneer* (New York: Macmillan, 1936; reprint, Russell and Russell, 1960), pp. 106–107. This is the well-written, painstaking, and frankly sympathetic standard biography. It has been supplemented of late by the numerous scholarly works of Ernest J. Burrus, s.j., among which is the elegant *Kino and the Cartography of Northwestern New Spain* (Tucson: Arizona Pioneers' Historical Society, 1965).

[2] These physical features of Father Kino are evident from his skeleton, which was exhumed during the spring of 1966 by a team of Mexican and American historians and archaeologists in Magdalena, Sonora, since renamed Magdalena de Kino.

[3] As he sailed for the New World, Kino was described succinctly on the passenger list: *"Buen cuerpo. Moreno. Pelo negro ensortijado."* Burrus, *Kino and the Cartography,* p. 10, n. 15.

[4] Shiels, "The Critical Period in Mission History," *Mid-America (MA),* Vol. XXI (1939), pp. 97–109.

arrived, one to the Philippines, the other to Mexico. Kino and a friend both wanted the Philippines. They cast lots, and Kino lost.

In Spain he waited two years, boarded a ship that ran aground before it had cleared Cádiz harbor, waited another six months, and finally prevailed. Because the king had restricted the number of foreigners to one third of the total in any Jesuit group bound for the Indies, and because Kino's group included more than the quota, several of them crossed as Spaniards. Kino for the moment became Eusebio de Chaves, a pseudo-*cordobés*.[5] It worked. He arrived in New Spain in the late spring of 1681. Still current were reports from the north — twenty-one Franciscans martyred in New Mexico, the entire mission frontier in peril.

Before Kino left Mexico City to join the Baja California expedition, he had met the two outstanding geniuses of seventeenth-century Mexico, Don Carlos de Sigüenza y Góngora and Sor Juana Inés de la Cruz. With the former he had exchanged tracts explaining the "Great Comet of 1680." Kino, who had no intention of provoking Sigüenza, naturally took the traditional, neo-medieval, Church view of the comet as a dire omen meant by God to strike holy fear into the hearts of men. The sensitive Don Carlos, who thought Kino patronizing, ungrateful, and arrogant, based his argument on mathematical proof and demonstration, divorcing for his purposes God and science.[6] Don Carlos plainly was a century before his time. Yet in retrospect the Sigüenza-Kino debate of the 1680s can be seen to foreshadow the monumental upcoming struggle between Church and secular interests, one round of which would see another Carlos with secular leanings banish from the Spanish empire every member of the dogmatic Society of Jesus.

After three years the Baja California venture failed, though not from a lack of effort on Father Kino's part. The Crown had withdrawn its support, and at this stage the Society of Jesus was unwilling to finance the entire project. Kino refused to give up. He requested and was granted permission to work in the missions of Sonora. If he could establish a base among the primitive Seris on the coast opposite, California might be saved.

---

[5] Burrus, *Kino and the Cartography*, p. 10, n. 15.

[6] Irving A. Leonard, *Baroque Times in Old Mexico: Seventeenth-Century Persons, Places and Practices* (Ann Arbor: University of Michigan Press, 1959), pp. 204–11; Bolton, *Rim of Christendom*, pp. 77–83.

First, however, he had to lay his plan before the local Father Visitor, superior of the Sonora missions. Arriving at Oposura late in February or early in March, 1687, the persuasive Kino must have talked long and hard to convince his new superior that the Seris and California were of first priority. But it was no use. The Father Visitor had other plans for Kino.

Ever since the Pueblo Indians had successfully reasserted themselves and had driven the Spaniards out of New Mexico seven years before, the natives all along the northern frontier had been restless and emboldened. Ópatas, Sumas, Janos, Tarahumaras, and others were plotting.[7] *Tlatoleros,* or native agitators, scurried back and forth in an effort to coordinate the risings. The Apaches were known to be involved. Only recently a Pima headman had been hanged for trafficking with hostile tribes.[8]

For a generation, since the early 1640s when Pimas living along the Río Magdalena repulsed Don Pedro de Perea, "conqueror of Sonora," and his New Mexican friars, these Indians had enjoyed a reputation among Spanish frontiersmen for treachery and thievery. They resisted enslavement. There was, nonetheless, reason to believe that the Pimas would welcome Jesuit missionaries. To go among them, to sample their mood, and, if God willed, to make them Christians, the Father Visitor chose Kino. California would have to wait.

Almost immediately Kino's efforts in Pimería Alta bore fruit. On a promontory near the ranchería of Bamotze, or Cosari, he presided as the adobe walls of mission Nuestra Señora de los Dolores went up. The Pimas seemed happy. They flocked in for gifts, and they listened to what he said through his interpreters about the one true God and Jesus and Mary. They helped plant wheat and set out orchards. They were impressed when he sprinkled water from a silver shell on the heads of their children; he said it had power. "God willing, hundreds, and later, thousands [of Pimas] will be gathered into the bosom of our sweet, most holy Mother Church. . . ."[9]

---

[7] A brief account of the persistent restlessness and native risings along the northwestern frontier during the 1680s is included in Navarro García, *Sonora y Sinaloa,* pp. 262–86.

[8] Bolton, *Rim of Christendom,* p. 242, n. 1. See also Edward H. Spicer, *Cycles of Conquest: The Impact of Spain, Mexico, and the United States on the Indians of the Southwest, 1533–1960* (Tucson: University of Arizona Press, 1962), pp. 118–19, 232–33.

[9] Quoted in Bolton, *Rim of Christendom,* p. 257.

Kino was an irrepressible expansionist. Mission Dolores, on "the rim of Christendom" just two days' ride from the Pimas of Guevavi, only whetted his appetite. "To various and even remote parts" he sent native runners with promises of gifts to those who would listen. In rapid succession he expanded his influence over nearby rancherías — San Ignacio, Ímuris, Remedios, and Cocóspera. When he had met the people, baptized their children, begun a church, spoken of God, and created among them a demand for the material benefits of living like Christians, he was ready to move on. Kino's temperament was that of a missionary conqueror, not that of a consolidator. He had no desire to be confined by the annoying everyday business of mission administration; more timid souls were better suited for that. Kino's place was in the vanguard, meeting the challenges of unexplored frontiers. There the rewards were greater.

In the language of the Pimas, Baboquívari meant something like Great Pinched Rock or Mountain-Tied-in-the-Middle. It described that towering desert landmark admirably. Most Pima place names, however, were less explicit, often bestowed casually; anything to make an Indian think of a particular place at a particular time — Where Snake Died, Coyote Sitting, Owl Cry, Turtle-between-the-rocks. Guevavi, *gi vavhia* it seems, meant Big Well or Big Spring, hardly a name that taken by itself can be identified in our day with any one particular place. Neither, on the basis of incomplete evidence, are the archaeologists yet prepared to say exactly where the people of Big Well lived just prior to the Padres' coming.[10]

The maps and diaries of the earliest missionary and military visitors seem to place the Indian village of Guevavi on the river now called the Santa Cruz some ten miles or so north of the present Arizona-Sonora border. In that area, near a wide fertile place where arroyos ran down to the river, the people built a cluster of huts that came to be know as *gi vavhia*. The water from the river, which meandered north, clear and

---

[10] A great deal of archaeological work remains to be done in the Santa Cruz Valley of southern Arizona. Excavations at the post-1732 Guevavi site, carried on during the winters of 1964–65 and 1965–66 under Dr. William J. Robinson, failed to uncover much evidence of a pre-mission ranchería nearby. The documents of the early contact period seem to suggest, however, that the village was located even then not far from the still-visible ruins of later construction at Guevavi.

shallow, except when the rains turned it into a surging, muddy torrent, gave life to their maize and to giant cottonwoods, to willows and mesquites. For the same reasons that this was a good place for their ranchería, it was also a good place for a mission.

His first coming was hardly a surprise. The natives of Guevavi had known for generations that a warlike new people was pushing up from the south, even into the lands of the Pimas Bajos and the Opatas. They had traded with other Indians for objects made by this people, and perhaps they had even begun to plant wheat, flax, and watermelons.[11] They knew about the slaving raids and of death from the smoke-belching weapons carried by mounted, leather-armored warriors. Perhaps they knew firsthand.

Then came word that one of the new people, an impressive man in black, was giving gifts to the Pimas only a few days south — strings of beads that light shone through, steel knives and scissors, bright ribbons, and huge, thick-horned animals heavy with meat. He claimed, too, to represent a potent new supernatural. The elders of Guevavi in council may have decided to join with their counterparts from several rancherías farther north in seeking him out. On their journey south they carried wooden crosses, knowing that these pleased him.

The year, according to the European calendar, was 1691. In Spain a pathetic monarch, the pallid imbecile Charles II — "the bewitched" — amused himself while his court seethed with intrigue and corruption. Had someone informed His Majesty of the delegation of Pima Indians on its way to a meeting with his representative in that outlandish place, the king might have mustered a stupid smile, but little else. In England William and Mary ruled by grace of Parliament in the wake of the recent Glorious Revolution. Never, they were resolved, would England submit to Louis XIV and his grandiose French design. On the continent of North America in fact, the first of the intercolonial wars, called King William's War, was now being waged intermittently between English and French colonials. It foreshadowed a contest that would last two thirds of the next century.

Spain's weakness at home pervaded the empire. In America she sought vainly to keep Carolina traders out of greater Florida and Frenchmen from extending Louisiana to include part of Texas. Though it was

[11] Castetter and Bell, *Pima and Papago Indian Agriculture*, pp. 73–74.

hardly a serious consideration in 1691, the whole of Pimería Alta lay within the sea-to-sea grant of the English Crown to the Carolina proprietors. But no such matters of intercolonial rivalry cluttered the heads of the Pimas as they followed the trail through the mountains and dropped down along the arroyo leading to Tucubavia. They had only one objective — to find this man in black and learn what he had to offer.

Even before he had met any Pimas, Father Kino was prepared to defend them. En route to found his mission of Dolores he had passed through the mining town, or *real,* of San Juan Bautista, then the seat of civil government in Sonora. For nearly a half century the *alcalde mayor* of Sonora, usually resident at San Juan, was to exercise nominal jurisdiction over Pimería Alta, though in fact he rarely interfered with the Jesuits in that little-settled territory. To the alcalde, Kino had presented the decree he carried exempting newly converted natives from mine and hacienda labor, and that official had gone through the appropriate ritual of compliance, kissing the document, then holding it over his head.

It was soon evident, however, that a mere piece of paper protected no one. Hardly had Kino been at his post a year when a Spanish officer wantonly slaughtered the Pimas of Mototicachi. Though that sadistic officer had fled a death sentence, other persons opposed to missionary protection for the Pimas stayed and resorted to rumors. These were frontiersmen who saw in the Jesuit advance a threat to their exploitation of the natives. These were, according to Father Kino, "persons of little loyalty." The Pimas, they maintained, were incorrigible liars, thieves, and plotters, no more worthy of the missionaries' attention than the savage Apaches. The Pimas opposed Father Kino and ran from him. Besides, there were really so few of them that the Jesuits were only wasting time that might be spent more profitably elsewhere. Before long the rumors had reached Mexico City and the ear of the new Father Provincial, highest-ranking Jesuit in all New Spain.[12]

The Jesuit hierarchy was simple and direct. In Rome sat the Father General, elected for life. In each of the several provinces he appointed a Father Provincial who served for three years, a *triennium,* and who was required to make periodic visitations of all the Jesuit establishments within his jurisdiction. In New Spain, so vast a territory, the Provincial appointed Father Visitors to preside in his behalf over designated areas,

---

[12] Spicer, *Cycles of Conquest,* pp. 118–21; Bolton, *Rim of Christendom,* pp. 258–63.

the missions of Sonora and Sinaloa, for example. At the bottom of the chain of command stood the Father Rector. He was superior of a relatively small community of his brethren, a Jesuit house, a college, or a grouping of missions, rarely less than three or more than ten, called a rectorate. As members of the Provincial's administration, the Visitors and Rectors also served three-year terms. Thus when he began to hear perplexing reports from distant Pimería Alta, the Father Provincial of New Spain acted accordingly.

"Square-jawed, hawk-nosed, clear-headed" Father Visitor Juan María Salvatierra arrived on Christmas Eve, 1690, at Nuestra Señora de los Dolores, mission of Father Rector Eusebio Kino. After a generous frontier feast, the Father Rector took the Father Visitor on a tour of the Pimería, so that the Father Provincial might know the truth about the Pimas. Whether Salvatierra realized it or not, he was now in the hands of a master promoter.

Received enthusiastically by hundreds of docile natives, the Father Visitor knew already that his report to Mexico City would be a favorable one. From the ranchería of Tucubavia on the headwaters of the Río Altar he and Kino had decided to turn back. Just then a native delegation from the heathen north appeared, painted and adorned in their fashion. More impressive to Salvatierra, they carried wooden crosses. The implication was clear. "The Father Visitor said to me," wrote Kino, "that those crosses which they brought were tongues that spoke much and with great force, and that we could not neglect going where they summoned us with them."[13] If Father Kino had arranged for their coming, he was gratified. The timing was perfect.

Farther north now rode the two trail-toughened Jesuits and their retinue, guided by eager heathens, across the present international border west of Nogales, then east through the mountains, and finally down an

[13] Kino, "Favores Celestiales de Jesus y de María SS^ma y del Gloriosissimo Apostol de las Indias S. Francisco Xavier Experimentados en las Nuevas Conquistas y Nuevas Conversiones. . . ." Parte I, Libro 2, Capítulo II; Archivo General de la Nación, México, D.F. (AGN), Misiones, tomo 27. All documents cited in this archive, unless otherwise stated, are on microfilm at the Bancroft Library, University of California, Berkeley (BL). Kino's *magnum opus,* compiled between 1699 and 1710, the "Favores Celestiales" was translated in its entirety by Bolton as *Kino's Historical Memoir of Pimería Alta,* 2 vols. (Cleveland: Arthur H. Clark, 1919; Berkeley: University of California Press, 1948).

arroyo into "the valley of Guevavi."[14] Instead of leading the caravan south to the ranchería of Guevavi, which at this point was closer, the natives beckoned north downriver toward the ranchería of Tumacácori. On the east bank of this river which Kino came to call the Santa María, on a half-moon-shaped bend lined with cottonwoods now bare, a congregation awaited them:

> At the ranchería of San Cayetano de Tumacácori, where there were some Sobaípuri headmen who had come 20 and 25 leagues from the north . . . they had prepared 3 shelters (*ramadas*), one in which to say Mass, another in which to sleep, and the third for cooking. There were more than forty houses close together. Some children were baptized and to all the Father Visitor gave bright hopes that they would obtain Fathers and Holy Baptism and their eternal salvation for which they asked. And having seen so many people, so docile and so friendly, with such lovely and such fertile and delightful valleys inhabited by industrious Indians, the Father Visitor said to me these words: "My Father Rector, the removal from this Pimería of any of the 4 Fathers already granted will not be considered; and furthermore, four others will come and I, by Divine Grace, shall try to be one of them."[15]

Salvatierra was convinced. Now they did turn back. For a distance of four leagues — one league equaled about two and a half miles — they rode again along the same stretch of river. But this time instead of veering to the west up the arroyo, they followed the river, passing on their left close by tan and looming San Cayetano Mountain and by the mouth of Sonoita Creek. The valley, trending at this point somewhat east of south, began to narrow as rounded hills pushed in from both sides. Still, cottonwoods and willows obeyed the river's every bend.

Two more leagues brought the Padres' caravan into the ranchería of Guevavi, which Father Kino mentioned only in passing. On this occasion, the earliest recorded visit by Europeans, the natives of Guevavi were no doubt curious, perhaps somewhat awed, but apparently willing. They accepted the trinkets given them, and they listened to what the Black Robes said as repeated by their interpreters. The sign of the cross

---

[14] For a discussion of the route taken by the Padres from Tucubavia to the Santa Cruz Valley, see Charles C. DiPeso, *The Upper Pima of San Cayetano del Tumacacori* (Dragoon, Arizona: Amerind Foundation, 1956), p. 8, n. 29.

[15] Kino, "Favores Celestiales," I, 2, II.

The valley at Guevavi

was easy to make. If they did not understand, that was of little concern — the Padres would be back. This brief visit in January, 1691, was only the beginning.

Over the next ten years, Kino transformed the trail along the river flowing north past Guevavi into an avenue of peaceful conquest. Though he came at the head of his laden caravans only once or twice a year, he and his helpers wrought more change in one decade than had native ingenuity in countless generations. All before Kino was prehistory, all after him history.

Though the changes were many during the initial decade, the inhabitants of Guevavi seemed to adjust readily enough.[16] By stages they learned to cultivate new crops, to herd sheep, to build an adobe-walled house and to sweep it out and stock it with food when they heard that the Padre was coming. They learned to use unfamiliar tools. When Kino and Captain Diego Carrasco, seven servants, the native governor of Dolores, and their pack train approached Guevavi in September of 1698 they were received "with the roads so cleared that many large trees must have been cut with an ax."[17]

The Padre's visits became welcome excuses to celebrate "with dancing and singing all night." The natives had no quarrel with Father Kino if he wished to call their ranchería San Gabriel de Guevavi,[18] their headmen *gobernador, alcalde* or *mador,* and their children Juan and María after the ceremony of the water. They were willing to listen to his talks and accept his gifts, even to go on campaigns with the soldiers

---

[16]An account of the Kino years at Guevavi and neighboring Tumacácori, including all available contemporary descriptions of both rancherías, is John L. Kessell, "Peaceful Conquest in Southern Arizona," in Fay Jackson Smith, Kessell, and Francis J. Fox, s.j., *Father Kino in Arizona* (Phoenix: Arizona Historical Foundation, 1966), pp. 53–95.

[17]Kino, "Relasion diaria de la entrada al Nordueste. . . ." AGN, Historia, 393. This Kino travel journal has been translated by Fay Jackson Smith in Smith, Kessell, and Fox, *Father Kino in Arizona,* pp. 8–29.

[18]Because "v's" and "b's" were entirely interchangeable in the Spanish documents of the time, the word Guevavi was frequently written "Guebabi," "Guebavi," or "Guevabi." It was accented on the *second* syllable, and thus, according to the rules of Spanish pronunciation, needed no written accent mark. Occasionally, just for good measure, a Padre did include the accent mark. See, for example, the facsimile of a page written by Kino reproduced as the frontispiece in Father Burrus' *Kino's Plan for the Development of Pimería Alta, Arizona and Upper California* (Tucson: Arizona Pioneers' Historical Society, 1961). For some reason Bolton and all the historians who have followed him have insisted, incorrectly, on accenting the word on the first syllable.

of His Majesty against the nomadic enemies of the province. These things they did more or less on their own terms and only intermittently. Though they celebrated more often and ate better, though they prized the new tools, crops, and animals, their day-to-day life, what they really cared about, remained much as it had always been. Not until the summer of 1701 did the people of Guevavi get a sample of what lay ahead.

As early as 1694 San Cayetano de Tumacácori, six leagues north of Guevavi, was considered a likely post for a resident Padre.[19] But when blissful young Father Francisco Xavier Saeta arrived on the frontier, he was assigned instead to more populous Caborca, where, soon after, the natives rose up and killed him.

As was so often the case, martyrdom only spurred the Jesuit advance. Like Salvatierra, Father Visitor Antonio Leal returned from a tour with Kino the promoter, convinced of the missionary potential of Pimería

Eusebio Francisco Kino

Alta. Leal, too, sought additional Padres for this neglected vineyard of the Lord, and by 1701 he had recruited four. Two he designated for service on the Río Santa María, one at San Xavier del Bac farther north, and the other, not at San Cayetano de Tumacácori, but at San Gabriel de Guevavi.

Probably Kino had discussed with the Father Visitor the relative merits of Guevavi over San Cayetano. For one thing, there now appeared to be more natives congregated at Guevavi. Where earlier, eighty or ninety souls had lived, in the spring of 1700 Kino counted two hundred. But he would not have known the difference if half of them were hungry, nonresident Pápagos in from their desert only temporarily.

Guevavi, to be sure, was more centrally located. A Padre living there could minister with little difficulty to the natives of two other village congregations on the river, San Cayetano, six leagues north, and

---

[19] Kino, "Inocente, Apostolica y Gloriosa Muerte del V. Pe. Francisco Xavier Saeta . . . 1695," Libro I, Capítulo I; photocopy, Bolton Research Papers (BRP), BL. Edited by Father Burrus, this tract appeared as *Vida del P. Francisco J. Saeta, s.j.: Sangre misionera en Sonora* (México, D.F.: Editorial Jus, 1961).

San Luis del Bacoancos, seven leagues south. Furthermore, at Los Santos Reyes de Sonoita, some five leagues to the east on Sonoita Creek, the Sobaípuri headman Captain Coro and his more than five hundred tribesmen had taken up residence, at least temporarily.[20]

These three native settlements then — San Cayetano, San Luis, and Los Reyes — would become Guevavi's *visitas,* or secondary mission villages. Guevavi itself would be designated the *cabecera,* the "head" mission village, and there the Padre would live. By the summer of 1701, it was set: like Dolores and San Ignacio and the rest, Guevavi was to become an operating Jesuit mission. "The Father for whom they asked" was on his way.

At about the same time as the summer rains, Juan de San Martín reached the Pimería. With the trails muddy and the washes aflood he was forced to lay over at mission San Ignacio, roughly sixty-five miles south of Guevavi "by the shortest route." His supplies had been packed on toward Guevavi ahead of him.

The annoying delay, however, need not have been lost time. Father Agustín de Campos, young protégé of Padre Kino, had served at San Ignacio since 1693. Whatever San Martín could get Campos to tell him about native behavior and customs was all to the good, for this was only the beginning of Father Juan's missionary career. He had crossed the Atlantic from his native province of Murcia in Spain at an early age and as a lad of eighteen or so had entered the Society of Jesus in Mexico City.[21] A dozen years of study and probation and his ordination behind him, he had requested and been granted a missionary assignment.

If only the cursed rain would let up he would get on with it. But "because nothing happens by chance as far as God is concerned," he wrote to Father Kino on June 30, 1701, "He arranged my detention so that I might receive the letter of Your Reverence and learn from it the great kindness Your Reverence shows me by offering to assist me with everything necessary for the new villages to which holy obedience summons me."[22] To a missionary just starting out, every head of livestock or cutting from a fruit tree, every ax, and every santo was a blessing.

[20] Kino, "Favores Celestiales," II, 1, III.

[21] Father San Martín was born in Caravaca, Spain, in 1670. He began his novitiate in 1688 and professed his final vows on the Sonora frontier in 1704. Alberto Francisco Pradeau and Burrus, "Los Jesuitas en Sonora," unpublished manuscript, Los Angeles, 1965.

[22] San Martín to Kino, San Ignacio, June 30, 1701, quoted in Kino, "Favores Celestiales," II, 2, XIII.

Practically nothing is known about the brief ministry of Guevavi's first resident Jesuit, except for the little Father Kino chose to tell. Did Father Campos ride up from San Ignacio to introduce San Martín to his charges? Were the Padres escorted by soldiers? How did the natives receive "the Father for whom they asked"? Were the roads cleared, were there arches of branches at the village entrance and the people lined up in two rows, was "the adobe-walled house" swept and stocked with food? Once they had seen their respective villages all four of the new missionaries, according to Kino, "were very pleased and had great hopes of building there in the interior some very flourishing missions. . . ."

With Kino's assistance, Father San Martín, it seems, got off to a good start. "At Guevavi in a few months we finished a small but neat house and church, and we laid the foundations for a large church and house." [23]

Small house and church aside, how did the people of Guevavi react to Father San Martín? Was it not a rude shock to them when the Padre did not get on his horse and ride out of their ranchería after his sermon and some refreshments? This Black Robe had come to stay.

Every day they saw him. Every day he and his assistants, likely *"Indios ladinos,"* "civilized" Yaquis or Ópatas, told them what they should and what they should not do to better themselves and their mission. Perhaps not quite yet, but the time would soon come when he who was caught participating in a cactus liquor bacchanal, no matter if it

had ceremonial significance, would be whipped. The village hechiceros cannot have been pleased when they found their magic curtailed or forbidden altogether. Yet these natives of Guevavi, whom later Jesuits accused of haughtiness, laziness, and ungratefulness, were, according to the propagandist Kino, docile, hard-working, and ever-desirous of becoming Christians.

---

[23] Kino, "Favores Celestiales," *ibid.*

Father San Martín lasted only a few months. On the evening of November 4 Kino found the Padre's house at Guevavi vacant. "On the 5th, having said Mass in the new and very neat little church that Father Juan de San Martín had built not long before (at this time His Reverence had left to restore his health), and having directed that it be roofed and whitewashed, I set out to the west. . . ." [24]

Sickness among the Jesuits of Guevavi was to become almost traditional; San Martín's case was the first of many. If he returned, it was only briefly. [25] When on February 5, 1703, Kino wrote to the viceroy, San Gabriel de Guevavi was again among villages lacking "the Fathers they hope to receive." [26]

When in the spring of 1704 Father Eusebio rode down to Guaymas, it was Father Juan de San Martín, formerly of Guevavi, who welcomed him and showed him "a thousand kindnesses" at the villages of San Francisco and La Santísima Trinidad del Pitiquín, near present-day Hermosillo. [27] For a decade or more San Martín seems to have left the frontier. But by 1726 he was back and serving as minister at Arivechi in east-central Sonora, where he remained for eleven more years and where he was accused by Father Christóbal Lauria, his immediate superior, of being a gossipmonger. On his way to Mexico City in 1737 to become Father Procurator for the province, Father Juan fell off his horse and badly injured his leg. A decade later, at the Jesuit College of Espíritu Santo in Puebla, on December 8, 1748, he died. [28]

The other missionary assigned in 1701 to the northern Pimería fared worse than San Martín. Twenty-five leagues beyond Guevavi at

[24] *Ibid.*, II, 3, II. The site of San Martín's "very neat little church" has not yet been identified.

[25] If he did come back to his first mission, Father San Martín, seeking more healthful surroundings, may have chosen to live in Tumacácori. A listing of *memorias,* annual financial statements and requests for goods, submitted by the Padres in 1702 cited one from San Cayetano. "Extracto de lo conducente á la demanda sobre Sinodos de Missiones. . . ." AGN, Misiones, 22.

[26] Burrus, *Kino's Plan,* p. 30.

[27] Kino, "Favores Celestiales," III, 3, VII and VIII.

[28] Pradeau and Burrus, "Los Jesuitas." In two vitriolic letters to the Father Provincial, San Martín seemed to be settling accounts with Father Rector Lauria and the other Italian Padres. San Martín to Father Joseph Barba, Arivechi, September 10 and November 21, 1735; Archivo Histórico de Hacienda, México, D.F. (AHH), Temporalidades (Temp.), legajo 17, microfilm, BL.

the much larger ranchería of San Xavier del Bac, young, enthusiastic Francisco Gonzalvo hoped and prayed for a bountiful harvest of souls. But he too reaped sickness, and in the hot, sticky month of August, 1702, they carried him south through Guevavi. Weak and feverish, he lay at San Ignacio in the house of Father Campos, his shipmate on the voyage from Spain. At four in the morning of August 10 he died, having done to the end "continuous acts of faith, hope, and charity." He was only twenty-nine.[29]

If the natives of Guevavi and Bac had lost their first resident Padres, they still had Kino. That fall of 1702 he rode again, presumably through Guevavi and Tumacácori on the way to begin "a very large church" at Bac, everywhere along his route "looking after the spiritual and temporal matters of the poor natives." But this was apparently his last trip to the north. Kino was now fifty-seven and slowing down.

Early the next year Father Eusebio by messenger exhorted his Pimas to go after marauding Apaches, and Father Campos promised to send to Guevavi twenty-five beef cattle to fill the warriors' bellies. Once again Kino, the Padre of Dolores, began inviting the Pimas of the north to come south and join in building and dedicating churches. Once again it was Christianity on their terms.

Eusebio Kino, foremost apostle to the Pimas, died in 1711. For nearly ten years before and twenty years after, the people of Guevavi seldom saw a Padre. The missionary frontier that had leaped forward with Kino fell back without him.

The lean years following his death might have been lost years had it not been for the labors of one man, a man whose ministry to the Pimas lasted nearly twice as long as Kino's. Not the propagandist or the promoter that the apostle was, Agustín de Campos operated persistently and effectively from mission San Ignacio, twenty-five leagues south of Guevavi.

A Spaniard born in 1669 in Sijena, province of Huesca, Campos had been a Jesuit since he was fifteen. He had sailed for the New World at age twenty-three, begun his ministry at San Ignacio at twenty-four,

---

[29] Mission San Ignacio, Libro de Entierros, 1697–1787; one of a number of Pimería Alta baptismal, marriage, and burial books "collected" by Alphonse L. Pinart and preserved today in the Bancroft Library as "Colección de Pimería Alta" (CPA).

and after eighteen years in the field was only forty-two when he buried Kino.[30]

During the early years in Pimería Alta the Jesuits relied for protection on their own devices and on the questionable allegiance of their neophytes. Military assistance, such as it was, often worked greater harm than good. Most frontier officers devoted more energy to exploiting Indians than to protecting Jesuits. Even Father Kino's frequent companion Captain Juan Matheo Manje lashed out in 1706 at the Jesuit missionary monopoly of lands and labor. The military escorts that accompanied Kino on his journeys of discovery went along less to protect the Padre than to verify, at his insistence, the Pimas' friendliness and their favorable disposition toward missionaries.

When the Pimas of Caborca murdered Father Saeta, soldiers arrived to punish the perpetrators and, as it happened, to bungle the job. The memory of their infamous slaughter of guilty and innocent alike at a place called El Tupo lived on in native tradition — and festered. A half century later, on the eve of the Pimas' bloodiest rebellion, vengeful tlatoleros could incite their fellows to kill with the cry "Remember El Tupo!"

In all the vast Pimería there was no permanent garrison, no presidio. The mobile company of Sonora, created in the early 1690s, made its headquarters at Santa Rosa de Corodéguachi, soon renamed Fronteras, about a hundred miles east and south of Guevavi. From there the soldiers, backed by Ópata and Pima auxiliaries, rode forth — all too infrequently, claimed the Jesuits[31] — to chase and only rarely to punish Apache raiders. Viceregal orders also called for periodic patrols to implant respect in the more settled natives and to encourage their loyalty, to remind them of their vassalage to the king in Spain.

---

[30] Campos, who often signed himself Joseph Agustín de Campos, served at San Ignacio until 1736, when, under most unfortunate circumstances, he was removed by his superiors. He died in July, 1737, at the Jesuit college in Chihuahua.

[31] The missionary closest to Fronteras claimed that in eight years and five months the garrison had scouted beyond the frontier only four times and waged only two "half-campaigns." It provided, as then constituted, virtually no protection. Father Ygnacio de Arzeo to Father Visitor Joseph María Genovese, Cuquiárachi, January 25, 1722; AHH, Temp., 278, microfilm, BL.

One such force dismounted at the mission of Father Campos on February 12, 1718. In command was a royal inspector, Don Antonio Bezerra Nieto, Captain of the presidio of Janos east of Fronteras. With the Padre's permission he addressed a gathering of Pimas from the north. "I offered for my part," dictated the Captain to his scribe, "to cooperate in bringing about with the least possible hardship the salvation of their souls. After several talks which I gave them so that they would persist in their faith they took their leave pleased." [32]

That many of the Pimas did persist or at least maintain contact with Christianity during the difficult years after Kino died was due not to the occasional urging of soldiers but to the continual efforts of Agustín de Campos. Almost annually Father Agustín organized expeditions reminiscent of Kino's, first to the west and then to the north. He was apparently neither geographer nor cartographer, and never did accept Kino's proof that Baja California was not an island. Nonetheless, he was, according to his co-worker Luis Xavier Velarde, eminently well prepared to save souls. One needed only to consider "his command of the native language, his saintly industry, the love and respect which the Pimas have for him, the various other means of conversion dictated by his prudence, zeal, and experience, and the knowledge he has of the Indians." [33] After Kino's death, when the people of Guevavi felt the urge for a change of scene or were hungry, they came to Campos and were baptized and married and fed.

Though nothing seemed farther from the Pimería than the issue of whether or not a Bourbon should sit on the Spanish throne, dynastic wars cost mighty sums of money. And when the Spanish treasury suf-

---

[32]Archivo de Hidalgo del Parral; photocopy, BRP. Bezerra Nieto was conducting an inspection of Sonora as *juez visitador general*. For a biographical sketch, see Francisco R. Almada, *Diccionario de Historia, Geografía y Biografía Sonorenses* (Chihuahua: Ruiz Sandoval, 1952), pp. 108–109.

[33]Velarde, Nuestra Señora de los Dolores, May 30, 1716; AGN, Historia, 393. Father Velarde's *relación* was incorporated by Juan Matheo Manje in his "Libro Segundo. Luz de Tierra Yncógnita. . . ." and forms most of Chapters 9, 10, and 11 of that work, along with various editorial observations by Manje. Separately, Velarde's relación was translated by Rufus Kay Wyllys as "Padre Luís Velarde's *Relación* of Pimería Alta, 1716," *New Mexico Historical Review (NMHR),* Vol. VI (1931), pp. 111–57; and with the second part of Manje's *Luz* by Harry J. Karns and associates as *Unknown Arizona and Sonora, 1693–1721* (Tucson: Arizona Silhouettes, 1954), pp. 221–67.

fered, missionary reinforcements to non-strategic areas were a long time coming.

Campos carried on without them. Between 1716 and 1720 he baptized 1,004 souls "most of them children at the breast, others up to twelve years of age, and fewer adults." During the same period Father Velarde, who succeeded Kino at Dolores, Remedios, and Cocóspera, but who apparently did not often trek much farther afield, welcomed his share of visitors from the north. "I have baptized sixty-six children belonging to these three villages, and one hundred and twenty-nine from other rancherías nearby to the north and from missions where there used to be Fathers."

So few Padres and so many heathens. Campos did admit that the native population of the Pimería was being "notably lessened" because of killing Old-World diseases. Many of the children he baptized on one expedition were dead by the next, carried off during epidemics of measles, smallpox, or typhus. If such plagues ravaged the Pimas in Father Kino's day — and there is no reason to believe they did not — the positive-thinking apostle kept the fact to himself.

Campos and Velarde dutifully concentrated on the spiritual salvation of the young and the infirm. There simply was not enough time to catechize healthy adults. "May God Our Lord favor us with the needed workers," prayed Father Agustín, "and me, now at age fifty-one, with the needed strength, mine having been somewhat broken by twenty-seven years in the Pimería."[34]

In 1720 two of the needed workers arrived, both Sicilians and both named Luis María — Fathers Gallardi and Marciano. Soon thereafter, the sound of hammers and saws was heard again in the west along the Altar Valley at Tubutama and Caborca. Meanwhile, "in eager anticipation" of one thing or another, the Pimas of the north continued to

---

[34] Campos, San Ignacio, September 9, 1720; Velarde, Dolores, September 10, 1720; printed in Francisco Javier Alegre, s.j., *Historia de la Provincia de la Compañía de Jesús de Nueva España,* ed. Burrus and Félix Zubillaga, s.j., 4 vols. (Roma: Institutum Historicum Societatis Jesu, 1956–60), IV, pp. 504–507. Father Velarde was born on August 25, 1677, in Valladolid, Castilla, Spain. He entered the Society of Jesus on April 20, 1697. Apparently he did not arrive in Pimería Alta until two years after the death of Father Kino, and thus never met the man he eulogized so earnestly. Velarde professed his final vows before Father Campos at Opodepe on March 25, 1715. Still in charge at Dolores he died there on December 2, 1737. Pradeau and Burrus, "Los Jesuitas."

range south. At Ímuris, near San Ignacio, on January 17, 1722, Father Agustín first baptized and then joined in Christian marriage María and Ignacio of Guevavi. For two of the children baptized that day Tumacá-cori's native captain was godfather. When the Padre felt up to it, he carried these services north to them.

At the head of an entourage of native officials, *justicias* they were called, and other helpers, and accompanied by Fray Joseph Durán de la Peña, "a lay brother of the Order of Saint Hippolytus,"[35] Campos rode into Guevavi on March 5, 1722, and proceeded to baptize *sin solemnidad*

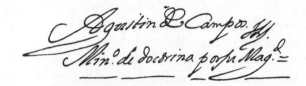

eighteen children. If Father San Martín's neat little church had crumbled and the wheatfields were overgrown, if the other signs of civilization had faded, still not all was forgotten. Salvador called himself alcalde, and Jacinto was mador.

Next day Father Agustín's party, swelled by natives from Guevavi and the other rancherías, trooped along the river to San Cayetano de Tumacácori. In that village on the half-moon-shaped bend twenty-seven more infants were baptized and named for Christian saints. As godfathers the native governors of both Guevavi and San Cayetano took part in the rite. Word raced ahead of the Padre. At San Xavier del Bac, twenty-five leagues farther north, delegations were gathering. They came from as near as San Augustín de Tucsón and as far as Casa Grande. Nearly a hundred children lined up for baptism. That rewarding task done "in the name of the Father, the Son, and the Holy Ghost" and good words spoken, the caravan now doubled back along the river trail to a point several leagues north of Tumacácori. From there Campos led

---

[35] The Order of Saint Hippolytus, or Order of Charity, grew out of the philanthropy of a pious Spaniard in mid-sixteenth-century Mexico. It was best known for its hospitals and sanitariums in the cities. See Mariano Cuevas, s.j., *Historia de la Iglesia en México,* 4 vols. (I-III, Tlalpan, D.F.: Asilo "Patricio Sanz," 1921–24; IV, Santa Julia, D.F.: Colegio Salesiano, 1926), II, pp. 446–50; III, pp. 331–33. What a lay brother of this order was doing on the distant Pima frontier is a good question.

them off to the southwest through Sopori and Arivaca to Tucubavia, where thirty-one years before some small wooden crosses had so impressed Father Visitor Salvatierra.[36]

"Because of the sicknesses which are spreading and the smallpox which is already on its way," wrote Campos in San Ignacio's book of baptisms, "I left this mission of San Ignacio on February 24 to visit my children of the north. . . ." Four days later he was at Guevavi, apparently ahead of the scourge. Through holy baptism he insured nineteen more children against death without hope. The year was 1724.[37]

Since his last visit Father Campos, like Kino, had ridden the six hundred leagues to Mexico City and back again — 3,000 miles in all — to explain certain rash and "intemperate" letters he had written to his Father Visitor and, while there, to further as best he could the cause of Pimería Alta.[38] He had explained to his superiors the urgent need for more Padres, and he had listened to their excuses. He had suggested in a report to the viceroy that a Spanish colony and one-hundred-man presidio be planted on the lower Gila. Kino, too, had advocated a town at this spot, which he called San Dionisio. It would serve as a link with California. To secure the Gila, furthermore, would have been to secure the northern Pimería. And from its banks upstream, the Black Robes could more easily penetrate the apostate Moqui, or Hopi, pueblos.[39] Kino would have been pleased.

Taking yet another page from his mentor's book, Campos summoned to San Ignacio in September, 1726, as impressive an assemblage

---

[36] Mission San Ignacio, Libro de Bautismos, 1720–1762; CPA.

[37] *Ibid.* Again traveling as far north as Bac, Campos then rode east to the San Pedro and south through the Sobaípuri rancherías. In all, he traveled 160 leagues, some 400 miles.

[38] Campos left San Ignacio on April 9, 1722, and returned on May 24, 1723. Fathers Marciano and Gallardi signed entries in the mission books during his absence. *Ibid.* Father Joseph Toral to Barba, Guépaca, March 25, 1736; W. B. Stephens Collection (WBS), Latin American Collection, University of Texas Library, Austin, 1747, ff. 25–34.

[39] Campos to the viceroy, México, January 24, 1723; AGN, Historia, 308. As early as 1711 and 1712, it seems, the Hopis had expressed to Campos through intervening tribes their preference for Black Robes. Not long after, Captain Bezerra Nieto had begun to recommend in earnest that the Jesuits accept the Hopis' offer. A royal cédula of February 11, 1719, decreed it. John A. Donohue, s.j., "Jesuit Missions in Northwestern New Spain, 1711–1767," unpublished Ph.D. dissertation, University of California, Berkeley, 1957, p. 13; Alegre, *Historia de la Compañía,* IV, pp. 308–309. For nearly half a century the feasibility of Jesuit missions among the Hopis was considered and reconsidered. Though several Jesuits set out from Pimería Alta to reach the Hopi pueblos none is known to have arrived there.

of northern Pimas as he could. They were going, he told them, to call upon a very important and holy man, one who could perhaps acquire Padres for them, not to mention food and gifts. Benito Crespo, Bishop of Durango, out on a heroic visitation of his immense domain, would not soon forget the sight of the dusty black-robed Campos trooping into the mining town of Motepore at the head of these colorful, obedient savages, "more than seventy" of them. The immediate need for Jesuit missionaries to the Pimas had never been so apparent to the Bishop. The Hopis could wait.[40]

The early 1720s were years of strife in Sonora; the Jesuits and an element of the military and civilian populace were at it again. Chief detractor of the Padres, and consequently their chief target, was the grafter Don Gregorio Álvarez Tuñón y Quirós, Captain of the garrison at Fronteras. He and his associates, apparently hopeful of a massive land grab and cheap Indian labor, petitioned to have the Jesuits removed and their missions secularized. Other men of Sonoran affairs rallied to the defense of the embattled Padres and an uneasy impasse resulted.[41] Not until late 1726 when the military Inspector General, Don Pedro de Rivera, reformed the presidio of Fronteras and ousted Don Gregorio did the missionaries breathe easier. The presidio's new Captain, Don Juan Bautista de Anza, was a staunch friend of the frontier Padres, as was his more famous son and namesake after him.

Meanwhile, in higher circles the Inspector General's frank praise of the Jesuit missionary effort in Sonora both scotched the talk of secularization and lent weight to the pleas for more Padres.[42] From Durango, Bishop Benito Crespo urged the Viceroy and the Father Provincial to send three additional ministers to Pimería Alta, even volunteering to underwrite the expense himself. When New World functionaries did not move fast enough for the Bishop, he sat down and wrote to the King. He described for His Majesty the delegation of heathens led out

---

[40] The Bishop inspected the records of Mission San Ignacio at San Antonio de Motepore on September 19, 1726. San Ignacio, Bautismos. The favorable effect of Campos' meeting with the Bishop is described by Donohue, "Jesuit Missions," pp. 22–23.

[41] The Jesuits' side of the controversy is well aired in AHH, Temp., 278. See also Donohue, "Jesuit Missions," pp. 38–49.

[42] Rivera to the Marqués de Casafuerte, Janos, February 14, 1727; WBS, 1747, ff. 21–24. Donohue, "Jesuit Missions," pp. 78, 104.

of the north by Campos, their desire for conversion, and the pitiful lack of missionaries to instruct them. Apparently the Bishop was convincing.[43]

Spain had emerged from the war of succession shorn of her European holdings, humiliated but better off. Internally she was more unified and externally less involved. Her new Bourbon king, Philip V, with the aid of French, Italian, and even Spanish advisers had begun to clear away the clutter left by the last Hapsburgs. José Patiño reformed the navy. Efforts were made to tie the empire more securely to the mother country. Despite fiascos in Italy and at Gibraltar, Spain seemed to come to life. There was a renewed feeling of assertiveness, a feeling that the age of Spain had not yet passed. If there were not enough Jesuits to secure the place called Pimería Alta, why were there not?

While the case for more missionaries was considered by the king's ministers, Fathers Campos and Velarde carried on as usual. During Holy Week of 1726, Campos on his way to the Gila paused to christen twenty-five natives at Tumacácori before a gathering of their kin. Just north of San Cayetano at a pleasant place on the river the Padre and his following took a siesta. Here, because another baby was brought forward for baptism, Father Campos recorded the name of the ranchería, perhaps for the first time. Tubac, it was called.[44] In less than a generation a garrison of His Majesty's troops would preempt this place and the name Tubac would be heard in Madrid.

To keep the heathens of the north coming to his villages, Father Velarde ordered from Mexico City a supply of gifts.[45] Between November 1, 1725, and April 20, 1729, he reported that "57 marriages have been celebrated *in facie ecclesiae* for the natives from the villages of Santa María and Guevavi and their adjacent rancherías. From the same villages and rancherías and others farther into the interior whose people frequent our villages from the end of November until the end of January,

[43] Royal cédula, Madrid, October 10, 1728; translated in George P. Hammond, "Pimería Alta after Kino's Time," *NMHR*, Vol. IV (1929), pp. 225–27.

[44] San Ignacio, Bautismos. Campos went on to San Xavier del Bac where he baptized forty-nine persons on Good Friday, April 19, and twelve more on Saturday, and where presumably he observed Easter Sunday. During the following week he reached the Gila, which he left on April 28 to return to his mission. On March 15, 1728, he baptized eighteen children at the ranchería of San Luis. Governor Francisco of Guevavi was *padrino* for at least two of them.

[45] Donohue, "Jesuit Missions," p. 108.

276 children have been baptized, most of whom have died of measles, but with the grace of baptism." With an escort of Pimas to protect him from roaming Apaches, Velarde planned to visit Santa María, Guevavi, and various other rancherías after Easter, "God willing."[46]

The long-awaited royal cédulas were dated October 10, 1728. In due course these gave rise to the Viceroy's instructions of April 27, 1730. "For the conversion of those heathen Indians to our holy Catholic Faith and for their education, three missions are to be erected and planted in northern Pimería Alta and entrusted to three religious of the Sacred Company of Jesus."[47]

Back in Europe a "mission" of twenty-six Jesuits was being assembled. They came from various parts of Germany, Italy, and Spain, recruited by a superior who was to act as their shepherd on the long trip and whose responsibility it was to submit accurate expense accounts to royal officials for lodging, supplies, and travel. Once they were gathered in Spain the eager missionaries-to-be resided in the large Jesuit hospice in Sevilla or at the Puerto de Santa María on the Bay of Cádiz where a spacious new house was being constructed specifically for Jesuits awaiting passage to the Spanish Indies. In some cases they were forced to wait several years for space on a ship sailing with the convoyed fleet. The foreigners utilized this delay to improve their Spanish, while all of them joined in developing skills they thought would prove useful in the missions. The Croatian Ratkay, who had waited with Kino, recalled that at Sevilla:

> We studied not only astronomy, mathematics, and other interesting
> fields of knowledge, but we ourselves made all sorts of trinkets and

---

[46] Velarde, "Cathologo de esta Mission de N.ª S.ra de los Dolores Nueva Conversion de Pimas Altos desde 1.º de Nov.re de 1725, en q. fue el ultimo, hasta la fha del presente," Dolores, April 20, 1729; AHH, Temp., 17. Velarde to Father Rector Marcos de Somoza, Cocóspera, March 15, 1729; *ibid*.

[47] El Marqués de Casafuerte, México, April 27, 1730; *ibid*.

worked at practical things. Some of us made compasses or sun-dials and others cases for them; this one sewed clothes and furs, that one learned how to make bottles, another how to solder tin; one busied himself with distilling, a second with the lathe, a third with the art of sculptoring; so that with those goods and skills we might gain the good will of the wild heathen and the more easily give them the truths of the Christian faith.[48]

Before they were allowed to embark each and every one of the Jesuits was ordered to appear before a board of examiners. It was standard procedure for preparing the detailed passenger list. Along with other information, a physical description of each man — forerunner of modern passport photos — was required. "We arrived quite early," wrote a German Padre,

and were lined up before the board. At a table sat several gentlemen who looked us over from head to foot. Each was asked to state his name and nationality, also his rank, whether priest or lay brother, how far he had advanced in his studies, and so on, all this being duly noted down on paper by the secretary. Next we were again stared at for a time by all of them, so that our lineaments and stature could be carefully described, to the end that no imposter might embark and thus illegally reach the Indies. I could hardly contain my laughter as these gentlemen so gravely regarded us and dictated to the scribe our entire physiognomies. . . . No butcher stares at a calf as these men looked at us.[49]

When His Majesty's ship *La Potencia,* alias *El Blandón,* put out to sea in 1730 they were aboard, all twenty-six of them, Spaniards and foreigners alike. The kings of Spain had been amply rewarded in the past for permitting foreign Jesuits to labor in the vast missionary fields of their empire. There were even those who claimed that the *extranjeros* made better missionaries than did the Spaniards themselves. When conflict arose within the order between the various national groups, as

---

[48] Father Ratkay quoted in Theodore E. Treutlein, "Jesuit Travel to New Spain (1678–1756)," *MA,* Vol. XIX (1937), p. 111.

[49] Treutlein, ed. and trans., *Missionary in Sonora: The Travel Reports of Joseph Och, s.j., 1755–1767* (San Francisco: California Historical Society, 1965), p. 17. A copy of the list of twenty-six Jesuits comprising the mission of 1730 is in the Archivo General de Indias, Sevilla, Spain (AGI), Contratación, legajo 5550; transcript, BRP.

occasionally it did, the Jesuits were usually able to keep it to themselves. If during their trying voyage the Italians got on the Germans' nerves or the Germans irked the Spaniards, surely all of them joined on the Day of the Purification of the Blessed Virgin, February 2, 1731, in joyous thanksgiving as *La Potencia* sailed into Havana harbor beneath the protective guns of El Morro.

In April the group crossed over to tropical, unhealthful Vera Cruz, where one of their number noted that the name bore a certain ironic aptness:

> I do not know why the Spaniards have called this city *Vera Cruz,* though it bears [the name] with full right, for the uncomfortable situation, the unhealthy air, the always unfriendly sky, stormy wind, sickness, especially the "black vomit" and the "cramps," allow little happiness to the inhabitants.... We see many corpses being carried to the grave and we are told that of the strangers — crews of ships and merchants — who come in numbers from Europe on regular business, hardly half get away with their lives to their home country. So dangerous and harmful is the hot air.[50]

They were not sorry to take their leave of Vera Cruz and begin the climb on muleback to México, metropolis of the New World.

When they had been in the capital only a short time, hardly long enough to see the impressive sights, three of the Jesuit reinforcements — one Swiss, one Moravian, and an Austrian — "the most zealous for the well-being of souls," were designated by their new Father Provincial for duty in the Pimería. Theirs was to be a challenging assignment, he may have told them, but the harvest of souls was potentially very great. Each was to receive the customary royal gift of vestments and altar furnishings for the church he would build in the wilderness. With trunks packed and transportation arranged, the three rode north from the city of México hundreds of leagues in the summer heat of mid-June, 1731. The roads to Durango were excellent: they might have ridden in a coach, had they felt they could afford such luxury.

Actually, four Jesuits arrived in Durango to meet and to confer

---

[50] Father Konschak quoted in Treutlein, "Jesuit Travel," *MA,* XIX, p. 121. For an exceptionally graphic description of the arrival of the annual fleet at Vera Cruz, see Leonard, *Baroque Times,* pp. 1–5.

with their patron, Bishop Benito Crespo. Father Gaspar Stiger was on his way to a mission among the lean Tarahumaras. The others, Phelipe Segesser, who had not been feeling well, Ignacio Xavier Keller, and Juan Bautista Grazhoffer, with the Bishop's special blessing set out on the second half of their journey in August, bound for the Pimería. Now the roads got worse.

Following the Camino Real north to the mining center of Parral, the little group of foreigners probably took the more westerly alternate, skirting the Sierra Madres through Satevó and Cusihuiriáchic in Tarahumara country, thence to Casas Grandes and the presidio of Janos. Due west they rode now to Fronteras, where Captain Anza almost certainly extended the weary trio a warm welcome. A half day's ride beyond, at the Ópata mission of Cuquiárachi, their superiors were waiting. There on October 7, 1731, they met Father Visitor Christóbal de Cañas, Father Rector Luis María Gallardi, and "the two eldest missionaries," doubtless the enduring Spaniards Campos and Velarde.

After the amenities and considerable discussion on the part of their seniors, the untried arrivals were matched with vacant missions. At Guevavi, San Xavier del Bac, and Santa María Soamca, they were told, hardship and the crudest conditions would be their lot. Nearly three decades without resident Padres had gone far toward obliterating the beginnings so carefully nurtured in those places by Father Kino.[51] Because the dwellings built during his time were now so dilapidated, it was decided that each of the newcomers should spend several months at the mission of a veteran learning what he could of the Pimas' language and of their ways. While the long-overdue reinforcements were thus engaged, Captain Anza personally supervised the building of a small house and the planting of a plot of wheat at each of their assigned posts.[52]

The natives of Guevavi grown used to Christianity on their terms were in for a change.

---

[51] For a comment on the deterioration of the northern missions after Kino's time, see Miguel Venegas, s.j., *Noticia de la California, y de su conquista temporal y espiritual,* ed. Andrés Marcos Burriel, s.j. 3 vols. (Madrid, 1757), II, p. 524.

[52] Father Christóbal de Cañas, *et al.,* to Bishop Benito Crespo, Pimería Alta, July 31, 1732, certified copy, Durango, November 19, 1733; AGI, Audiencia de Guadalajara (Guad.), legajo 135; microfilm, BL. A translation of another copy of the above is included in Hammond, "Pimería Alta," *NMHR,* IV, pp. 227–35.

*"Through a skilled interpreter he delivered to more than a
thousand Pimas who gathered [at Guevavi] that day ... a
pious and effective oration explaining to them the cause,
purpose, and motive of his coming."*

Father Christóbal de Cañas, *et al.,* 1732

3.

The Padres Come to Stay
From Grazhoffer to Torres Perea, 1732-1744

TALL AND BROWN-HAIRED, his face pitted with pockmarks, Johann
Baptist Grazhoffer the Austrian, now in his forty-second year, was
finally going to see his vow fulfilled.[1] Within the week he would be
a practicing missionary, on his own *entre infieles,* among infidels, in
every sense of the term. Presumably he now knew that Guevavi meant
"big spring" in their language. He had for several months served as
apprentice to Father Rector Gallardi at Tubutama. Having recovered
from a "fever" that nearly killed him, he was, in the spring of 1732, fit
and anxious to begin his ministry.

At "the place called Quino" they rendezvoused — Fathers Grazhoffer, Segesser, and Keller, Captain Anza, a military escort, the native
captain general of the Pimas, and assorted mixed-breeds and Indians.[2]

---

[1] Grazhoffer, a native of Bleiburg, Carinthia, in extreme southern Austria, was born on
June 5, 1690. He was admitted to the Society of Jesus on October 27, 1710, and professed his
final solemn vows at Commotau in Bohemia on February 2, 1728. Alegre, *Historia de la
Compañía,* IV, p. 353, n. 33; Pradeau and Burrus, "Los Jesuitas." Determined to serve as
a missionary among heathens, Father Johann left Commotau on May 12, 1729, presumably
traveling overland to Genoa, and from there sailing across to Spain. AGI, Contratación, 5550.

[2] Cañas, *et al.,* to the Bishop, July 31, 1732.

[45]

Lashed to pack rigs on the backs of stamping mules the Padres' baggage reflected the hopes they held for the months and years ahead. There were carpenter's axes and blacksmith's tongs, magnificent damask vestments in the five colors, sickles and pruning hooks, and silver vessels for the altar.[3] Perhaps the pleas of Father Visitor Cañas for alms from the established missionaries in Sonora had begun to bear fruit — a broken-down mule, a few baskets of wheat, some peach-tree cuttings, a whipsaw, a heavy iron griddle; they could use them all.

In the early dawn of May 3 they celebrated Mass. The day likely was clear and dry; one had the feeling it was going to be hot. Even the first rays of the sun were warm to the skin. Above the voice of the celebrant, those who knelt to receive Communion could hear the cooing of the white-winged dove.

If one of them preached that morning he had no difficulty choosing a theme, for it was the feast of the Finding of the Holy Cross, "the glorious standard that we desired to plant in fields so barbarous and uncultivated."[4] Then, out of the milling, groaning animals, the yelling muleteers, those persons who mumbled their prayers and those who swore, somehow the Captain formed an expedition. For God and for king, the missionary reconquest of the northern Pimería had begun.

If drawn on a map the river on which all three of their missions were located resembled a giant fishhook. From its point in the Huachuca Mountains it extended south past the village of Santa María Soamca,[5] below which it began a big bend westward, then straightened up to push its long shank north by Guevavi and San Xavier del Bac to the Gila. Father Kino had called it the Río Santa María, presumably giving to it the name of the first major ranchería by which it flowed. Five years after Kino's death, however, Father Velarde termed it an unnamed arroyo. Throughout most of the eighteenth century sections of it were given local names — Río de Soamca, Río de Guevavi, Río de Tubac — but

---

[3]All of these items were listed on inventories of the scant wealth of Guevavi and Bac compiled five years later. See Appendix II.

[4]Cañas, *et al.,* to the Bishop, July 31, 1732.

[5]Also spelled Suamca, Soanca, Suanca, etc. Father Kino seems to have called the same ranchería Santa María de Bugota. Today the village of Santa Cruz occupies nearly the same site.

Approaching the Santa Cruz River near Guevavi

apparently not until the late 1780s when the presidio of Santa Cruz replaced the abandoned mission of Santa María did the cartographers begin to apply to it its present name — the Santa Cruz.

In early May earth colors still dominated the scene through which they passed. Tan, dry grass covered the hills. The ground was reddish brown and strewn with rocks. It was dusty. As members of the reconquering expedition of 1732 approached the river somewhat south of Guevavi, they could see a meandering green column of cottonwoods and willows before they glimpsed the shallow running water that sustained it. Building missions along this river's banks, the Padres may have concluded prematurely, would surely not be so difficult or unpleasant.

Their coming was heralded. Hundreds of Pimas flocked in to Guevavi to see the show. They were painted and wore "blankets and feathers." On the fourth of May the reconquering expedition made its grand entry into the village. As his future charges clamored for gifts, Father Grazhoffer may have looked around this clearing atop the small mesa and tried to visualize the mission he would build here. With any luck at all — he would have called it divine providence — a fine adobe house and chapel would soon replace the makeshift shelter, and where the plot of wheat was coming up mission fields and orchards would yield plentiful harvests for his neophytes. Whether the ruins of San Martín's little church stood nearby, a reminder of earlier beginnings, has not been determined. But apparently from the time of Father Juan Bautista Grazhoffer, for the next forty years mission "Los Santos Ángeles Gabriel y Raphael de Guevavi o Gusutaqui" occupied this one site atop a rise on the east bank of the river.[6]

Father Kino had called Guevavi San Gabriel. Father Grazhoffer now added San Rafael. Still another Jesuit, a dozen years later, began calling the mission San Miguel. Over the years then, all three of the

---

[6] If ever a specific report by Captain Anza describing the improvements he made at Guevavi, Bac, and Soamca is found, it may well provide clues tying the Kino-era sites to the post-1732 sites. Writing in 1737, Anza recalled sending such reports to the viceroy. He hinted, however, that for the purpose of "giving him an account of the sites and locations of the missions, the number of their Indians, and their suitability for subsistence," he had merely forwarded the report of Father Visitor Cañas, *et al.*, which he, too, had co-signed. Anza to the viceroy, Corodéguachi [Fronteras], January 14, 1737; AGI, Guad. 185, microfilm, BL; translated by Donald Rowland in "A Project for Exploration Presented by Juan Bautista de Anza," *Arizona Historical Review (Ariz HR)*, Vol. VII (1936), pp. 10–18.

principal archangels — Los Santos Ángeles — were invoked to protect and nurture this mission among the Pimas. But even at that, it did not prosper. The Pima name "Gusutaqui," meaning "big water," evidently was first recorded by Captain Juan Matheo Manje in 1699. In the years to come it was to appear and reappear as a synonym for Guevavi.[7]

Captain Anza, mindful of the natives' love of pageantry, formally introduced to them their new Padre with all the pomp and dignity circumstances would allow. A symbolic replanting of the Holy Cross and the firing of muskets were appropriate to the occasion. The natives reciprocated with races, dancing, and singing. Then,

> through a skillful interpreter the Captain delivered to more than a thousand Pimas who gathered that day from its cabecera and visitas a pious and effective oration explaining to them the cause, purpose, and motive of his coming, which was to present to them, in the name of the king our lord, Philip V, whom God guard, a Father Minister to teach and impress upon them Christian obligations, to baptize their children and instruct adults so that they might gain the same benefit and partake of the rest of the services offered, as do the natives in the other missions. At this all showed great happiness and offered to be prompt and obedient.[8]

It was next the turn of "Don" Eusebio Aquibissani, native "captain general of all the Pimas," who harangued his brethren "with energy and authority." Yet the people of Guevavi may have resented Don Eusebio, namesake of Father Kino. They were not used to having someone from another village tell them how to behave, even if he was a Pima. But the Spaniards, the conquerors, were indisposed to wait while a

---

[7] In 1699 Gusutaqui may have been a smaller ranchería two leagues north of Guevavi at the mouth of Sonoita Creek in the vicinity of a later visita called Calabazas. But because of Manje's ambiguous statement, "we arrived at the ranchería of Guevavi or Gusutaqui, to which they give the name because here the river is joined by another stream," the word hung on as a synonym for Guevavi. See Smith, Kessell, and Fox, *Father Kino*, p. 81.

[8] Cañas, *et al.*, to the Bishop, July 31, 1732. About the copy of this report that he translated Dr. Hammond commented, "There are some obvious copyist's errors in the manuscript, but they are not especially significant...." "Pimería Alta," *NMHR*, IV, p. 225. One such error concerned the number of Pimas present at Grazhoffer's installation. Dr. Hammond's copy read "more than ten," certainly not enough to brag about. From the AGI copy it is apparent that *more than a thousand* attended. Nine hundred and ninety Pimas surely add up to an error of significance.

hundred separate village councils met and discussed a course of action. Instead they elevated a single Indian and told him what to do. That they bestowed upon Don Eusebio the military title "captain general," rather than the civilian title "governor," is indicative of what the Spaniards wanted from the Pimas as a nation — a fighting buffer against the Apaches. If the system also engendered personal ambition among a people whose tradition had guarded against it, that could not be helped. Thus twenty years later, another captain general, Don Luis, would pervert the power given him, and make the conquerors pay.

Because Francisco of Guevavi was an old, capable, and "active" Christian, who was also popular, he was allowed to retain his baton of authority as governor of Guevavi. When the lesser justicias had been appointed and the natives admonished again, the Captain gave the order to mount up. "Leaving Father Juan in possession, we set out for San Xavier, twenty-two leagues to the north."[9]

Like San Martín a generation earlier, Grazhoffer had come to Guevavi to stay. If he did not tread lightly, he should have, for he was by no means among friends. His charges, inconstant at best, were curious, not convinced. When they realized he was moving in, some among them, particularly the hechiceros, showed open hostility toward him. In God's time, he thought at first, even they might be won over.

If he had read a description of the Pimas by Father Kino, Father Grazhoffer soon must have questioned whether these were truly the same Indians. Kino failed to mention their drunkenness, their orgies, their plural wives. But then he had every reason not to. Only by convincing the authorities that these Indians were docile, hard-working, and eager to become Christians could he save the Pimas for the missionary. Only by countering reports that they were vicious, untrustworthy, and reprobate could he protect them from the secular exploiters. Kino wrote about the Pimas only what served his purpose. If he could not praise the characteristics that made them Indians, he could stress those qualities that a European would appreciate. Kino was a propagandist, not an anthropologist. By deliberately misrepresenting the Pimas he was, in a sense, doing a disservice to the missionaries who came later. Yet, but for Kino, they might never have come at all.

---

[9] Cañas, *et al.*, to the Bishop, July 31, 1732. San Xavier was more usually given to be twenty-four or twenty-five leagues north of Guevavi.

Father Grazhoffer's task at Guevavi was infinitely more difficult than Kino's had been. Grazhoffer had to confront the customs of the people, he had to oppose and to destroy if he could whatever obstructed their conversion to Christianity. Because he did not come among them as a guest bearing gifts but instead moved in as the new authority in the village, only once did he experience the spontaneous excitement, the celebrations, the dancing and singing all night. Afterwards, the people grew sullen. The visits of Kino and Campos had led them to believe that Christianity involved little more than a few symbolic gestures, in turn for which they always received steel knives or bright ribbon. Now, as Father Grazhoffer's Ópata or Yaqui assistants moved among them telling them what to do, the natives of Guevavi resented it.

At Grazhoffer's bidding a small physical plant began to take shape. Thanks to Captain Anza he already had a "little house," modest though it must have been. Nearby the natives built for him a sturdy, well-roofed ramada beneath which he had the altar set in place. During services it provided shade for him, for Francisco, and for some of the other justicias, but the majority of his congregation stood around outside. Such was the cabecera or seat of his mission. Beyond lay four specified visitas, representing some changes from the day of San Martín — Sonoita a half day's ride to the northeast, Arivaca a greater distance to the west, Tumacácori six leagues north downriver, and Tubac a league beyond Tumacácori. In all, he estimated that his mission contained "something over 1,400 souls,"[10] in which figure he may or may not have included a guess at the number of heathens living in dozens of unnamed, movable rancherías scattered over the vastness surrounding him.

South of Guevavi in what came to be called the San Luis Valley, Spaniards and mixed-bloods had settled the fertile big bend of the river, evidently preempting the lands around the mission's former visita of San Luis del Bacoancos. Prominent among them was Don Nicholás Romero, who had arrived, he claimed, in the early 1720s.[11] Others may have preceded him.[12] These frontiersmen were *gente de razón*, that is, free and rational persons subject to the laws of the land and to the jurisdiction

----

[10]*Ibid.*

[11] Testifying in 1752, Romero said he had settled in that area some thirty years before. San Ignacio, February 25, 1752; Ortiz Parrilla testimonies, Quaderno 8, AGI, Guad., 419, microfilm, BL, more fully cited below in Chapter IV, note 14.

[12] A member of the Romo de Vivar family seems to have operated a stock ranch at San Lázaro even before the coming of Father Kino. Bolton, *Rim of Christendom,* p. 358, n. 2.

and tithe of the secular clergy. They were, in other words, not wards of a mission. But because they lived so far from the nearest secular priest, the settlers and their families turned for spiritual needs to the missionary of Guevavi. Most of the time, it seems, he welcomed their presence. It was a comfort to him, knowing that he was not entirely alone among heathens on the Pima frontier.

Few details of Grazhoffer's initial successes and failures are known. Thirteen to fourteen leagues southeast of him Father Keller struggled to survive at Santa María Soamca. "All I received," Keller recalled some years later,

> were uncivilized and scattered Indians. I had the winds to breathe, with nothing more for sustenance. I had the open country in which to sleep, with no cover but the heavens.... My neophytes had no oxen, nor did they know how to plow, until two years later when I acquired four.... Because of the lack of provisions I was not able to go ahead with the building of a church, not even a house. Thus I persevered living for years in a straw-thatched hut like the natives, sustaining myself and them on the alms I would go out to beg for, and devoting to them the annual stipend with which His Majesty (whom God guard) favors us.[13]

Father Grazhoffer left Guevavi temporarily in mid-summer. He had never known such heat in Germany. Sweating, he rode the twenty-five leagues to San Ignacio to join with his brothers in observing the feast day of Ignatius Loyola, July 31. On that special day the three new missionaries together concluded an account of their progress to date in the northern Pimería. Fathers Cañas and Gallardi, and Captain Anza co-signed as witnesses. The result was propaganda that would have done justice to the pen of Father Kino — none of the hardship, none of the disillusionment, only the prospects of a glorious harvest of souls. But how else could they show their appreciation to that pious gentleman, the Bishop of Durango, their patron?[14]

As guests at San Ignacio of aging Father Campos, then in the thirty-ninth year of his ministry to the Pimas, the assembled Jesuits

---

[13]Keller to Father Visitor Joseph de Utrera, Soamca, November 30, 1754; Biblioteca Nacional, México, D.F. (BNMex), carpeta 46/724. This and succeeding documents cited in BNMex are on microfilm belonging to Father Norman M. Whalen, Benson, Arizona.

[14]Cañas, *et al.*, to the Bishop, July 31, 1732.

satisfied their annual obligation to perform the Spiritual Exercises of Saint Ignatius, which amounted to an eight-day retreat. While there they may also have read and acknowledged the latest decrees of the Holy Office of the Inquisition, another annual requirement. Thereby refreshed and edified, Fathers Grazhoffer and Keller returned to their crude missions. Phelipe Segesser, whom Campos referred to as "the ragamuffin native of Lucerne," stayed on to look after the crusty veteran, who was suffering at the time from "a persistent kind of dysentery." For the next several months Segesser seemed to divide his time between San Ignacio and San Xavier, fifty leagues apart, no doubt passing back and forth through Guevavi.[15]

Late the following spring Segesser rode into the village to find Grazhoffer languishing. From Guevavi on May 1, 1733, Father Phelipe wrote to one of his brothers, apparently in Genoa.[16] The circumstances of Father Juan Bautista's sickness were unusual, and serious. His condition grew worse. Then on May 26, in Segesser's arms, Guevavi's Padre died. When the body was buried, and Grazhoffer's "innocent soul was delivered up to its precious Creator," Segesser accused the natives of murder. They had poisoned their missionary, "a fact which they later admitted."[17]

But the mystery surrounding Father Grazhoffer's death did not end there. In a cursory report written "a few years" later, the following comment appeared: "Juan Bautista Grazhoffer, deceased, whose cadaver was preserved fresh because the place of his burial was extremely moist."[18] Fresh or not, Guevavi's Padre was dead.

---

[15] San Ignacio, Bautismos. Segesser performed baptisms at San Ignacio during every month from July, 1732, through March, 1733, when Campos apparently recovered.

[16] A whole series of letters written home to Europe by the observant Father Segesser, from the time he embarked for the New World until his death in Ures, Sonora, in 1762, has been preserved in the Segesser von Brunegg family archive in Lucerne. Microfilm copies, some nearly illegible, have been obtained for the Bancroft Library and the University of Arizona Library. In addition to the letter of May 1, 1733, from Guevavi, there are several others from San Xavier and San Ignacio written during the Padre's Pimería Alta period, 1731–1734.

[17] Treutlein, "The Relation of Philipp Segesser: The Pimas and Other Indians" [1737], *MA*, Vol. XXVII (1945), p. 142. This is a classic description of the daily life and trials of a missionary in Sonora. The date of Grazhoffer's death is given in Alegre, *Historia de la Compañía*, IV, p. 353, n. 33.

[18] "Razon de las Missiones que administra la Compª en esta Provª de Nueva Spna."; WBS, 79 and 1746.

When the Father Visitor had weighed the sad tidings, he assigned Segesser to Guevavi and called Father Gaspar Stiger from Tarahumara Alta to fill the vacancy at Bac.

The third of seventeen children born to a "senator and provincial governor" of Lucerne, Philipp Segesser von Brunegg was forty-three years old and of medium build.[19] He had blue eyes, light brown hair, a patchy beard, and, fortunately, a sense of humor. He was an astute

Phelipe Segesser

observer and a capable missionary. Yet at Guevavi, Father Phelipe succeeded little better than his hapless, short-term predecessors. He did manage to plant some fruit trees, as he had done at Bac. Then one day he ordered the natives of Sonoita to come to Guevavi and help clear additional acres for planting. When they failed to arrive he rode over to find them uproariously drunk. Furthermore, to the Padre's chagrin, they invited him to join in.

> "Father, what do you say! Taste the wine, how sweet it is. It is certainly a fine drink." Thereupon some Indians brought a gourd dish filled with wine, to propitiate me. Since I wished to have nothing to do with the intoxicated Pimas, I sat cautiously to horse so as to be ready any instant for flight. Thereupon the magistrate [headman] called his companions to greet me, according to the custom of the region. Then one should have seen the capers they cut! Some, who could not even walk on their quaking knees, were dragged up by the others, and all shouted very tearfully: "Father, the drink is good! Get off your horse and join us, the wine is good!"
>
> I did not consider it advisable to tarry longer with those drunkards. So although I could hardly contain my laughter I turned to the magistrate and said, very earnestly, "Tomorrow, we will look into the matter."[20]

---

[19] Segesser, born on September 1, 1689, had entered the Society of Jesus on October 14, 1708. He professed in 1726. For a biographical sketch, see Treutlein, "Relation of Segesser," *MA*, XXVII, pp. 139–40.

[20]*Ibid.*, p. 150.

Rather than trying to reason with his already drunken neophytes, Father Phelipe wisely rode back to Guevavi. Unintentionally, it seems, their Padre had arrived at Sonoita during the annual rain ceremonial, the time of communal drinking, the beginning of the native year. Thus it must have been July, just before the summer planting. For several weeks at "cactus camp" the women had harvested the fruit of the giant saguaro using long poles; the fruit had been crushed and the juice boiled; and finally in a ceremonially prescribed manner the boiled juice had been fermented. The end product was "a crimson-colored sort of cider with a slightly nauseating taste, which, when drunk in the ritual quantity, induces vomiting."[21] Because it spoiled quickly, they drank it all within a day or so. "We drank it," said a native woman, "to pull down the clouds." They got "beautifully drunk . . . like plants in the rain" and they sang "for happiness."[22]

Had the revelers of Sonoita succeeded in getting their Padre drunk, thus bringing into play the power of the new God, surely it would have poured.

As the conquest proceeded, as more and more of them died of disease or were culturally disoriented, the Pimas seemed to resort to drink more frequently. Among the Padres they gained a reputation for drunkenness. The Bishop even threatened natives who participated in these bacchanals with excommunication. But Father Segesser knew enough to be lenient. At the least provocation his charges were wont to flee into the mountains leaving him to minister to an empty village.

When some of the native boys caught a medium-size snake in his house and cut it open, Father Phelipe marveled that a maw so small could have encompassed a rabbit whole. Their Padre, it appeared, was interested in everything. He even noted some of their customs. When, for example, the governor of the rowdy natives of Sonoita died, his body was borne to the grave on a horse. The horse was then, as a part of the ritual, supposed to be set free. In this case, however, Father Phelipe wanted very much to have the horse for himself, "but they did not wish to give it to me," and apparently they did not.

---

[21] Castetter and Underhill, *The Ethnobiology of the Papago Indians,* University of New Mexico Bulletin, Whole No. 275 (1935), p. 26.

[22] Underhill, *The Autobiography of a Papago Woman,* Memoirs of the American Anthropological Association, No. 46 (1936), p. 11.

On another occasion, while he was still at San Xavier, he had gone out to visit his natives at a place he called Tubac. Where the ranchería had once stood he was alarmed to find only the charred remains of their huts, completely deserted. After a search he found the people. They had moved away, they told him, after the death of their governor, as was their custom.[23] Like most Indians of the Southwest the Pimas got rid of the property of dead kin. A ghost who returned for his horse or his house might just as easily take back with him one of the living.

His neophytes, Segesser was quick to discover, were far from irrational. When he asked some Pima women why they bit and ate the lice they picked off their children, "they asked me whether I hadn't noticed that hens also eat their lice."[24]

Not many months after he had buried Grazhoffer, Father Phelipe, too, lay miserably ill, "though at San Xavier," he asserted, "I had been as healthy as a fish in water." It may have been malaria, but he suspected the village hechiceros. Now it was Father Keller's turn to act as nurse. Fearful that Guevavi might claim a second Padre's life, the missionary from Soamca ordered Segesser placed on a makeshift litter. Thus began a painful nine-day journey south to mission Cucurpe. Along the way Keller and some Spaniards in the party shifted the litter to their own shoulders "at dangerous places," Segesser recalled, "so that the incautious though painstaking Pimas would not let me roll down into a gorge."[25] After an illness of five months he was back at Guevavi.

As July 31, 1734, approached, Segesser arranged with Father Keller to observe that joyous feast of Saint Ignatius at Soamca. Father Stiger,

---

[23] Treutlein, "Relation of Segesser," *MA,* XXVII, pp. 187, 158–59. Segesser may have meant Tucsón rather than Tubac. If the incident occurred while Father Phelipe was at Bac, Grazhoffer should have been ministering to the natives of Tubac.

[24] *Ibid.,* p. 149.

[25] *Ibid.,* p. 142.

who might have joined them, had recently been recalled from San Xavier del Bac by the Father Visitor, which was depressing news to all three of them. Nevertheless, the two remaining Black Robes made ready. Then, without warning, "the Devil prevented the desired result, perverting to his own use the proverb, 'Mourning taketh hold of the ends of joy.' For the fathers . . . beheld the feast of our Founder not with joy, but with tears."[26] The Indians of Soamca had deserted them.

Segesser hastened back to Guevavi to find that his own charges had fled into the hills driving the cattle and horses before them. At Bac, in the absence of Stiger, the natives had simultaneously broken into the Padre's house stealing everything, "including the new, beautiful, and precious vestments in five colors and all appurtenances which our viceroy had given to us when we were sent to these new missions."[27] Again Stiger hurried northward. This was rebellion.

Had the Pimas of the north wished to set back the Spanish advance mightily, this was truly the time. The three precarious missions, mere tokens of the new authority, were extremely vulnerable. Certainly there were not enough settlers to stand against the rebels, and as yet no presidio in all the Pimería. Moreover, the Jesuit superiors had begun to doubt again if the Pimas could ever be converted, and they feared for the safety of their missionaries laboring among such a restless people.[28] But, for lack of will or lack of organization, the Pimas, this time, did not follow through.

Hearing of the trouble, Captain Anza and his soldiers rushed to the scene. Already the three missionaries had begun negotiating the peaceful return of their neophytes. Once before, Father Segesser had brought back his flock from the mountains. Again he persuaded them to return. To San Xavier repentant natives carried back all they had stolen, though much of it was broken and torn. The cause of the flight, the Padres discovered, was a rumor that the Captain was coming to kill all of the Pimas. The rumor, it seemed, had been conceived and spread

---

[26] Stiger to Father Francisco Xavier Halaver, San Xavier del Bac, November 9, 1734; original cited by Bolton in Bavarian Hauptstaatsarchiv, Munich, Jesuitica 283; transcript and translation from the Latin "by Reynolds," BRP.

[27] Treutlein, "Relation of Segesser," *MA*, XXVII, p. 164.

[28] Stiger to Halaver, November 9, 1734.

by malevolent Spaniards who wished to frighten the Indians and turn them against their missionaries. Back of it, however, the Padres discerned the lurking figure of the Devil, the ubiquitous "Father of Lies."

From San Xavier in November, Father Stiger reported each of the three missionaries "now with his own flock," though Segesser "is ill with the fever; last year he almost died of it; apparently, this country is not good for his health."[29] This time, weak and disconsolate, Father Phelipe was escorted from Guevavi by Anza who happened to be there "on business." At Fronteras the experienced Señora de Anza (who, ironically, was herself to be buried at Guevavi twenty-six years later) restored the Padre's health "with her household remedies." This time Segesser did not return to Guevavi. Instead, his superiors assigned him to the more healthful mission of Tecoripa in Pimería Baja.[30] There, they felt, Father Phelipe would be safely beyond the reach of what he knew to be "the baneful influence of mission Guebavi."[31]

For a couple of years after Segesser's final exit, Mission Los Santos Ángeles de Guevavi was relegated to the occasional care of an absentee Padre. During 1735 tall, dark-haired Stiger of Bac, who bore the scar of an old wound between his eyebrows, ministered whenever he could to the needs of the spiritually orphaned children of Guevavi. Yet the compassionate, courageous Father Gaspar, who claimed that he was "wholly content" with his calling, more than had his hands full at San Xavier. Thrice the fearsome shamans cast curses upon him. They would have killed him had it not been for the intercession of Father Campos. Even at that, he suffered ill effects for the rest of his life.[32]

When the elderly Campos, whose mind had begun to cloud, was

---

[29]*Ibid.*

[30] For a description of Tecoripa, on a tributary of the Río Yaqui in south-central Sonora, see Paul M. Roca's unique *Paths of the Padres Through Sonora: An Illustrated History and Guide to Its Spanish Churches* (Tucson: Arizona Pioneers' Historical Society, 1967), pp. 245–48.

[31] Treutlein, "Relation of Segesser," *MA,* XXVII, pp. 142–43. Many leagues south of Guevavi, Segesser served with distinction until his death at Ures on September 28, 1762.

[32] Stiger was born in northern Switzerland in the village of Oberriet near St. Gallen on October 20 or 21, 1695. Ordained on Whitsunday Eve, 1719, Father Stiger served as a parish priest in his native country for more than six years before entering the Society of Jesus on October 9, 1725. He was Padre at the mission of Cárichic in Tarahumara Alta before being summoned to the Pimería. San Ignacio, Entierros. Pradeau and Burrus, "Los Jesuitas."

finally dislodged from San Ignacio by order of his superiors,[33] Father Stiger rode down from Bac to replace him. For the next quarter century, until his own death at two in the afternoon of April 24, 1762, Father Gaspar was Padre of San Ignacio.

Thus with Stiger gone south, the entire northern Pimería fell to Keller — Soamca, Guevavi, and Bac, ten thousand square miles of territory, a challenge he readily accepted. Ignacio Xavier Keller, a strong-willed individual, tall and fair, with a scar on his lip, was as tough and zealous as they came.[34]

Keller, like Kino, got along well alone. He resented other missionaries closing in on him. He liked to ride, to have the heathens flock out to meet him. As early as February 12 and 13, 1736, he was preaching and offering holy baptism to the people in and around Guevavi. He seemed to prefer the name Gusutaqui to Guevavi, sometimes calling their village "Gusutaqui, alias Guevavi."[35]

To keep Christianity alive at the Fatherless mission, Keller returned in early May, twice in July, once in September, and perhaps again in December, 1736, and in January, February, and March, 1737. On one occasion he baptized "en Gusutaqui" three Pima baby girls and a boy he called a "Nijorita." Nijora, or Nixora, was a term used on the Sonora frontier for an Indian sold by other Indians to the gente de razón, a Yuman-speaking captive, for example, sold by the Pimas to a settler. The Nixoras were not a tribe but a class.[36] Since they were virtual slaves

[33] Father Joseph Toral to Father Provincial Joseph Barba, Guépaca, March 25, 1736; WBS, 1747, ff. 25–34. A detailed treatment of Campos' sad finale is Dunne, "Captain Anza and the Case of Father Campos," *MA*, Vol. XXIII (1941), pp. 45–60.

[34] Born on November 11, 1702, in Olomouc, Moravia, Keller had been a Jesuit since October 17, 1717. Pradeau and Burrus, "Los Jesuitas." While missionary of Soamca, the only mission at which he served regularly, he professed his four solemn vows in 1736. Burrus, *La Obra Cartográfica de la Provincia Mexicana de la Compañía de Jesús, 1567–1967* (Madrid: Ediciones José Porrúa Turanzas, 1967), 55.

[35] Keller, Informe, Soamca, July 9, 1744; "Cartas de las Misiones de la Compañía de Jesús en la Baja California y Norte de México," a collection of documents found by Father Burrus in Barcelona, Spain; microfilm, University of Arizona Library (UAL). According to this informe, Keller took possession at Soamca on April 20, 1732, a couple of weeks before he joined the expedition of reconquest. Between that date and the date of the informe he had, he claimed, baptized more than 2,000 persons. On an undated sketch map he drew of his immense domain, he used only the name "Gussutaqui" not Guevavi.

[36] Henry F. Dobyns, *et al.*, "What Were Nixoras," *Southwestern Journal of Anthropology*, Vol. XVI (1960), pp. 230–58. The term *genízaro* was used in New Mexico in almost the same way.

among the natives, Spanish law permitted their purchase as slaves by the colonists. In this case little Francisco was probably the property of Vicente Figueroa who served as his godfather at the baptism. Keller also baptized gente de razón on his visits to Guevavi — a son of Luis Pacho and Juliana Romero, a daughter of Juan Núñez and María Rosa Samaniego, a son of Augustín Fernández and María Antonia Romero.[37]

Evidently more and more settlers were moving in along the river south of Guevavi. Keller seemed to encourage these gente de razón to act as godparents to the irresolute natives. Besides bearing witness to the

baptism and assuming responsibility for the nurture of a new Christian, godparents were joined to parents as well by a social bond which permitted them to address each other by the endearing terms *compadre* and *comadre*. Entering into the union of *compadrazgo* with Indians, however, was all too often regarded by gente de razón as a magnanimous gesture on their part toward hopeless inferiors, a gesture not to be taken seriously but rather to be taken advantage of. Some of the soldiers who accompanied Keller, Campos, or Kino, and who became godfathers dozens and dozens of times, more often than not never again saw their native godchildren or their native compadres.

When Father Keller approached Guevavi from the north on New Year's Day, 1737, leading a large entourage, the natives must have been reminded of the visits of Father Campos. Keller had been to the Gila. He had been joyously received in the rancherías of "Haivani muquit" and "Tushonimo," where he had baptized twenty-six females, bestowing on all of them the name Catalina "in order to avoid confusion." For the same reason, and with a keen sense of proportion, he left behind him as well twenty-six new Ignacios.[38]

Early in the spring Father Visitor General Andrés Xavier García

---

[37] Mission Santa María Soamca, Libro de Bautismos, 1732–1768; CPA.
[38] *Ibid.*

and his retinue reined up at Keller's poor mission of Soamca.[39] Apparently the Visitor General made no effort to visit Guevavi or Bac since at neither was a missionary in residence. Father García, who had recently brought over from Europe forty-nine Jesuits, recognized the Pimería's urgent need for missionaries. Vacant missions served neither God nor king. While praising Keller's heroic circuit rides, Father García may also have told the lone missionary that two hardy newcomers would arrive in the next few months to lighten his burden. Keller would, of course, do all he could to see them properly installed.

Meanwhile, to the southwest of Guevavi, an incredible discovery had been made. Near Captain Don Gabriel de Prudhom Heyder Butrón y Muxica's mining camp of Arizonac, or Arizona, toward the end of October, 1736, the son of Antonio, a Yaqui Indian prospector, had stumbled upon the first of some amazing chunks of virgin silver lying on the surface. Word leaked out. Wealth without digging! Frantic but short-lived, the rush for the *planchas de plata* was on. The size of the silver balls grew with every telling. Some a team of oxen could hardly budge. Some surely weighed more than a ton, almost two. But very soon the supply was exhausted. Hundreds of disappointed late arrivals, adventurers, merchants, and vagabonds, took to the hills of the Pimería. There had to be more.

As *justicia mayor* of Sonora under the new governor of Nueva Andalucia, or Sinaloa, Captain Anza had arrived at the scene a few weeks after the initial discovery. He was to conduct an investigation and determine if he could just what sort of phenomenon these balls of silver represented — the product of mining by ancients, a mysterious hidden treasure, a gift of Nature. Not until a determination had been made could the king's share be assessed. But it was little use. Most of the silver had been spirited away. What remained were tenaciously clung-to hopes

---

[39] The office of Father Visitor General had been created in 1725 as a regular rung in the Jesuit hierarchy. Its holder, sort of a Vice Provincial, oversaw the entire northwest missionary empire and outranked the various local Father Visitors, e.g., of Sonora, Sinaloa, or Baja California. It was his responsibility to tour all the missions at least once during his three-year term. For a discussion of the role and duties of the Visitor General, see Donohue, "Jesuit Missions," pp. 71–75. Father García baptized two persons at Soamca on April 2, 1737. Soamca, Bautismos.

of new finds, many more gente de razón in the Pimería, and the name Arizona, now synonymous with quick wealth.

A thousand miles south in Guadalajara the investigation continued, perhaps to insure the royal treasury its due from future planchas strikes. One Don Juan Nicolás de Tapia, testifying on July 13, 1737, told of other wealth in the Pimería. He had with his own eyes, he claimed, seen at San Ignacio a marvelous gift brought to Father Stiger, a knife of gold crudely fashioned with rock implements to resemble Saint Francis Xavier. There was more — a lake of mercury and pearls along the coast.[40]

Commenting from his mission of Tecoripa on all the lusty excitement of the planchas strike, Father Segesser wrote: "It is quite possible that I rested on the very spot where the discovery was made at the time that I was sent to the silver mines of Arizona. However, I did not discover the treasure, for through holy baptism I searched for another kind of treasure — for souls."[41]

Before 1737 no Padre had lasted more than a few months at Guevavi; after 1737 all of them did. Gradually the village came to resemble a mission community rather than a native ranchería. For the next thirty years neither disease nor revolt nor Apaches could keep the Jesuits away. During this period the heathen wilderness became a Spanish frontier. More settlers and cattlemen moved in on the Pimas' lands. First one presidio, nineteen leagues from Guevavi, then another, only seven leagues away, was built at royal expense. The soldiers helped to keep the Pimas in line. They brought in Pápagos to replace the many neophytes who died in the mission villages, and they tried to fend off hostile invaders.

Though the next two Padres each lasted more than three years at Guevavi, their administrations belong more to the wilderness phase of the mission story than to its more prosperous frontier phase. Their greatest contribution to Guevavi's future was their own tenacity.

The first of these longer-term Padres to take up residence at Guevavi was an irrepressible individualist. In spite of a dozen years of Ignatian discipline, Alexandro Rapicani spoke his mind. Born in the town of

---

[40] The documents concerning the planchas de plata strike are in AGI, Guad., 185. Some of the planchas were said to have been reburied or never found; the quest for them is still very much alive today.

[41] Treutlein, "Relation of Segesser," *MA*, XXVII, p. 183.

Zeven in the Duchy of Bremen on November 3, 1702, of a Swedish mother and a Neapolitan father, he must have been a memorable-looking young man. He was sound of body and fair of skin. His hair and beard were very blond, and his eyes were blue.

Like Father Jacobo Sedelmayr of Bavaria who also left the protective walls of a Jesuit college that spring to seek his fortune in foreign missions, Father Alexandro bid *Vale* to his classmates on April 14, 1735, and journeyed from Westphalia across most of Germany.[42] His route presumably led him up and through Brenner Pass and then down to the port of Genoa where he negotiated passage to Spain. The ensuing voyage of two weeks or a month provided a rigorous if not nauseating initiation for a landlubber missionary-to-be. Once his ship had anchored off the picturesque city of Cádiz, he and his fellow passengers were subject to an annoying quarantine period, usually lasting from five to ten days. Then he disembarked on Spanish soil.

Across the Bay of Cádiz at the Puerto de Santa María a fine new hospice had been built to house the Jesuits while arrangements were made for their ocean crossing. "The quadrangular house is beautiful to look at," wrote another temporary resident several years later. "[It] is three stories high with two towers on the sides, and contains more than a hundred spacious rooms all of them provided with alcoves. The court with a beautiful alabaster fountain standing in the middle of it is completely paved with white and black Genoa marble laid in checkerboard pattern, and the entire building rests on twenty-four white marble pillars."[43] Here, Alexandro Rapicani met Father Andrés Xavier García, superior of the group readying itself for departure. And here, also, he met Father Sedelmayr, Brothers Juan and Thomás Tello, sixteen and fifteen years of age respectively and more than forty other members of the mission to New Spain of 1735. At two in the morning of November 22, crowded aboard the warship *Santa Rosa*, they sailed with the westbound fleet.

It was a miserable crossing. Then, on February 18, 1736, "the last

---

[42] AGI, Contratación, 5550. For a biographical sketch of Father Sedelmayr, the best-known Jesuit to serve in Pimería Alta after Kino, see Dunne, *Jacobo Sedelmayr: Missionary, Frontiersman, Explorer in Arizona and Sonora* (Tucson: Arizona Pioneers' Historical Society, 1955), pp. 1–11.

[43] Treutlein, *Travel Reports of Joseph Och,* p. 7. See also Treutlein, "Jesuit Travel," *MA,* XIX, pp. 107–109.

and unluckiest day of our voyage . . . God was pleased to reveal what he might have done when we were in mid-ocean." Within sight of port the *Santa Rosa* ran aground and foundered off the island of San Juan de Ulúa in Vera Cruz harbor. Over the side went a number of the frightened Jesuits abandoning ship pellmell. Some lost the trunks which contained their few guarded belongings. Fortunately, none drowned.

Resuming their journey on firm ground, the now travel-wise Black Robes pushed on toward Mexico City. At Puebla de los Ángeles in the cathedral Bishop Benito Crespo, recently promoted from the see of Durango, received them warmly. Father Sedelmayr was particularly impressed that the Bishop "told us from memory the names of all the German missionaries in his extensive province, and informed us, too, as to the province and diocese in which each of them was born." [44] On the basis of past performance Benito, Bishop of Puebla, had nothing but praise for German missionaries. The Germans present were resolved that he would not be disappointed in their future performance. When later Rapicani and Sedelmayr learned that Benito Crespo, patron of the Pimería, had succumbed to the ghastly plague of 1736 it was with a sense of deep personal loss.

"On June 1, 1737, I turned over that which is set forth in this inventory," declared Father Keller. "I received it on the same day and in the same year," confirmed Father Rapicani. "This transfer was made

Alexandro Rapicani.

in my presence," attested their Father Rector, Gaspar Stiger. It was standard procedure. Each time a mission changed hands an *entrega,* or transfer, was drawn up and signed by both the incoming and the outgoing Padre as well as by a witness, often their superior. So it was in the summer of 1737 that Alexandro Rapicani received by formal inventory the scant wealth and the many burdens of him who would serve as Minister of Doctrine for His Majesty at Guevavi.

Five years had passed since the reconquest began, yet this was still a very poor mission. A meager assortment of tools — axes, saws, a small

---

[44] Sedelmayr to Father Magnus Amman, México, May 10, 1736; translation in BRP.

hammer, a gouge — and kitchen utensils — copper pots and a large skillet, majolica and earthenware plates and a large china cup, two napkins and a chocolate cloth — gathered dust in the Padre's house. The religious paraphernalia, donated by the king, were more complete, even to a pair of "large or tower bells," presumably hanging from a cross-bar elevated on poles until the day there was a tower. According to the inventory, the mission owned the following livestock: 240 cattle, 150 sheep, 50 goats, 8 oxen, 12 horses, 10 mules, and a few mares. Perhaps if he proved to be an able ranch supervisor Father Alexandro would succeed in raising a surplus of meat, maize, or grain and would sell it to supplement the annual royal stipend of three hundred and fifty pesos. If he hoped to improve his mission, he would need additional operating capital.

Jesuit San Xavier del Bac rarely had a resident Padre. During the seventy-five years from the advent of Kino in 1692 to the banishment of all the Black Robes in 1767, the Father's house at Bac stood vacant on the average of four out of every five years. When Father Rapicani took over Guevavi in the summer of 1737 he also took over San Xavier del Bac. This "farthest and most populous" of the missions in Pimería Alta was administered by him and his successors for a dozen consecutive years essentially as a visita of Guevavi.[45] Some of the time they were granted an extra two hundred pesos annually for their trouble.[46]

The inventory of items at Bac showed even fewer tools and furnishings in the Padre's house. Though the religious objects were the same in number and kind as those of Guevavi they bore the marks of the abortive uprising of 1734. The altar lamp had been smashed to bits, the vestments "rather abused," and the altar cloths "torn into pieces that could not be gathered up." Captain Anza had taken the damaged processional canopy and censer with him to have them repaired. There were exactly the same number of cattle, sheep, and goats listed for Bac

[45] One Father Joseph Favier, a native of Cologne and like Rapicani and Sedelmayr a member of the mission of 1735, was assigned in 1737 to Kino's old mission of Dolores. Because the climate there did not suit him he was soon reassigned to San Xavier del Bac. Apparently death prevented him from ever reaching Bac. His burial was recorded by Father Stiger at San Ignacio on October 25, 1737. See José Pabier in Pradeau and Burrus, "Los Jesuitas."

[46] Father Joseph Garrucho of Guevavi reportedly received the additional two hundred pesos for looking after Bac in 1745, 1746, and 1747. "Quaderno de Missiones donde se relacionan las que estuvieron corrientes hasta el año de 1753"; AGN, Misiones, 22.

as for Guevavi — which indicates that these figures were only estimates — but fewer horses, mules, and mares, and no oxen.[47]

Alexandro Rapicani, whose subsequent career is well documented because of the polemics he engaged in, seemed to start out quietly enough. Virtually nothing is known about his first two years at Guevavi. He did seem to be away for several months during the winter of 1737–1738.[48] By June of 1739 he was complaining to the Father Visitor that he had not received the items he had ordered from the Father Procurator in Mexico City, particularly a heavy cassock for the cold winters at Guevavi. In response, the Father Visitor suggested to the Father Provincial that the Father Procurator be admonished. Such oversights should not be allowed to occur. Father Rapicani had every right to be annoyed. After all, "he is at one of the new missions of the Pimería and lacks everything of necessity unless Providence provides him with it."[49]

At each mission, just as in all the parishes throughout the Roman Catholic world, every baptism, marriage, and burial was entered in books maintained by the Padre in accordance with the decrees of the Holy Council of Trent. Periodically these books were examined for conformity. In all likelihood just before Christmas of 1737 Rapicani had journeyed down to San Ignacio with the books of Guevavi in his saddlebags, there to present them to Bishop Martín de Elizacochea for inspection. Unless Father Alexandro had lapsed into some error of format, it was customary and routine for the Bishop's secretary to enter a statement for the prelate's signature, complimenting the Jesuit on his "apostolic and assiduous zeal" and urging him to continue the good work.[50]

Unfortunately most of the pages filled by Rapicani in the Guevavi books are missing, as are all those used by his resident predecessors. The

----

[47] The original entregas, both in Father Rapicani's hand and dated June 1, 1737, are in WBS, 1744, ff. 67–68, 71–73. They are translated in their entirety, along with two later ones, as Appendix II of the present study.

[48] On January 19, 1738, Father Keller baptized six persons in Gusutaqui. Phelipe, native governor of the village, became little Aniceta's godfather. The following week Keller was at San Xavier to celebrate another twenty-three baptisms. Back in Gusutaqui on February 22 he baptized still another native for whom Phelipe was godfather. At no time did he mention the Padre Ministro of Guevavi. Soamca, Bautismos.

[49] Father Visitor Joseph Toral to Father Provincial Juan Antonio Oviedo, Banámichi, June 26, 1739; AHH, Temp., 17.

[50] Soamca, Bautismos. Donohue, "Jesuit Missions," p. 158.

✝

En 6 de Octubre de 1766 .se casaron in facie Eccl.ª, echas las diligencias, que prescribe el Conc. Tridentino Pedro vivdo por muerte de Christina, y Jpha Maria Viuda por muerte de Miguel; ambos de Guevavi. Fueron testigos el Alcalde, y Jph.

Ante mi
Custodio Ximens

En 3 de Noviembre se casaron in facie Eccl.ª echas las diligencias, que prescribe el N.C. Tridentino Francisco del Eccson, Viudo por muerte de Chatarina, con Lorenza, de Tumacacori, Viuda de Christoval. Fueron testigos Mador y Jph.

Ante mi
Custodio Ximeno

Ano 1767

En 8 de

En 8 de Febrero de 1767 se casaron in facie Eccl. Jacinto, Viudo de Luisa con Jpha, Soltera, echas las diligencias, que manda el Tridentino, Ambos de Tumacacori. Fueron testigos el Mador y Jph.

Ante mi
Custodio Ximens

En 26 de Abril de 1767 se casaron in facie Eccl. echas las diligencias, que prescribe el Tridentino, Manuel, viudo por Muerte de Maria con Isabel Soltera del Pueblo de Sonoita. Fueron testigos Mador y Alcalde.

Ante mi Jhs
Custodio Ximeno.

En 26 de Abril de 1767 se casaron en facie Eccl. echas las referidas diligencias Migl. Viudo de Isabel con Massa Viuda de Felipe Ambos de Sonoita. Fueron testigos Mador y Alcalde.

Ante mi
Jhs Custodio Xim.º

En diez de Mayo de 1767 se casaron in facie Eccl., echas las diligencias que prescribe el Conc. Tridentino Andres. Viudo por muerte de Inas Maria, y Rosa Viuda por muerte de Agustin. Ambos de Calavasas. Fueron testigos Mador, y Jph.

Ante mi
Custodio Ximeno

En 14 de Junio de 1767 se casaron in facie Eccl. Juan Antonio Alcalde Viude con Maria Antonia Soltera, echas las diligencias, que prescribe el Tridentino del Pueblo de Tumacacori. Fueron testigos su Mador y Jph. Ante mi

Jhs
Custodio Ximeno

From the Libro de Casamientos,
the last surviving entries by a Jesuit at Guevavi

earliest entry extant records the marriage of a native couple, Lorenzo Mumurigca and Antonia Sipinimuhbi, both of Guevavi, by Father Alexandro on August 16, 1739, with local gente de razón, Phelipe Santiago de Luque and Isabel Valenzuela, as witnesses. From this date forward, the surviving pages of baptisms, marriages, and burials form the most valuable single source for the history of Jesuit Guevavi.[51]

Alexandro Rapicani, who later hired an architect and stone mason to build for him at Batuc "without doubt the most beautiful church in all Sonora,"[52] had not the wherewithal at Guevavi to build even an adobe chapel. During his time at the wilderness mission he did, however, learn the Piman tongue, apparently well. But even this did not win over the village hechiceros, who continued to call down their evil magic and to obstruct his ministry. Rapicani, it seemed to his superiors, was doing his best under trying circumstances. When in the spring of 1740 there arrived from Rome a list of Jesuits deemed by the Society's Father General proven and ready to profess their final solemn vows, Father Alexandro's name was on it.

Notified of the good news the Padre of Guevavi rode south in mid-April to San Ignacio. There he was joined by his former shipmate Jacobo Sedelmayr, also come to profess. To prepare themselves the two missionaries to the Pimas may have put themselves through the purifying annual eight-day Spiritual Exercises there at San Ignacio. Then on May 1, 1740, together, with Father Visitor General Joseph Xavier de Molina presiding, they professed at a public Mass solemn vows of poverty, chastity, obedience, and willingness "to go whithersoever the pope might wish to send [them]." As "professed" Fathers, Rapicani and Sedelmayr

[51] Bound in a single manuscript volume and labeled "Tubaca y Otros," the remaining pages of the Guevavi books, 1739–1767, are kept today in the Archives of the Roman Catholic Diocese, Tucson, Arizona. A companion volume, "De Calabasas Bautismos," contains the surviving Franciscan records from Guevavi-Tumacácori, 1768–1825. Both are on microfilm at UAL and at the Arizona Pioneers' Historical Society, Tucson (APHS). Some years ago Father Victor R. Stoner tediously made handwritten transcripts in pencil of the Guevavi books, which he hoped eventually to have published. These, too, are at APHS.

[52] Roca, *Paths of the Padres,* p. 201. Rapicani's impressive, vaulted, cut-stone church was inundated in the mid-1960s by the waters behind El Novillo dam. Only the façade was salvaged. See Juanita Ruiz, "Farewell, Batuc — A Lost Historic Site," *Journal of Arizona History* (*JAH*), Vol. VI (1965), pp. 152–54; also Pradeau, *La expulsión de los Jesuitas de las Provincias de Sonora, Ostimuri y Sinaloa en 1767* (México, D.F.: Antigua Librería Robredo, 1959), pp. 202–203.

had reached the culmination of all their years of study and probation. As missionaries they had just begun.[53]

Before leaving San Ignacio to return to their missions they must have discussed with the Visitor General the worsening situation to the south. For six weeks there had been sporadic outbreaks of violence among the Yaquis and neighboring tribes. Alarmists were saying that the entire Northwest would soon be enveloped by the flames of native revolt; Yaqui agitators had even been reported in Pimería Alta. Responsibility for this dire state of affairs, the Jesuits agreed, lay with one man — Governor Don Manuel Bernal de Huidobro.

Since 1734 the five northwestern coastal provinces — Rosario, Culiacán, Sinaloa, Ostimuri, and Sonora (including Pimería Alta) — had been administered as a single jurisdiction under Bernal de Huidobro. From the moment he took over, the Governor's pretensions to rule instead of reign over mission Indians had involved him in a continuous feud with the Jesuits. Now the pernicious effects of his policies had come home to roost, and everyone would pay.[54]

As if this were not enough. Hardly had Rapicani arrived back at Guevavi when news of a wholly unexpected tragedy reached him. Captain Anza, friend and protector of the Jesuits, was dead.

It had happened near Soamca. Father Keller, knowing that Apaches had recently scouted the area, cautioned the Captain to be on his guard. Heeding the Jesuit, Anza closed up the ranks of his column as they rode through broken terrain. When they reached open country, however, the danger seemed less and Anza rode on ahead of the column. Hidden by the chaparral, the Apaches lay in ambush. Without warning they were upon him. Before his men got to him, the valiant officer was slain. In an instant the hostiles had claimed their trophy — the crown of Anza's scalp.[55]

---

[53] Rafael de Zelis, s.j., *Catálogo de los sugetos de la Compañía de Jesús que formaban la Provincia de México el día del arresto, 25 de junio de 1767* (México, D.F., 1871), p. 72. On April 17, 1740, Rapicani baptized five children at San Ignacio.

[54] For details of the Yaqui revolt and Bernal de Huidobro versus the Jesuits, see Navarro García, *La Sublevación Yaqui de 1740* (Sevilla: Escuela de Estudios Hispano-Americanos, 1966).

[55] The details of Anza's demise are provided in *Apostólicos Afanes de la Compañía de Jesús* (México, D.F.: Luis Alvarez y Alvarez de la Cadena, 1944), 426–27 [originally published in Barcelona: Pablo Nadal, 1754]. The year is generally given as 1739. It appears, however, the Captain died on May 9, 1740. Navarro García, *Sublevación Yaqui*, p. 97, n. 16.

Not only had this champion of the Jesuits been Captain at Fronteras and justicia mayor of Sonora, but as leader of the flourishing Basque community on the northern frontier he had exercised great influence in the councils of the province.[56] Anza's place in the pro-Jesuit ranks, Rapicani knew, would be difficult to fill.

The summer of 1740 was a long, hot one. By June the fierce Yaqui and Mayo rebels had severed all communications between Sonora and the south. Governor Bernal de Huidobro was holed up in Álamos unwilling to take the field. It appeared that the contagion was spreading north. To hold the line in Sonora, the Governor felt constrained to call upon a man he did not regard highly, the *sargento mayor* of that province, Don Augustín de Vildósola. At the time Don Augustín, *paisano,* close friend and associate of Anza, was settling the latter's estate.[57] Laying aside this task, he now entered the fray, and over the next few months not only successfully defended Sonora but also took the offensive against the rebels, emerging, to the Governor's consternation, as the hero of the entire Northwest.

Pimería Alta remained quiet but nervous. Toward the end of August, Vildósola sent a detachment among the Pimas to ferret out Yaqui infiltrators. Later, soldiers executed four Yaquis and an Apache, whom they suspected of plotting a rising of the whole Pimería.[58] Rapicani, who had endured the summer at Guevavi, was now preparing to leave. Sometime after August 27, 1740, when he had united in a Christian service Andrés Warsuwo and María Huworihuosi of the ranchería of Tutup "previously married according to their law," Father Alexandro departed for the Seri mission of Pópulo on the Río San Miguel 140 miles south.[59]

Not a year after he had left Guevavi, Rapicani clashed with Governor Don Augustín de Vildósola, newly elevated to succeed the disgraced Bernal de Huidobro. The Governor, it seemed, needed wheat for his

[56]*Ibid.,* pp. 21–22.

[57]*Ibid.,* pp. 96–97. For a biographical sketch of Vildósola, see Almada, *Diccionario,* pp. 825–26; also Dunne, *Juan Antonio Balthasar, Padre Visitador to the Sonora Frontier, 1744–1745* (Tucson: Arizona Pioneers' Historical Society, 1957), pp. 65–72.

[58] Navarro García, *Sublevación Yaqui,* pp. 112, 128.

[59] "Entrega que de orden del Pᵉ Visor. grl. Jsph. Xav. de Molina haze al Pᵉ Alexandro Rapicani el Pᵉ Nicolas de Perera de la Mission de Nᵃ Sᵣᵃ del Populo en 28 de Octubre del Aᵒ de 1740"; WBS, 1744, ff. 123–26.

horses since there was no maize that year. Father Alexandro, then serving at the Ópata mission of Batuc, refused to sell, saying that if he did, he and his Indians would soon have none. One thing led to another. Don Augustín resorted to certain "indecorous epithets" to describe the stubborn Jesuit. Rapicani in turn labeled the demanding Governor an Attila, a Scourge of God. Writing in Latin to the Father Provincial he asserted that Vildósola, a wolf in sheep's clothing, "intolerably arrogant and vain, treats everyone, including us, like slaves, expecting us to obey and to carry out his desires while he vigilantly attempts to acquire everything for himself." [60] Curiously enough, at the same time the bitter, deposed Bernal de Huidobro was calling Vildósola an "ally, retainer, and creature" of the Jesuits. [61]

Concerning the behavior of Rapicani, Father Juan Nentuig two decades later wrote hopefully: "Because of his zeal, Father Alexandro Rapicani has seemed rather indiscreet to some persons. In the past he has given his superiors trouble and has suffered greatly because of it. Since he was restored to the mission of Batuc he has behaved in such a manner that not the least complaint against His Reverence has reached me . . . he is indefatigable even though now old and ailing." [62]

But his enemies persisted. The *teniente político* of Batuc gathered testimony against Rapicani and submitted it to Governor Juan Claudio de Pineda. In his defense, Father Visitor Manuel Aguirre argued that the testimony was illegal. To prevent the Governor from making a hasty decision in the case, the Visitor on Christmas Day, 1764, delivered the coup:

> I feel that it is my obligation to inform Your Lordship just who Father
> Alexandro Rapicani is. He is, if one considers his birth, the son of

---

[60] Rapicani to Father Provincial Matheo Anzaldo, November 16, 1742; quoted in Latin and Spanish in Pradeau, *Expulsión,* pp. 203–204. Toral to Vildósola, Guépaca, January 29, 1742; AHH, Temp., 17. Keller was also engaged in a bitter quarrel with Vildósola at this time. Letters of Keller, 1740–1742; *ibid.* See also Father Visitor Balthasar's frank indictment of Governor Vildósola in Dunne, *Balthasar,* pp. 97–107.

[61] Navarro García, *Sublevación Yaqui,* p. 141, n. 7.

[62] Nentuig to Father Provincial Francisco Zevallos, Opotu, July 18, 1764; AHH, Temp., 17. Rapicani had been removed from Batuc for several years, presumably for disciplinary reasons. In his absence, Father Bernardo Middendorff carried on the construction of Father Alexandro's beautiful stone church.

the favorite of the great Queen Christina of Sweden.[63] As a priest and religious of the Company of Jesus, because of his excellent virtue and instruction, he is professed of the four vows. As a missionary with more than twenty years of service to His Majesty (whom God guard) in discharging the royal will, instructing both Pimas and Ópatas as well as Eudeves, he has mastered the three different languages and is one of the most zealous workers for the glory of God and the wellbeing of souls. . . . Furthermore, he is a man of such great honesty, frankness, and known simplicity that one can with assurance give more credence to one simple statement of his than to all the sworn declarations of those who oppose him.[64]

Weighing the facts, the Governor concluded discreetly that there really was "nothing in the whole uproar contrary to the good reputation and honor of the Father."[65]

Joseph de Torres Perea was the youngest missionary ever sent to Guevavi. He was also the only Mexican-born Jesuit to serve regularly at that difficult post. A native of Chalchicomula, Puebla, Torres Perea had entered the Society of Jesus in 1729 at the age of sixteen. By 1737 he was studying second-year theology at the Colegio Máximo in Mexico City. Soon after his ordination, Father Joseph set out for the missions. He must have noted as he traveled north through Mayo and Yaqui country the devastating results of native rebellion. The Indians involved had been made to burn their weapons publicly as an act of submission, yet resentment persisted.

Arriving at Arizpe on the upper Río Sonora, young Torres Perea presented himself to Father Visitor Carlos de Roxas on the last day of January, 1741.[66] The missions of Guevavi and San Xavier del Bac among the northern Pimas were now vacant and had been for some

---

[63] During the reign of Christina, 1644–1654, Sweden by the Treaty of Westphalia gained territory in northern Germany which included the Duchy of Bremen, Rapicani's birthplace. Christina abdicated in 1654, shortly afterward converting to Catholicism and moving to Rome. Though she died in 1689, thirteen years before Alexandro Rapicani was born, the fact that the Jesuit's father had been the queen's favorite lived long after her, and apparently warranted respect.

[64] Aguirre to Pineda, Bacadéguachi, December 25, 1764; BNMex, 45/723. The Father Visitor was exaggerating a bit by claiming three *different* languages for Rapicani. Eudeve, or Southern Ópata, was a dialect of the Ópata.

[65] Pineda to Aguirre, quoted in Pradeau, *Expulsión,* p. 209.

[66] Pradeau and Burrus, "Los Jesuitas."

months, Father Roxas explained. They were his if he thought he could handle them.

By mid-February, Joseph de Torres Perea, this inexperienced, newly ordained Father in his late twenties, who wrote with the beautiful hand of a notary and signed his name like a grandee, was in residence at

Guevavi.[67] Father Keller of neighboring Soamca, veteran of nearly a decade and, if not already, soon to be named Father Rector of the Pimería, doubtless saw to the youngster's proper installation. From then on it was up to him.

Judging from his entries in the Guevavi books, Father Joseph's ministry was an active one.[68] In addition to his neophytes at Guevavi and its four visitas and at San Xavier he offered his services to the natives of many and widely scattered rancherías — Bacocut, Tutup, Toacuquita, Concuuc, Sopoc, Taupari, Bacuacucan, Toaczoni — either inviting them to come to him or riding out in search of them. Several dozen consented to holy baptism during his initial months. Others, he later admitted, ran and hid from him.[69]

The first marriage ceremony he performed for his charges as Padre of Guevavi must have been a gala affair. Joseph Tutubusa, native governor of Tumacácori, took as his bride on May 23, 1741, Martha Tupquice

[67] Torres Perea baptized young Augustín on February 19, 1741. There are three earlier entries on the same page dated only "the same day" referring to a date on the previous page, now lost.

[68] A number of pages of Father Joseph's entries are missing. It can hardly be a coincidence, noted Father Stoner, that the baptismal, marriage, and burial records for the same period, January, 1742, to December, 1743, have been torn out.

[69] Torres Perea, "Informe de la Mission de los Angeles de Guebavi alias Guzutaqui de la Pimeria alta del Norte," Guevavi, March 16, 1744; "Cartas de las Misiones. . . ." cited above in this chapter, note 35. Of the many reports required of the Padres at Guevavi this is the only one that has yet turned up.

of San Xavier. Among the witnesses to this union were the governor of San Xavier, Ygnacio Jocumisa; his mador, Domingo Cussu; and a number of settlers with Spanish names. The young missionary used the occasion to exhort those natives married only by their rites "to renew their consent" in the Christian way. One venerable couple agreed the following month. Eusebio was eighty or ninety years old and his bride, who knew she had been baptized but could not recall her Christian name, was about seventy. This namesake of Father Kino and his forgetful wife may well have experienced the magic of the apostle himself, half a century before.

Like magnets, the planchas de plata had drawn northward to the very margins of Guevavi all the loose human scraps of a mineral-oriented frontier society. Some of them stayed, planted a few crops in the fertile bottomlands, and let their stock graze the hills. Most prospected. Because of this influx, the settlement pattern of gente de razón within the mission's jurisdiction had changed. No longer were settlers confined to the area along the river south of Guevavi, though, to be sure, Don Nicholás Romero continued to preside over a large and expanding family at Buenavista, and at San Luis, Santa Bárbara, and Divisadero other families now lived — the Tapia, Grijalva, Bohórquez, Barba, Amésquita, Gallego, Samaniego, and more.

Seven leagues north of Guevavi at Tubac there were others. On Saint Valentine's Day in 1740, Father Rapicani had performed a double marriage ceremony for Francisco de Ortega and Gertrudis Barba, and Luis Villela and Rosalía Durán, all of whom he termed *"vecinos de Tubaca,"* loosely, citizens or settlers of Tubac. By the fall of 1741 the Villelas had a son for Father Torres Perea to baptize. They called him Miguel Ignacio, and the Padre called them "Spaniards of Tubac."

Also near Arivaca, westernmost visita of Guevavi, non-natives had begun preempting watered land and good pasture. There Don Antonio de Rivera maintained an *estancia,* or stock ranch, with a large household of Yaqui and Nixora servants, a foreman, and vaqueros. Between Arivaca and Tubac near Sopori lay "the Captain's estancia," the property of a prominent Spanish frontiersman, Captain Don Bernardo de Urrea.[70]

---

[70] Don Bernardo de Urrea was a conspicuous figure on the Sonora scene for nearly four decades. Born about 1710 in Culiacán, he served in a bewildering succession of military and political capacities. Three times interim governor of Sonora, he died in 1777 at Altar. Almada, *Diccionario,* pp. 805–806.

Even the foreman of Guevavi, Andrés Martín Covarrubias, was evidently not an Indian.

In theory at least, all of these gente de razón belonged to the parish of Nacosari, one hundred and twenty miles southeast of Guevavi. To the curate of Nacosari they owed their tithes. But because the seat of their parish was days away by horseback, when their newborn needed baptizing, their lovers marrying, or their dying the last rites, they sought the services of Father Joseph. In payment he collected no set fee, but instead, if the gente chose to offer them, a few chickens, a bushel of wheat, or perhaps some very fine squash.

Juanico Ssaritutu, former *topil* of Guevavi, succeeded Francisco Covoazic as governor of the village in 1741.[71] For this and the various other offices filled by neophytes, Father Torres Perea and his predecessors had tried to choose natives who commanded the respect of their brethren and who might have been headmen among them even in their heathen state. As governor of the mission village it was the duty of Juanico to act as intermediary between Father Joseph and the people. He must convey the Padre's orders and oversee the activities that resulted. He must judge their lesser disputes, and see that the other justicias did their jobs. He must not, however, administer punishment without the consent of the missionary, in whom for all practical purposes resided the final authority — executive, legislative, and judicial.

Francisco Wuicho, alcalde of Guevavi, was Juanico's right-hand man. He carried on in the governor's absence. The village *fiscal*, Joseph, saw to it that everyone attended Mass. In the event of a village meeting called by the Padre, Joseph summoned them again. And he reported who was absent. Juan Sags, the mador, assembled the children for daily instruction and made the rounds of the village to find out if anyone were ailing, in which case he reported to Father Joseph. A tried warrior and hunter, Francisco served as *capitán*, or war leader. He led the men of Guevavi when they were called upon to join campaigns as auxiliaries to the king's soldiers.

Rarely did the Padre himself whip his charges. It was poor psychology. Had Father Joseph meted out punishment with his own hands he soon would have found himself the sole object of native resentment.

---

[71] As topil Juanico Ssaritutu witnessed a marriage on June 1, 1741, and as governor he was godfather at a baptism on November 26, 1741.

Instead, through governor Juanico he handed down a sentence suited to the transgression and Manuel, now topil, administered with gusto the lashes so necessary, to the Padres' way of thinking, if even a semblance of order was to be maintained in the mission.

As heathens the Pimas had managed to govern themselves without corporal punishment, except for the occasional execution of an evil shaman. A council of all the experienced men had made decisions; and a ceremonial leader had told the people what was good and what was bad. Now in the mission school of civilized government they were learning a new way, a way that depended on lashes, a way that permitted a clever native to throw off the old communal restraints and lord it over his fellows. As a justicia of the mission he had symbols of authority and prerogative of which he was unusually proud — a baton with silver knob on the top, a special place in church. These gave him esteem and set him apart from the others.[72]

With a small detachment of soldiers from distant Fronteras and some of his justicias and helpers, Father Joseph jogged on horseback along the trail beside pleasant Sonoita Creek. He was on his way a week before Christmas in 1741 to call upon and to marry in the eyes of the Church governor Antonio of Sonoita. It had long been the opinion of the Padres and the frontier citizenry alike that a presidio was needed in the Pimería. Fronteras was simply too far away to send an escort every time Father Torres Perea rode to Sonoita, or every time the Apaches stole a few head of mission stock. Almost daily, word of the Apaches' growing boldness was heard in Sonora. A year and a half had passed since a party of these savage hostiles had ambushed and scalped Captain Anza. Without him the frontier lay all the more exposed.

Though Father Joseph may not have realized it as he rode on toward Sonoita, plans for the founding of a new presidio, decreed six months earlier by the viceroy, were being acted upon at that very moment by the royal bureaucracy. The garrison was to be of the usual strength, fifty

---

[72] For the duties of the various native officials and the functioning of village government, see Treutlein, *Travel Reports of Joseph Och*, pp. 166–70, and Ignaz Pfefferkorn, *Sonora, A Description of the Province*, trans. and ed. Treutlein (Albuquerque: University of New Mexico Press, 1949), pp. 266–68. What imposition of this foreign form of government meant to the mission Indians is treated by Underhill, *Social Organization*, pp. 83–89, and Spicer, *Cycles of Conquest*, pp. 384–88.

Sonoita Creek

men, commanded by the veteran Captain Don Joseph Gómez de Silva. Nineteen leagues southeast of Guevavi and five southeast of Soamca, at the place known locally as San Mateo de Terrenate, the construction of adobe quarters for the soldiers would soon begin. Because the Viceroy had suggested that the new garrison be placed somewhere near Guevavi, and in his decree had referred to it as the presidio of Guevavi, that name stuck and proved a source of confusion to officials in Mexico City.[73] Perhaps on his next visit to Sonoita, Father Joseph would feel more secure in the knowledge that the royal presidio of San Phelipe de Guevavi, alias Terrenate, stood on a bluff only nineteen leagues away, hardly a day's ride.

As minister of Guevavi, Father Joseph spent a good part of the time in the saddle. During July of his first summer the young missionary rode over to Soamca to repay a visit by his superior Father Keller. As was customary for a visiting Padre, he baptized several Indian children while there, embellishing the Soamca book with his lovely penmanship and ornate rubric. Again the following year "in the absence of the Father Rector," he was back at Soamca, this time burying two women, one "just to the side of the doorway of the church toward the north," and the other "nearby the bells toward the north."[74] Then again when Padre Keller was asked to be the godfather of little Juana Bartholoméa San Román, whose father Don Diego had died, once more Father Joseph called for his horse, and at Soamca on October 13, 1743, he performed the service.

In the meantime he had his own vast territory to look after. Like a number of his successors, Torres Perea felt that this sprawling mission should be divided in two.[75] He tried, nonetheless, to cover it all, to visit regularly all of his villages and those of Bac as well, even though the realization that he could not hope to provide for the spiritual or the temporal needs of so many scattered children weighed heavily upon him. With Kino he would have agreed — Christianity spread thin was better than none at all.

Before, after, or during one of his regular visits to San Xavier del

[73] Despite the name, the new garrison was never stationed at or near the mission of Guevavi. Kessell, "The Puzzling Presidio: San Phelipe de Guevavi, alias Terrenate," *NMHR*, Vol. XLI (1966), pp. 21–46.

[74] Soamca, Libro de Casamientos y Entierros, 1735–1768; CPA.

[75] Torres Perea, Informe, March 16, 1744.

Bac, Father Joseph — this time escorted by soldiers from the new presidio of San Phelipe — rode into the village of Santo Thomás Apóstol Supquituni, wherever that may have been, and on December 18, 1743, married eight couples. Four of the soldiers "and the whole village of Toamuqui" were witnesses to the ceremonies.

By the twenty-ninth the party was at Guevavi's visita of Santa Gertrudis de Arivaca. There the Padre properly married five more couples and baptized half a dozen children. Heading then for Guevavi they followed the trail northeast to Sopori, where on the first day of 1744 the youthful missionary had the unpleasant task of recording five deaths. These he attributed to vomit, yellow vomit — two had died of this — retention of urine, and inflammation of the throat. Annoyed that he had not been informed earlier, Father Joseph wrote spontaneously in the book of burials, "I have reprimanded the native officials often because they do not call me to confess the sick or even tell me about the dead, and finding out for myself hit or miss requires real effort."

When he got back to Guevavi he learned that María, wife of Christóval the oxherd, had died giving birth to a dead child whom they had buried in the cemetery "far from its mother." Another small boy was dead. He simply could not be everywhere at once.

Just before his superiors transferred him from Guevavi in the spring of 1744, Father Joseph de Torres Perea set down on paper the state of his mission and that of Bac as well. Every Jesuit who served in an administrative capacity — from missionary to Provincial — was required to submit periodic reports; yet from Guevavi only this one is known to have survived.

First Father Joseph supplied the distances to neighboring missions — thirteen or fourteen leagues to Soamca, twenty-five to San Ignacio, and twenty-five to San Xavier — over roads made perilous by "the ferocious enemy Apache." Since the mission's refounding in 1732, he continued, there had been recorded in its books 978 baptisms. Many more were to be found recorded in the books of other missions whose Padres had passed through Guevavi. At the time he wrote, only twenty-three families, not counting "some native boys from elsewhere," were living in the cabecera of his mission. Even at that the population was declining, which gave the Padre cause for alarm. For more than a page he attempted to explain it.

Guevavi's climate was unhealthful for one thing, "to which may be added the absurdities which the natives of the place practice both in good health and in sickness." They were accustomed to eat raw fruit and then wash it down with almost-poisonous water. They bathed any time, even just after a meal. All the Father's vigilance was not enough, for they paid no attention to what he told them for the sake of their health.

A second cause of the population decline in Guevavi, Father Joseph believed, was the sterility of the women. He left the men out of it. Whether the cause was some occult local disease or again the unhygienic practices of the women themselves he was not sure. The fact that the milk of those few who did give birth dried up and that they bathed immediately after delivery, then carried on as before, caused their babies to die.[76] This, he noted, was not the case in other villages of similar climate. Quite understandably it did not occur to him that the natives of the other villages might have enjoyed better health because their lives had been less interfered with and because they had no Padre to tell them what was good for them. As a people they had survived for dozens of generations without outside advice. But he had yet another explanation, one which demonstrated that a well-educated Jesuit missionary of the mid-eighteenth century shared with his neophytes a strong belief in the mysterious powers of shamans. It was, of course, the Devil in them.

Two famous hechiceros had shown up in Guevavi in 1741. Because Father Joseph opposed them, they resorted to "the arts of their witch-craft" and made sterile the women. One of them had admitted as much. "The women, and *sensim et sine sensu* [gradually and without its being perceived] the weather, and the yearly sicknesses seemed to be extinguishing the people." In such subtle ways the shamans worked their evil. Not until lowered into the grave were native officials who cooperated with Father Joseph free from the tyranny of these sinister malefactors. They even terrorized their own kin. But was it not possible, reasoned Torres Perea, that God working through him had already begun to nullify and to correct these evils? Certainly the Padres were not going

---

[76] Nearly two hundred years later a Pápago woman recalled her own experience: "The children came so fast. I was always nursing one while another was coming, and then the nursing one died." Underhill, *Autobiography of a Papago Woman*, p. 48.

to give up. They would continue opposing the hechiceros; they would continue guiding their neophytes toward the Christian way of life, no matter the cost.

> So it is natural that they are exposed to travail for the sake of Christ, whose comforting presence is not lacking in the enormities which are suffered and which the Lord permits for the greater glory of his Ministers in this new field of conversion. So it was with the Fathers who were my predecessors. Of them the first, who [re] founded this mission, died in a year, and many believe that he died of a spell (only God knows). If it were so, he died doing his duty.
>
> The other Fathers lasted only a short time in the mission. There were three of them. Two were bewitched. All labored at the risk of their lives, much less their health, apostolically experiencing the effects of Holy Poverty in dress and in ordinary sustenance. For the sake of one soul they paid no heed to the inclemencies of the seasons, going forth to suffer the rigors of cold, the miseries of hunger, the distress of thirst, the risks and fatigues of the road, and the other hardships that the life of a missionary entails.[77]

Then, almost as if he felt that he had been too harsh on the Indians, he reversed himself. In Guevavi at least, his children were throwing off their heathenish ways. They were becoming less crude. They accepted baptism and attended daily instruction. At the exhorting of their Padres they had given up their bacchanals, and now they danced only occasionally, without abuses. They had taken to Christian marriage and were opposed to concubinage. They were even attempting to remove the public hechicero from their midst. Above all, he pointed out, they were obedient to their Padres, whom they venerated and imagined were not men from earth but come down from heaven to be with them.

Conditions were, Father Joseph was forced to admit, quite the opposite in the mission's visitas and rancherías. The distances, scarcity of water, and the danger of the roads made it difficult for the Padre to minister to them. The farther from him, the more backward the natives. He did not resent them — he pitied them. It filled him with compassion to see them subsisting in the hills by a muddy waterhole, subject to the

---

[77] Torres Perea, Informe, March 16, 1744.

whims of the weather and with hardly enough to eat.[78] They had neither baptism, Mass, instruction, nor anyone to confess them when they died. Most of them, in fact, did not know that there was a hell, and thus did not understand the necessity of conversion. "We need royal assistance to expand Christianity and to bring out of the hills the many heathens." Surely if the king were informed he would send more Padres.

San Xavier del Bac, where over four hundred families resided, had to be considered just one great heathen ranchería. Though the names of 2,142 persons had been entered in the mission's books of baptism since 1732,[79] there had been virtually no change in their mode of life. Few if any of them, Father Joseph noted, were "inclined to submit to the gentle yoke of Christ." They knew not how to pray, not the Pater Noster, nor the Ave María, nor even how to make the sign of the cross. Some fled baptism. Nearly all resisted Christian marriage, attempting to deceive their Padre by telling him that his predecessors had married them. Yet the book of marriages showed that they were lying — not thirty of them had been married in the eyes of the Church.

"Because of the distance and the dangers of the country it is not possible for the Fathers of Guevavi to do all that is necessary for the full instruction and proper administration of the Indians of this mission." Until they were provided with a Padre of their own, whom apparently at this stage they were *not* asking for, the natives of Bac would regrettably remain "Christians in name rather than in fact."[80]

Ildefonso de la Peña, another Jesuit born in Mexico, was having a difficult time as a missionary. He had served at Caborca, but "the superiors had to remove him," in the words of Father Sedelmayr, "because of his insuitability for the missions and because of certain disagreements which the Indians had with him."[81] In the opinion of Father

---

[78] Ruth Underhill goes to the other extreme to describe the Pápagos in their native state: "Poor as the Papago country was, its economics were those of abundance. Papago did not hoard property; they did not quarrel about land boundaries; they were constantly giving, as though from an inexhaustible supply. The answer is that the supply, meagre though it was from the modern point of view, was sufficient, for their simple needs and more." *Social Organization,* p. 90.

[79] Except for a few loose pages, all of San Xavier's books of baptisms, marriages, and burials from the Spanish and Mexican periods are missing.

[80] Torres Perea, "Mission Sⁿ Xavier del Baac," Pimería Alta, March 16, 1744; BL, Mexican Manuscripts (M-M) 1716, doc. 48, with a transcript and translation in BRP.

[81] Sedelmayr to Anzaldo, Tubutama, October 25, 1742; AHH, Temp., 17.

Keller, Peña was "not a good Father for Pimas or the Pimería; he is very tender for all this barbarity." [82] Yet in February, 1744, Peña came to Guevavi.

He may have been sent by his superiors to observe and to learn from Father Torres Perea. Or perhaps the latter had after three years fallen victim to Guevavi's unhealthful environment and needed the care of a companion. Whatever the case, Father Joseph, when he had recorded the marriage of Juan Miguel Martínez to one of the Romero girls on

February 9, turned over to Father Ildefonso the responsibility for the mission books. [83] Later that spring he got together his personal belongings and rode out of the village.

Father Torres Perea was on his way to Caborca, hardly a less unfortunate or less baneful post than the one he was leaving. Perhaps on the basis of a potential demonstrated in his realistic yet compassionate reports of conditions at Guevavi and Bac, Father Torres Perea was nominated by Father Visitor Duquesney on July 8, 1744, for the office of Father Rector of the rectorate of Los Santos Mártires del Japón in east-central Sonora. [84] Had he assumed this position, which apparently he did not, he would have become the immediate superior of his predecessor at Guevavi, the difficult son of Queen Christina's favorite, Alexandro Rapicani. Three years later, on August 8, 1747, a pall hung over Caborca. The young and fervent Mexican, Joseph de Torres Perea, was dead.

Through the spring of 1744 the gentle Father Peña survived. In mid-May he had illustrious company. Not since the days of Father Kino

---

[82] Keller to Father Visitor Luis María Marciano, February 16, 1741; quoted in Pradeau and Burrus, "Los Jesuitas." Peña, born in Saltillo in 1709, had been a Jesuit since 1727. He died at Onapa in July of 1745, just over a year after leaving Guevavi.

[83] Peña recorded no marriages while at Guevavi. He wrote his first baptismal entry in February, but failed to give the day, and his last on May 14. His burial entries, if he made any, are missing.

[84] Pradeau and Burrus, "Los Jesuitas."

had such a high-ranking Jesuit come to Guevavi. Father Visitor Juan Antonio Balthasar, a Swiss destined six years hence to become Father Provincial of New Spain, was touring the missions.[85] Because of the notable lack of facilities for guests at Guevavi he and his entourage probably did not tarry long. Nevertheless, native delegations flocked in from the mission's visitas, presumably to see the "Padre Grande." On May 13 Father Peña baptized six children from Sonoita and one from Tumacácori. The next day, while he performed the same service for still another child from Sonoita, the Father Visitor hinted in a letter to the Father Provincial that the interim Padre of Guevavi was not staying on.

"If per chance missionaries are on their way [from Europe]," wrote Balthasar, "I beg Your Reverence to bear in mind this province of the Pimería where there are two vacant missions and where two zealous and healthy laborers are needed."[86] Ildefonso de la Peña, who for one reason or another did not qualify, evidently left with the Father Visitor's party. Once again the Padre's house at Guevavi was closed up and vacant.

The following July the natives of Guevavi recognized a familiar figure riding along the river toward their village. When he had stayed several days and then ridden on, seven more children, two of them gente de razón, enjoyed the grace of holy baptism. Once again Ignacio Xavier Keller, the durable "cacique" of Soamca, bore the burden of three missions. Thus, temporarily, Father Visitor Balthasar informed the Father Provincial, the stipends for Soamca, Guevavi, and Bac should be sent to Keller. If, however, "Father Carlos Neymayr, whom I have assigned conditionally to the latter two missions, should arrive, their stipends can be turned over to him."[87] But Neymayr did not arrive.

---

[85] See Dunne, *Balthasar*, for a biographical sketch of the Father Visitor and for the circumstances of his inspection tour. Father Dunne apparently did not know that Balthasar visited Guevavi.

[86] Balthasar to Father Christóbal de Escobar y Llamas, Guevavi, May 14, 1744; AHH, Temp., 17. In the margin someone else noted the need for two "strong and healthy subjects for the Pimería."

[87] Balthasar to Escobar, "De algunas Missiones de esta Prov.ª de Sonora vacantes y de aplicacion de su lymosna [1744]"; *ibid.* Father Neymayr ended up in Baja California instead of the Pimería. On July 8, 1744, Father Visitor Duquesney listed Guevavi and San Xavier as vacant. His report from Babiácora, *ibid.*

In early November Don Joachín Félix Díaz, curate of Nacosari and one of the few secular priests who dared brave the dangers of the Pimería to visit his scattered parishioners, recorded in the Guevavi book the baptism of Juana Gertrudis de la Luz Rita Ramírez. Don Nicholás Romero and his wife María Ephigenia Perea, the valley's most popular godparents, had another little godchild to keep track of. Father Keller was present too. In the marriage register he scribbled for Father Díaz's signature a notice of the union of Juan Nicolás de la Higuera and an Apache woman. Again at Christmas time Keller was back in Guevavi baptizing, marrying, and listing the burials of those who had died since his previous visit.

Meanwhile, the Jesuit destined to serve longer than any other at Guevavi, to bring to the mission relative prosperity, and to arrange for the building of a real church, was having his trouble getting to the New World.

"From Santa María I traveled on to the mission of Guevavi, which is cared for by Father Joseph Garrucho. With his great zeal and concern for souls he has much enlarged the village, gathering many Pimas who used to live in the barrancas and reducing them to life together beneath the bell."

Father Visitor Carlos de Roxas, 1748

4.

Prosperity at a Price
The Administration of Joseph Garrucho, and Revolt, 1745-1752

WELL PROPORTIONED, though somewhat slender, he stood at the ship's rail that day in February, 1744, and surveyed for a last time the busy port of Cádiz, gateway to Spain's New World. His black hair matched his cassock and contrasted with his light skin. His eyes were a definite blue, his beard sparse. Born Giuseppe Garrucio at Castel Aragonese on the island of Sardinia, he was a young priest, a Jesuit. For three years he had been waiting to sail for America. Now at long last he had embarked on the *San Francisco,* alias *La Peregrina.* Would the tide never change? As her crew made ready, neither they nor the young Jesuit suspected how apt their ship's alias would prove this crossing.[1]

No voyage across the Atlantic in the eighteenth century was without risk. In 1744, in the wake of the naval war the English called Jenkins'

---

[1] At his embarcation in 1744 Garrucho was reported to be twenty-eight years old. Elsewhere, however, his birthdate is given as March 27, 1712, which is apparently correct, making him thirty-two instead. Father Joseph had entered the Society of Jesus on January 6, 1731, and had sailed from the port of Alghero, Sardinia, bound for Spain on October 23, 1740. AGI, Contratación, 5550. Zelis, *Catálogo,* pp. 20–21. Because the Jesuits of Sardinia were joined to those of Spain in the internal organization of the order, a considerable number of Sardinians found their way to the missions of the Spanish New World.

Ear, it was even riskier. Furthermore, it would be uncomfortable. Nine years earlier aboard the ill-fated *Santa Rosa* Fathers Rapicani and Sedelmayr had endured a constant struggle "with hunger and thirst, with [sea] water in the ship, with heat, with crowded quarters, and above all, with swarms of vermin," only to be shipwrecked in Vera Cruz harbor.[2] With their names now conveniently hispanicized, Father Joseph Garrucho and his nearly twenty fellow Jesuits might well have echoed Sedelmayr's initial bid to his ship: "May she stoutly defend her Americans against the English!"[3]

It happened off the north coast of Cuba, almost within sight of haven. Captain Tovar had guided the *San Francisco* safely across the Atlantic and to the relief of his passengers had brought her once again into coastal waters. But just then his ship was set upon and successfully boarded by Englishmen. The daring captors, finding themselves with too many mouths to feed, decided to put ashore excess passengers.

News of their unceremonious arrival preceded the two castaways inland to Puerto del Príncipe, today Camagüey, where by chance certain of the leading citizens had been earnestly requesting the services of Jesuits. Welcomed as an answer to prayers, Fathers Garrucho and Juan Cubedo rested and then engaged in a "fervent and very fruitful" twenty-day ministry, after which, amid tears and regrets, they set out for Havana and from there booked passage to the mainland. Thanks in part to the reports of two Sardinians, Garrucho and Cubedo, the people of Puerto del Príncipe in Cuba soon boasted a Jesuit college.[4]

To his superiors in Mexico City, Joseph Garrucho had appeared sufficiently "zealous and healthy" for assignment to the Pimería. Early in 1745 he had arrived on that far frontier and had met the "severe and difficult" Father Keller. Now, together, they rode beside the shallow river, shaded by immense cottonwoods whose fresh spring foliage was set to rustling by the slightest breeze. To their left, rounded, dry grass- and mesquite-covered hills descended almost to the river's bank. Across the arroyo-cut valley to the east were similar hills farther away, and to the north, seemingly isolated, stood the mountain that came to be called

[2] Sedelmayr to Father Magnus Amman, México, May 10, 1736; translation, BRP.

[3] Sedelmayr to Amman, Puerto de Santa María, November 21, 1735; translation, BRP.

[4] Alegre, *Historia de la Compañía*, IV, pp. 404–405. Forty-one-year-old Father Cubedo (Giovanni Cubeddu) later served for many years at the mission of Chínipas, on a tributary of the upper Río Fuerte in extreme western Chihuahua. *Ibid.*, p. 404, n. 31.

San Cayetano. Beyond and to its right the impressive Santa Rita peaks rose in the distance.

It was a familiar scene to Ignacio Keller. If, as they approached the mission that was to be his first, the newcomer craned for a glimpse of bell towers like the hundreds he had passed on the Camino Real from Mexico City, he was disappointed. There were signs of life all along the river, but he could see nothing that resembled a mission.

Suddenly they mounted a rise on the east bank and were there. Without the cross and the bells and the crowd of curious Pimas, he might have taken this several-acre clearing and its poor buildings for another rancho. The Padre's adobe house, perhaps somewhat enlarged, was apparently the same one that Captain Anza had begun for the hapless Father Grazhoffer. The church, and they used the word loosely, was nothing more, it seemed, than a brush roof on posts, which his predecessors may have ordered walled with adobes. Not long before Father Torres Perea left Guevavi, he had buried one of the unfortunate babies of the village "in the *enramada* between the first and second posts to the east." Doubtless the new Padre noted the various improvements, whether adobe storage huts, a cemetery wall, chicken coops, or corrals. But this mission at best was crude — a worthy challenge for Joseph Garrucho.

To the throng of brown faces Father Keller introduced another Father Joseph come down from the heavens, or at least over an ocean to be with them. The forceful Padre of Soamca spoke of obedience. They must let their new minister know when someone lay ill or dying. They must plant and work the fields of the Church. And they must convince all of their relatives to come and live in the mission and receive instruction and baptism. In return they would be granted the greatest gift of all — eternal salvation. The Pimas listened attentively and were agreeable: they may have even smiled at these words.

Once Father Keller's scribe[5] had entered in the book of burials

---

[5] This scribe, perhaps a resident of the presidio at Terrenate, made numerous entries in the books of Soamca for Father Keller, who was indeed a very poor penman. Because Garrucho signed some of these entries while visiting Soamca (e.g., baptisms on June 4, 1746, and October 19, 1747) several historians have taken the scribe's graceful studied hand for Garrucho's and thus have erroneously implied that Soamca not Guevavi was Father Joseph's station from 1744 to 1748, for example Pradeau, *Expulsión*, p. 150. By comparing the entries Garrucho actually did write (e.g., Soamca, Libro de Bautismos y Casamientos de los Pueblos de Visita, 1743–1755, September 4, 1746; Pinart, CPA; and Guevavi, "Tubaca y Otros," 1745–1751) with those of the scribe it is obvious that they were indeed two different men.

those seven persons who had died since Christmas, Joseph Garrucho on May 5 in a pinched but legible hand made his first entry as resident Padre, noting the burial in "this church" of a girl servant formerly in the employ of Captain Urrea.[6] Next day Keller performed a marriage, and on the seventh Father Joseph baptized four children. One couple had

brought a son all the way from Baboquívari in the shadow of that great pinched-rock mountain. For him — called Phelipe — Juanico Cipriano Cavosstuitoc, latest native governor of Guevavi, was godfather.

Perhaps because May 8, the feast of San Miguel's fifth-century appearance at Monte Gargano,[7] was at hand, the patronage of the village, previously entrusted to Los Santos Ángeles Gabriel and Raphael, was henceforth given over to the third of the principal archangels. Until the Black Robes were banished, the warrior angel prevailed as patron saint, and dark little Miguels and Miguelas padded around the village.

Almost before Father Joseph got to know his neophytes, they subjected him to an initiation they had practiced before. They deserted him. In response to the alarmed Padre's plea, Captain Pedro Vicente de Tagle Bustamante and a detachment of soldiers hastened north from the presidio of San Phelipe at Terrenate — founded not only to chastize Apaches but also "to curb such recurring restlessness among the Pimas."[8] Father Keller rode with them. Reining up in Guevavi, they found Garrucho in the company of all those who remained — two houseboys and a vecino. The Captain was all for bringing the faithless fugitives

---

[6] Though we have not a shred of Father Garrucho's correspondence from Guevavi, nearly all of his entries in the mission books remain. Between May 5, 1745, and November 21, 1751, he and an occasional visiting Padre recorded 306 baptisms, 163 marriages, and 156 burials.

[7] Until recently the occasion of Saint Michael's alleged appearance at Monte Gargano in Italy was observed as one of that saint's two feast days. The other, September 29, has prevailed.

[8] Lieutenant Francisco Xavier de Escalante, Cuquiárachi, September 5, 1754; Utrera testimonies, AGI, Guad., 419, microfilm, BL. These are testimonies recorded by the Jesuit Father Visitor General, Joseph de Utrera, August-December, 1754, concerning the Pima rebellion of 1751.

down from the hills and punishing them forthwith. The two Padres protested. Without resort to bloodshed they succeeded "with their kind words, cajoling, and flattery, and some gifts," in returning the wayward children and livestock to the mission.[9] These Pimas were by no means content and loyal neophytes, reported Garrucho to the Father Visitor, who reported to the governor of Sonora, who did nothing.[10]

Even when they stayed in the mission, Garrucho soon learned, their numbers decreased. Measles and smallpox, far more than the feared Apaches, were the scourges of the Pimería. During Garrucho's six years, at least three killing epidemics visited Guevavi.[11] In October, 1747, he returned from Bac or one of his other villages to find ten children dead, all of whom he buried in "this church," such as it was.

To replace those who died, Father Joseph had to bring in new blood from native rancherías in the barrancas and hills nearby. At this he was very successful, as the mission books reflected and his superiors noted.[12] It was almost like hoarding a gradually disappearing commodity; as the overall supply decreased, one's particular stockpile increased. By whatever means he found at his disposal the Padre attempted to attract natives into the mission. If he succeeded, as Garrucho did, the population — and thus the potential prosperity of the mission — grew even as the total number of Pimas diminished. Yet long before the end of the mission period in Pimería Alta, the Padres found themselves caring for more and more gente de razón and fewer and fewer Indians.

"If the Fathers of the Pimería had soldiers to help bring heathens and [backsliding] Christians out of the barrancas," wrote Father Visitor Roxas, "Christianity and the mission villages would be greatly

---

[9] Their flight on this occasion was supposed to have been caused by a false report spread by a malevolent Pima. Christóbal de Osef, Real de Todos Santos, September 16, 1754; *ibid.*

[10] Juan Ygnacio Rodríguez Soto, San Miguel de Horcasitas, November 15, 1753; "Testimonio de los Autos formados en orden de Rl. Cedula de 4 de Octre. de 1752, sobre la averiguazn. del origen que tuvo el Alzamiento de los Pimas Altos, en la Provincia de Sonora"; AGI, Guad., 418, microfilm, BL. Testimonies taken by Governor Pablo de Arce y Arroyo, November, 1753–January, 1754. Cited below as Arce y Arroyo testimonies.

[11] From the bunching of burials at Guevavi during certain months in 1747, 1749, and 1751, Dobyns noted the lethal effect of these epidemics in "Tubac Through Four Centuries: An Historical Resume and Analysis," unpublished report for the Arizona State Parks Board, 1959, pp. 94–100.

[12] Father Carlos de Roxas to Father Provincial Andrés Xavier García, Arizpe, December 29, 1748; AHH, Temp., 278.

augmented. The Pimas are easily brought together and just as easily led astray again. . . ."[13] The need for military assistance was obvious. But reduction, the uprooting and transplanting, cannot have been a pleasant business, either for the Indians or for Garrucho.

Most of Guevavi's population, Father Stiger later admitted, was reduced by force.[14] It took the prodding of soldiers and Christian Indians to provide converts. On his tours of inspection even Governor Vildó-sola helped congregate the heathens in "more convenient places."[15] Luis Oacpicagigua, soon to become the most infamous Pima of them all, listed among his good works the reduction of two rancherías of his brethren to Guevavi and two more to its poorly populated visita at Arivaca. This he had done, or so he later claimed through his apologists, not for pay but for love of God and king.[16]

As Father Segesser had observed, "Indians do not come to Christian service when they do not see the maize pot boiling."[17] To a people whose existence had from time immemorial revolved around the quest for food, certainly it, above the new God, was the most attractive feature of mission life. Upon the Padre's ability to supply food for his neophytes depended the expansion of his mission. As a provider, Garrucho was also very successful. To put his practical and theological ranch school on a productive basis, Father Joseph employed a division of labor. He named foremen and vaqueros, shepherds and oxherds, mule boys, plowmen, irrigators, gardeners, and a cook and a baker. The king had decreed that natives be made to work no more than three days each week in the mission fields. Depending on the jobs to be done, however, they worked

[13]*Ibid.*

[14] Father Gaspar Stiger to Segesser, San Ignacio, November 29, 1751; Ortiz Parrilla testimonies, Quaderno no. 1, AGI, Guad., 419, microfilm, BL. This legajo contains the documents assembled by Governor Diego Ortiz Parrilla during and immediately after the Pima rebellion of 1751, November, 1751–March, 1753.

[15] Vildósola to Viceroy Revillagigedo, México, February 6, 1749; BNMex, 28/706. This is the former governor's defense of his administration written shortly after his removal from office.

[16] Luis Oacpicagigua, San Ignacio, March 24, 1752; Ortiz Parrilla testimonies, 8. The names of the rancherías reduced to Guevavi were recorded as "Upiatuban" and "El Concuc"; and those of the rancherías reduced to Arivaca as "El Toamuc" and "El Suctuni." Perhaps the latter was the same ranchería referred to by Father Torres Perea in 1743 as "the village of Santo Thomás Apóstol Supquituni."

[17] Treutlein, "Relation of Segesser," *MA*, XXVII, p. 161.

sometimes more than three days and other times less. After all, "the sky was high and the king far away."

Under Garrucho's general supervision the mission ranch at Tubac began to produce. At the other visitas there were crops to harvest and cattle to brand. In the village of Guevavi proper, Father Joseph made it a practice to keep a supply of maize during most of the year in the center of the plaza in a *tapestle,* a large open cage on stilts, where it served as a convenient reminder to all of a full stomach.[18]

The Padre's day was an endless round. Perhaps in describing the hectic routine for his relatives in Europe, Father Segesser crowded too much into a typical day. Nonetheless, his account of the missionary's life, written at Tecoripa but applicable to Guevavi under Garrucho, provides a rare glimpse of the mundane tasks that occupied most of his time.

> Every day I must awaken the houseboys and supervise the morning prayer, because the Pima is so careless that he no longer knows on one day what he was ordered to do the day before. For that reason an old father missionary in Puebla de los Angeles said to me jestingly during my journey to Mexico: "Since the Pope ordered one to believe that the Indians have a rational soul, one would have to believe it; but one had not seen it."
>
> After the morning prayer a bell is rung as a signal for Mass, the choir master prays the rosary with the people and afterwards sings the All Saints Litany. Besides the prayers which the Indians say in their own languages, the king and the superiors of the Order have directed that the Indians learn also in Spanish the Christian doctrine and the necessary prayers. The missionary must, therefore, know Spanish. A knowledge of Spanish is also required of the missionary so that he may hear confession of the many Spaniards settled in this country. With Spanish, the missionary may also do business with the merchants of this nation. . . .
>
> After Mass the Christian doctrine is prayed or sung, although if there is pressing work to be done the latter is sometimes omitted. Afterwards the father and his ever-present guests partake of a breakfast of chocolate. . . .
>
> After breakfast the father has to give the cook his directions for the mid-day meal and must provide him with the wherewithal for it

---

[18] Captain Gabriel Antonio de Vildósola, Cuquiárachi, September 9, 1754; Utrera testimonies.

from the storehouse. To give the cook the keys to the storehouse would mean, according to the Pima custom, to give him leave to eat everything available, and all at one time. An entire ox seems meager fare for a three or four day period for my Pimas. . . .

The houseboys have to take care of feeding the hens, ducks, and geese. The housemaster is supposed to provide wheat for the feeding, but since he is often not at his post the padre has to take care of this business himself. The padre must also give the gardener his orders for gathering in the produce and must direct the herdsmen to care for the stock. Meanwhile, he may get a report that there are children standing at the church door waiting to be baptized, that a magistrate [native official] has made a request for seed maize, or that someone is ill or dying. And so it goes the livelong day.

Besides spiritual duties the missionary has continually to take care of worldly business which he by no means dare neglect. . . . Providing food for the Indians seems very laborious to many fathers for they had an entirely different view of things when they left their beloved province to devote themselves to missionary work. . . .

It happens that I left my paternal hearth to enter a spiritual station principally because I saw that business and agriculture were not for me, but in this mission I encountered much more of that sort of anxiety than I would ever have had in my fatherland. . . .

Thus there remains little time to the father missionary for the performance of his spiritual labors (unless we wish to say that the entire day is spent in spiritual business, even though it may be temporal). In order to write these fugitive lines — as I promised to do — I had to set aside other business with which I will, however, immediately catch up.

In the meantime, we shall view further how the daily order or better said, disorder, is carried on. Let us imagine that the above-mentioned business has been attended to and that I think I have earned an opportunity to say my horary [breviary] prayers. Along comes the cook and demands pepper, ginger, and saffron. The house servant announces that two messengers have arrived . . . I order that for the time being they be fed and promise to give them tobacco when I have finished my prayers. Then the cook comes once more and asks for lard and eggs which he had earlier forgotten to request. While I say my prayers the houseboys set the table for luncheon. Again much is forgotten. Now knives, and at other times forks, are not placed. . . .

After luncheon prayers are said. Then the cook is given directions to send food to the homes of the sick. He is instructed not to leave the dishes with them. Dishes must be returned at once to be washed and dried.

Then the father goes to the chicken-coop with the houseboys to gather eggs, and to see whether a bird of prey has carried away any hens.

Now comes the siesta, the time when it is customary here for everyone to take his afternoon repose, except the father who uses this most quiet hour of the day to write or read whatever seems necessary. Birds also sleep during siesta. When they awaken the turmoil begins again. Then the cook demands meat for the evening meal, the *fiscus* requests maize for *posoli* [posole], and the baker flour for baking. And finally, after instruction in the catechism (held every day except Sunday), it is necessary that the father go, shovel in hand, to the garden and work there until the Ave Maria chime so that things do not go to ruin. Then when one returns home tired out the servants are assembled to pray the rosary, the Litany, the Salve Regina (which I have taught them to sing as we do), as well as the *Alabedo* [alabado]. . . .

Evening meal follows the prayers, after which I record the day's sales and purchases, supplies used, and any noteworthy occurrences. All these items are recorded in special books so that no shortages will be found at the customary visitation of the superiors. When all these things have been attended to the rest hour at last arrives for the missionary. During this time he is somewhat in communion with God, and expects throughout the night to be called to a sickbed.

This is the schedule which remained the same from the first moment of my arrival here until the present, and it will remain this way until God bestows better understanding upon the Pimas so that they will take hold of things tolerably well without being admonished and ordered to do so. They do nothing for the church and for the house of the missionary without receiving an order. Unless directed to do so, they would not even feed or water a tethered horse or mule. Their attitude is the more noteworthy because they are able and mindful in their own affairs. Today on the feast of St. Jacob, when I think especially of my father professor, Jacob Begler, I ordered the sexton to place six candlesticks on the altar. But because I did not also fix him up with candles I found when I went to the altar that the candlesticks were empty and unlighted. So it goes with everything. Even the houseboys would not go to sleep in their proper places if the father did not watch them and seek them out from other nooks.

One can easily realize from this presentation what the missionary's work consists of and what the difference is between a European and an American pastor.[19]

---

[19] Treutlein, "Relation of Segesser," *MA*, XXVII, pp. 160–64.

Involved as they were for much of the year with the many temporal details of operating their individual missions, the Jesuits looked forward to their annual Spiritual Exercises. Eight days of disciplined rededication tended to restore their perspective and rekindle their zeal. On the eve of the feast day of Saint Ignatius Loyola in 1748, Father Garrucho evidently joined Father Keller at Soamca for this welcome break.[20]

For more than seventeen years Joseph Garrucho had been a member of the Society of Jesus. After a two-year novitiate and his first simple religious vows, he had begun the long prescribed course of study and examination, presumably in his native country — two years of collegiate studies, three years of philosophy, several of teaching, three years of theology, ordination, a fourth year of theology, and a year-long tertianship which was, in effect, a third year of novitiate, a "final test of his humility and obedience." With all that behind him, Father Joseph, like many of his brethren, had set out for foreign missions. Now, in 1748, as he observed the feast of the Society's founder, only his final solemn vows remained unsaid. Not until the Father General of all Jesuits, on the recommendation of Garrucho's superiors, gave his approval would the missionary of Guevavi be permitted to profess.

When Father Visitor Carlos de Roxas had seen for himself how well Garrucho was managing difficult Guevavi, he lauded the slender missionary.[21] By this time Father Joseph had acquired a degree of proficiency in the Indian language, which though variously enforced was required of a missionary before his final profession. Late in 1748 the word he waited for arrived.

More than a hundred miles he rode to get to Arizpe, the mission of Father Roxas. There in the church on December 10 during the celebration of Mass, before "Almighty God and in the presence of His Virgin Mother and the whole heavenly court and to all here present," which included Father Visitor Roxas representing the Father General in Rome, Joseph Garrucho professed his final solemn vows of perpetual poverty, chastity, and obedience. Then, as a Jesuit, he made his fourth vow: "I further promise my special obedience to the Supreme Pontiff."

---

[20] At Soamca on El Día de San Ignacio, July 31, 1748, Father Joseph baptized a boy for whom Father Ignacio was godfather.

[21] Roxas to García, December 29, 1748.

When Mass was over, Father Joseph retired to the sacristy with his superior where he repeated five simple vows. These included his promises to uphold the Society's regulations regarding poverty, never to promote his own election to any higher office inside or outside the Society, never to refuse to listen to the advice of his brethren, and only to obey such advice if he judged it better than his own as a Jesuit fully conscious of the laws of the Society. Thus fulfilled, he rode north once again to Guevavi, grateful that at long last he was indeed in the fullest sense of permanence, a Jesuit.[22]

In 1749 Garrucho almost enrolled in the ranks of Jesuit explorers. First, however, he was called upon to calm a distraught brother. The ill-disposed natives at Caborca, it seemed, had all but unnerved Father Bartholomé Sáenz. Replaced by the diminutive Father Tello, whom the Caborcans subsequently martyred, Sáenz was sent to Guevavi, where his superiors hoped that "being in the company of Father Garrucho, who has a light-hearted disposition, he might put aside all of his apprehensions."[23] Father Joseph's tonic seemed to work, so well in fact that he considered leaving Sáenz in charge at Guevavi while he went off to alter the course of empire.

---

[22] It was customary for a Jesuit to profess his final vows on one of the various feast days of the Blessed Virgin Mary. December 10 was the feast of the Transfer of the Holy House of Loreto (traditionally the house in which the Annunciation took place, later moved from the Holy Land to Loreto, Italy). Although Father Garrucho's profession was dated at Arizpe on December 10, he himself signed an entry in his mission book stating that he had baptized five children at Guevavi that very same day. In one or the other instance the date was an approximation or a slip, for it is extremely doubtful that Father Joseph was in both places on a single day. A copy of Garrucho's profession is listed in AHH, Temp., 16. An English translation of the profession of Father Henrique Ruhen, Tubutama, August 15, 1751, is included in Ronald L. Ives, "Mission San Marcelo del Sonoydag," *Records of the American Catholic Historical Society of Philadelphia*, Vol. LXVI (1955), pp. 220–21.

[23] Roxas to García, Arizpe, August 8, 1749; AHH, Temp., 278. Sáenz had accepted Caborca on November 29, 1748, and had given it up on July 10, 1749. Entregas; WBS, 1744, ff. 271–72, 295–96. He was apparently to have been installed at San Xavier del Bac in April of 1749, but when a military escort was denied the plan fell through. Arriving at Guevavi during the summer he seems to have remained in the salutary company of Father Joseph until fall. Shortly thereafter, he was reassigned to Cuquiárachi. Father Salvador Ignacio de la Peña also was assigned to San Xavier, it appears, but before he got there his mission was changed to Cucurpe. Father Thomás Miranda to Balthasar, Ures, June 16, 1749; *ibid.* José Rafael Rodríguez Gallardo to Ortiz Parrilla, Mátape, March 15, 1750; AGN, Historia, 16.

Since the days of Kino, the Padres and their advocates had looked
beyond the Pimería, to the lands of the Yumas, the Gileños, the Hopis
and farther. Keller had seen the Salt River in 1737 and had called it the
Río de la Asunción. Six years later he had penetrated the country north
of the Gila on his way to contact the Hopis. On that occasion, however,
the rugged Jesuit and his escort rode straight into an Apache ambush,
and at least one soldier died as a result.

At about the same time, a fond and frequent dream of Father Kino's
was revived. The king wished the Jesuits to extend their missions to the
lower Gila and Colorado River heathens, thus linking Pimería Alta and
ill-supplied Baja California.

The war-loving Yumas had not exactly made Father Sedelmayr feel
at home on the Colorado in 1748.[24] Yet he had resolved to go back. This
time he planned to take Garrucho and show him the tall comely people
and their great silty river. By early October the entrada was "conceived,
arranged, and prepared," only to have the acting governor deny the
necessary military escort. The soldiers, he claimed, were needed in the
wars against the Seris and the Apaches.[25] The Jesuits were not convinced. Repeatedly their plans, even the king's will, had been foiled by
imperious, unimaginative New World functionaries who paid more
attention to saving a few pesos than to active propagation of the Faith.[26]
Thus, the restored Father Sáenz was not left alone at Guevavi, and
Garrucho missed his chance to meet the Yumas.

Father Joseph was a congenial sort. Unlike some of his brethren
farther south, he seemed to get on well with most of the gente de razón
he served. It was more than just congeniality, however. For Garrucho,
it was a matter of self-preservation. He occupied the most advanced
position on the entire Jesuit frontier. Exposed as he was to Apache raid-

[24] Sedelmayr mislabeled an account of this trek to the Yumas "Entrada á la nacion de
los yumas Gentiles el año 1749. por el mes de Otte y Nov," Tubutama, January 15, 1750.
Original manuscript in APHS; translation in Dunne, *Sedelmayr,* pp. 55–64. He actually
made the trip in 1748. In 1749 his plans to go again were thwarted as described above.
Furthermore, he admitted that for six weeks during October and November of 1749 he was
flat on his back with *un tabardillo recio.* Sedelmayr to García, Tubutama, January, 1750;
AGN, Historia, 308.

[25]*Ibid.* Rodríguez Gallardo to Ortiz Parrilla, March 15, 1750.

[26] See for example Burrus, ed., *Misiones norteñas mexicanas de la Compañía de Jesús,
1751–1757* (México, D.F.: Antigua Librería Robredo, 1963), pp. 41–45.

ing and Pima restlessness, it behooved him, and the settlers, too, for that matter, to cooperate. Moreover, Guevavi's immense territory was big enough for both. The corrupting influence of the Spaniards' frontier way of life, the clamoring for Indian labor and mission lands, the bitter disputes with parish priests of mining towns — all of which combined in the long-established southern missions to make the Jesuit's life "a constant battle" — these were not yet well-defined issues at Guevavi.[27] Common defense and isolation drew Padre and settlers together.

Just how the land was distributed between the gente de razón and the mission, however, is something of a puzzle. The mission does not seem to have had a land grant as such. Apparently the allotments to Indian pueblos so carefully delineated in the Laws of the Indies did not apply to the Jesuits' frontier missions of penetration. The Black Robes' enemies in Sonora claimed, of course, that the missionaries had turned the province into a private domain. Only the king and the Indians, they pointed out, were rightful owners of the lands, yet, in fact, the Jesuits controlled all the best of it.[28]

While Don Antonio de Rivera and Captain Urrea probably held formal title to their estancias, it is doubtful that each of the motley settlers scattered along the watered valleys of Guevavi's vast jurisdiction had been legally granted his plot. Perhaps they entered into informal agreements with the Padre and paid him token tribute for the use of mission lands. Some no doubt simply enjoyed squatters' rights. Even if the ill-defined mission boundaries were considered to be contiguous with those of the neighboring missions, thus encompassing thousands of square miles, only a small percentage of the land was arable. As Spaniards or half-breeds preempted the river bottom acres and the most reliable waterholes, the Indians sulked. It was no secret that they resented these

---

[27] For an excellent summary of the areas of conflict between the missionaries and the civilian population, from the Jesuit point of view, see *ibid.*, pp. 81–83. The economic basis for Jesuit-civil discord is considered by Treutlein in "The Economic Regime of the Jesuit Mission in Eighteenth Century Sonora," *Pacific Historical Review,* Vol. VIII (1939), pp. 289–300, and by Navarro García, *Sonora y Sinaloa,* pp. 161–234.

[28]*Ibid.,* pp. 203–208. Though land ownership during the Jesuit years in Pimería Alta remains unclear, this is not the case in the later Franciscan period, when land grants, including the mission's, were carefully surveyed and duly recorded. See Ray H. Mattison, "Early Spanish and Mexican Settlements in Arizona," *NMHR,* Vol. XXI (1946), pp. 273–327.

intruders.[29] Yet, to Joseph Garrucho, the congenial and realistic Sardinian nine thousand miles from home, these fellow Europeans, or at least gente de razón, proved of no small comfort and assistance.

Meanwhile, behind the Padre's back, certain of his natives plotted their revenge.

His last months at Guevavi were the most eventful of his administration. Under his supervision the mission had prospered as never before. There had been a surplus, enough to permit consideration of a long-overdue improvement — a proper church. Several times during 1751 Garrucho was gone from Guevavi, apparently making arrangements farther south. His *memoria* for the year, a list of Guevavi's needs sent to the Father Procurator in Mexico City, almost certainly reflected the mission's new affluence. A new church deserved new ornaments.

Late in the summer Don Joachín de Cásares, master builder from Arizpe, arrived in Guevavi to take charge of the project. Plans called for, or at least came to include, a rectangular church whose inside dimensions were not particularly impressive, about fifteen by fifty feet. The new structure was to be built on the extreme east edge of the mesilla with its long axis lying roughly north-south and its main doors facing south onto the village plaza. Tabular slabs of local conglomerate rock cemented with mud mortar, Don Joachín and Father Joseph agreed, would provide a solid foundation. The walls of sun-dried adobes set in mud mortar were to be all of three feet thick, plastered with mud, whitewashed, and finally decorated inside in various colors. The flat roof would rest on *vigas,* large beams spanning the building's short axis. A door through the west wall of the church was to lead out into a patio enclosed on the other three sides by rooms one deep with their doors opening onto the patio. In this *convento,* measuring overall some 90 by 105 feet, Father Joseph would have his quarters, perhaps a small personal chapel, the Indian school, a kitchen, refectory, and whatever storage and work rooms space permitted. Here at Guevavi Joseph Garrucho would leave, if nothing else, a house of God where none comparable had previously stood.

Presumably master-builder Cásares brought with him to Guevavi artisans and assistants. For unskilled labor, he depended of course on the mission's neophytes. They would supply the muscle, albeit at their own

---

[29] Stiger to Segesser, November 29, 1751.

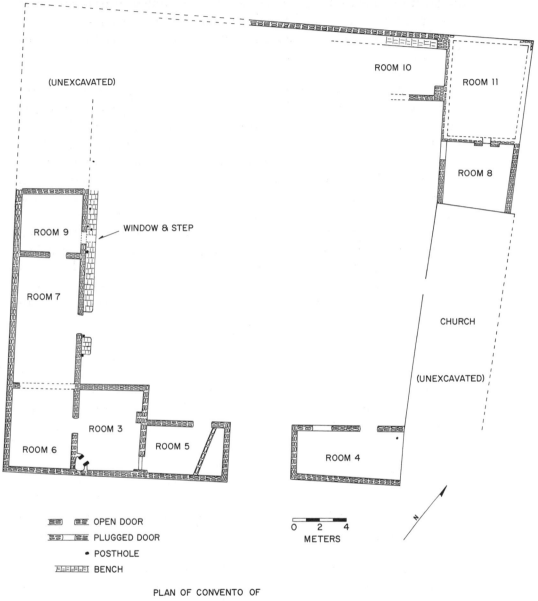

(UNEXCAVATED)

ROOM 10

ROOM 11

WINDOW & STEP

ROOM 9

ROOM 8

ROOM 7

CHURCH

(UNEXCAVATED)

ROOM 3

ROOM 6

ROOM 5

ROOM 4

N

⊟⊟ ⊟⊟ OPEN DOOR

⊟⊟) ⊟⊟ PLUGGED DOOR

• POSTHOLE

⊞⊞⊞⊞ BENCH

0 2 4
METERS

PLAN OF CONVENTO OF

MISSION GUEVAVI

less-than-frantic pace. Commenting on native building crews, Father Sedelmayr once wrote: "Their manner of working was to gather between eight and nine and to quit about four. The ones who dug the earth did so seated. Those who carried two small balls of mud did so, then sat down to rest. The others also worked at this pace. But because there were many of them, something was accomplished."[30]

Though normally compliant, the Pima was by no means unwarlike. Given the chance to fight as an auxiliary at the side of Spanish regulars he demonstrated considerable skill and ferocity — and against the normally defiant Apache, the Spaniards needed all the help they could muster.

As part of the annual fall offensive, in 1751 a contingent of Pimas was to join with the soldiers of the presidio of San Phelipe on a routine search-and-destroy campaign down the San Pedro and back through the Chiricahua Mountains. From Sáric on the upper Río Altar, Luis Oacpicagigua, captain general of all the Pimas and a hero of the Seri wars, set forth with a large band of warriors. Their route took them through Guevavi, where Father Joseph's maize pot boiled continuously for three days. The Padre himself told how he welcomed the famous Luis, treating him as if he were a vecino and entertaining the Indian in his own quarters. And when the warriors were ready to leave, Garrucho sent them on their way with fifteen head of the mission's cattle.[31]

At Soamca their reception was less cordial. "Don" Luis arrived dressed and armed as befitted a Spanish officer, and perhaps he was overbearing. Father Keller may have suggested that since Luis was more

---

[30] The quotation is from Sedelmayr's oft-cited apology of November 29, 1754, supposedly written from Guevavi. The copy in AGN, Historia, 17, does indeed read "Guevavi." Quite understandably, historians have accepted the fact and have claimed for Guevavi the distinction of Sedelmayr's presence (e.g., Hazel Emery Mills, "Father Jacobo Sedelmayr, s.j.: A Forgotten Chapter in Arizona Missionary History," *ArizHR,* Vol. VII (1936), p. 17; Dunne, *Sedelmayr,* p. iii, and *Balthasar,* p. 49; and Pradeau, *Expulsión,* p. 232). But the AGN copyist erred. Sedelmayr wrote from his mission of Guásavas, more than 150 miles southeast of Guevavi. Sedelmayr [to Father Visitor Joseph de Utrera], "Guassabas," November 29, 1754; apparent original in the Huntington Library, San Marino, California (HM 22238). Cásares alleged that his *peones,* as he called the workers, came to work late, took a long lunch hour, and quit early. Joaquín de Cásares, Arizpe, September 20, 1754; Utrera testimonies.

[31] Captain Santiago Ruiz de Ael, Diario, September 21 to October 11, 1751; Ortiz Parrilla testimonies, 7. Vildósola, September 9, 1754. Garrucho to Utrera, Oposura, December 6, 1754; BNMex, 43/721.

familiar with native weapons he would enjoy greater success with them.[32] Or, as some witnesses later asserted, he launched into the proud Indian, calling him a Chichimec dog whose proper attire was a coyote skin and a loincloth and whose proper pastime was chasing rabbits and rodents in the hills.[33] Whatever really took place at Soamca that day, it was enough to offend Luis, who now abandoned the campaign and went home nursing black thoughts.

This Indian Luis, the Padres had already concluded, was a bad sort, vain and ambitious. Worse, he was a creature of Sonora's new Governor, Diego Ortiz Parrilla, and as such he enjoyed extraordinary civil and military protection. Ortiz Parrilla had in fact elevated Luis to the rank of captain general suddenly, without consulting the missionaries. In so doing, the Governor had overridden the opinion of his *juez político* for the Pimería, Don Joseph de Olave, who considered Luis unworthy of consideration for such a high post, in short, "a very ordinary Indian." The Jesuits had for months expressed their concern over Ortiz Parrilla's unilateral dealings with the Pimas. "The Governor," Father Stiger had observed as early as April of 1750, "told the Pimas that they would come to see their lands extend to the Río Colorado. What we are seeing is that during the [Seri] campaign he flattered them greatly and they now return most haughty and averse to the Padres."[34]

The fiesta at Guevavi in honor of the principal feast of San Miguel, September 29, promised to be the best ever, with dancing and singing, aguardiente, and this year, bullfighting. It was a chance to dress up, to eat candy, to shoot off firecrackers. If construction had proceeded apace, San Miguel's new church would be filled to overflowing. To his table Father Joseph invited the gente de razón for leagues around. The Romeros came in force, led of course by Don Nicholás, "older than fifty" and illiterate, but nonetheless a gentleman.

Nearly everyone recognized Miguel Valenzuela. Only recently he had retired as sergeant of the Terrenate garrison "because of his illnesses," which obviously were not disabling enough to keep him away

[32] Antonio de Rivera, San Miguel de Horcasitas, December 5, 1753, *et al.*; Arce y Arroyo testimonies.

[33] Miguel Siarituc, San Ignacio, March 14, 1752, *et al.*; Ortiz Parrilla testimonies, 8.

[34] Olave and Stiger quoted in Roxas to Arce y Arroyo, Arizpe, January 18, 1754, unsigned draft; WBS, 1744, ff. 347–50, and 40, ff. 163–64.

from the fiesta. Juan Manuel Ortiz had ridden all the way from Agua-caliente, a mining camp four leagues from Sáric. He was, incidentally, the godfather of one of Luis Oacpicagigua's children. Garrucho may have noticed with displeasure that Francisco Padilla had joined the group. A prospector and thoroughly unsavory character, Padilla had been run out of New Mexico by the authorities.

Reining up in the crowded, noisy plaza now was no less a personage than Don Gabriel Antonio de Vildósola, son of the former governor and owner of hacienda Santa Bárbara.[35] From the newly endowed mission at Sáric, Luis' home village, a tall, slender Bohemian Jesuit who had been there since June rode over to take a break and join in the festivities. His name was Nentuig; a dozen years later when nearly blind he would write an enlightening description of all Sonora.[36] Another missionary arrived, a countryman of Keller's with an unusually thick nose. He was determined little Francisco Xavier Pauer, one of the several Padres assigned to relieve Garrucho of San Xavier del Bac, but the first to actually get there.[37]

The celebration was in full swing when a native troublemaker known as Pedro Chihuahua came looking for the Padres. Pedro, who considered himself Luis' right-hand man, was carrying the baton of sergeant major of the Pima nation, apparently granted to him by the governor of Sonora without the missionaries' knowledge. A dispute arose. Either Garrucho suggested that the haughty Pedro was not author-

---

[35] Young Vildósola, who became an excellent frontier officer and Indian fighter, was born in June, 1722, in the Basque town of Villares. With his father Don Augustín, Governor of Sonora (1741–1748), the lad Gabriel traveled to the New World. In 1754 he was named Captain at Fronteras where he served for thirty years until his death in 1784. Almada, *Diccionario*, pp. 826–27.

[36] "Descripcion Geografica, natural, y curiosa de la Provᵃ de Sonora . . . 1764"; AGN, Historia, 393. This important but hurriedly compiled document was most recently published in English as *Rudo Ensayo by an unknown Jesuit padre, 1763* (Tucson: Arizona Silhouettes, 1951). See also Pradeau, "Nentuig's 'Description of Sonora,'" *MA*, Vol. XXXV (1953), pp. 81–90. The Padre's name was also spelled Nentvig or Nentwig.

[37] Father Pauer apparently arrived in the Pimería late in the spring of 1751. During the last week of May he baptized eight children at San Ignacio. Soon after, he rode up to San Xavier to become that mission's first resident Padre in fifteen years. A day before the feast of Saint Ignatius he was back at San Ignacio. From that date, July 30, until the uprising in November he seemed to divide his time between San Ignacio and Bac. Father Stiger was probably ailing. Having baptized two boys at San Ignacio on November 19, Pauer must have barely got back to San Xavier in time to flee the uprising. San Ignacio, Bautismos.

ized to parade around Guevavi with his baton,[38] or he grabbed the baton away and ridiculed the Indian before the assembled crowd, snarling that if Pedro set foot in Guevavi ever again he would be rewarded with a hundred lashes. Now Pedro went away unhappy, not even pausing to watch the bullfights which had already begun.[39]

In November Father Garrucho rode out to Arivaca to hear the confession of a sick woman. He heard even more. Thieving natives had got away with a herd of mission horses. Immediately he dispatched governor Lorenzo and his village justicias, as well as mission foreman Juan María Romero and Joseph de Nava, just to make sure. Twenty-year-old Manuel Bustamante, son of Bártholo the tailor, went along for the ride. The trail led toward Baboquívari Peak near which, at the place known as El Mesquite, the thieves were surprised and taken into custody. That evening on the way back, tempers flared over squash for supper. In the resulting scuffle, either provoked by an insolent old thief,[40] or by the cruel Romero,[41] the former was lanced and the latter stabbed with an arrow, though neither wound was serious. By the time the prisoners were delivered at Guevavi and put to work on the church, Luis knew of the incident and Garrucho suspected that he was up to no good. Even the beef cows Father Joseph had sent as alms to Father Henrique Ruhen at the new mission of San Marcelo nearly fifty leagues west had been stolen.

These episodes in the fall of 1751 were typical of an active mission frontier. They actually took place, though the details varied greatly depending upon whom the reporter wished to blame for the shocking event which followed.

Sunday, November 21, began peacefully enough at Guevavi. If he fulfilled his obligation, Father Joseph preached at least part of his sermon in the Piman tongue. A small boy awaited baptism. Governor Juanico was to be his godfather, just as he had been six and a half years earlier for the first child Garrucho baptized at Guevavi. Don Joachín

---

[38] Father Juan Nentuig to Father Joseph de Utrera, Tecoripa, December 3, 1754, *et al.*; Utrera testimonies.

[39] Francisco Padilla, San Ignacio, February 4, 1752, *et al.*; Ortiz Parrilla testimonies, 8. Juan Manuel Ortiz, San Ignacio, December 9, 1751, *ibid.*

[40] Joseph Antonio de Ortiz Cortés, Cuquiárachi, September 12, 1754, *et al.*; Utrera testimonies.

[41] Juan Manuel Ortiz, December 9, 1751, *et al.*

de Cásares after three months was still in residence, indicating that the church or convento was not yet completely finished. A gold mine "very near the village" accounted for Don Antonio de Rivera's presence in Guevavi that day.

With little warning the routine Sunday activities of the mission and its guests came to an abrupt halt. Near panic ensued.

Into the village had stumbled a beaten and bloody Juan de Figueroa, mission foreman at Tubac. The Indians had gone crazy, they had set upon him and tried to club him to death. In his haste to save himself and carry the word to Guevavi he had left his wife behind. Later he learned that she had been hidden by a youthful native compadre, and that she had survived. At Arivaca, rumor had it, all was smoldering ruin and carnage. Don Antonio shuddered.

As if possessed, the natives of Guevavi grabbed up their weapons and fled while they could, paying no heed to the pleadings of their Padre. Rivera and the dozen vecinos he could muster rode out to Arivaca. Met by two hundred menacing Indians, they fought their way out, having verified the awful truth of the first report. Foreman Romero, Nava, and young Bustamante were among the dead.

On the advice of the sympathetic native governor at Bac, Father Pauer and a small escort made a dash to Guevavi where Garrucho had all but given up the hope that his neophytes would come back. A warning had reached Keller by this time and he had passed it on to San Ignacio. Rumors of all-out revolt and martyred Padres, of Luis allying himself with the Apaches, added to the dreadful reality of this thing that had happened.

Without its neophytes, Guevavi could not be defended. When Rivera and the vecinos returned, preparations to abandon the mission were already under way. The stock was rounded up, and most of the *santos* and church furnishings were lashed to pack animals. On Wednesday the retreat began. Garrucho apparently never returned to Guevavi.[42]

---

[42] There is some question as to whether word of the uprising reached Guevavi on Sunday, November 21, or Monday, the 22nd. There is no question as to the effect it produced. This account of Garrucho's last days at Guevavi is based on the various declarations and letters in AGI, Guad., 418 and 419, and on the Padre's own defense, Garrucho to Utrera, December 6, 1754. For a general treatment of the uprising, see Russell C. Ewing, "The Pima Uprising, 1751–1752: A Study in Spain's Indian Policy," unpublished Ph.D. dissertation, University of California, Berkeley, 1934; and his "The Pima Outbreak in November, 1751," *NMHR*, Vol. XIII (1938), pp. 337–46; and "The Pima Uprising of 1751," in *Greater America: Essays in Honor of Herbert E. Bolton* (Los Angeles, 1945), pp. 259–80.

Along the river through the San Luis Valley the caravan of refugees made its way, swelled by frightened families of vecinos at every cluster of adobe buildings. On five leagues past Soamca they pushed, seeking asylum at the presidio of San Phelipe, considered by one officer "a vagueness without any defense."[43] Laying over at Soamca, Garrucho confessed Pedro Chihuahua an hour or so before this Indian was summarily executed by Don Pedro Menocal, Captain of Fronteras, as an example to other followers of Luis. Not many days later Father Joseph hastened southward to present to the Father Visitor General the Padres' version of what had happened.[44]

Already Don Diego Ortiz Parrilla, "Lieutenant Colonel of the Royal Armies, Proprietary Captain of the Dragoons of Vera Cruz, Commandant of the detachments in the city of [Puebla] de los Ángeles, Governor and Captain General of this kingdom of Nueva Andalucia, Provinces of Sinaloa, Sonora, and the others adjoining, their presidios, frontiers, and the coasts of the Southern Sea," had begun to lay the blame squarely on the Jesuits.[45] His initial report of the revolt to the viceroy, which he dispatched on December 1 from San Ignacio, intimated that Garrucho's foreman and Nava had precipitated the whole thing. That report was in turn sent to the king himself. Now in the highest councils of the realm the name Guevavi was heard, and in a most unfavorable context.[46]

Yet Don Diego had only begun to fight. By the time he completed his investigation, the charges against Garrucho of Guevavi ranged

[43] Ensign Joseph Fontes to Ortiz Parrilla, Terrenate, *ca.* December 17, 1751; Ortiz Parrilla testimonies, 2.

[44] Lieutenant Ysidro Sánchez de Tagle to Ortiz Parrilla, Terrenate, *ca.* December 10, 1751; Ortiz Parrilla testimonies, 1. Father Augustín Carta to Ortiz Parrilla, "Benatmitu," December 16, 1751; Ortiz Parrilla testimonies, 2.

[45] Don Diego had enlisted in Spain in 1734. Six years later he shipped out to Cuba to fight in the War of Jenkins' Ear. Not long after that, he turned up in Vera Cruz with the rank of captain of dragoons. In 1749 he put down a revolt in Puebla, and that same year was named governor of Sonora. Concluding his controversial administration of that province Ortiz Parrilla took part in the ill-starred San Sabá project in Texas. Robert S. Weddle, *The San Sabá Mission, Spanish Pivot in Texas* (Austin: University of Texas Press, 1964), p. 38, *et passim*. From Texas he went on to serve as governor of both Pensacola and Coahuila, according to the somewhat confused biographical sketch in Almada, *Diccionario*, p. 542. He died on a visit to Spain, in Madrid in 1775. Navarro García, *Don José de Gálvez y la Comandancia General de las Provincias Internas del Norte de Nueva España* (Sevilla: Escuela de Estudios Hispano-Americanos, 1964), pp. 217, n. 30, 272, also 101–102, 197, 532.

[46] Ortiz Parrilla testimonies, 1; also AGI, Guad., 137. Royal cédulas, Buen Retiro, October 4, 1752; AGI, Guad., 418 and 137.

from wanton whipping of loyal Pimas to the kidnapping of native children. It remained for subsequent pro-Jesuit investigators to demonstrate that the administration of Father Garrucho had been, in reality, an exemplary one.[47]

Once they learned that their Padre was not coming back, the people of Guevavi split up. Some willingly joined Luis. Others were content to wait out the struggle in the mountains. Within a week or so of Garrucho's departure, a band of rebels held a *tlatole,* a native rally, at the mission and let off steam. "Unhinging the doors of the Father's house they ransacked it, then began in the church, tearing, throwing down, and abusing the few santos that remained."[48]

At dusk the day after Christmas of 1751, a Spanish patrol arrived at the scene to report that in addition to sacking the church and Padre's "house," mangling the santos, and smashing the tabernacle, the vengeful natives had killed all of Garrucho's chickens and pigeons.[49] Even at that, Guevavi had fared better at the hands of the *sublevados* than did San Xavier del Bac, where the *"capilla o enramada"* and the Padre's house were totally demolished. Nothing movable at either place was spared. Because they were more substantial, the church at Guevavi — presumably the new one — and Garrucho's house, or his quarters in

---

[47] One of the most remarkable pro-Jesuit accounts of the uprising and its aftermath for a decade, has been all but overlooked by recent historians, probably because a cataloguer mislabeled it. Seventy neatly written pages, it was set down in 1760 by Father Salvador Ignacio de la Peña. As one might expect, Peña praised rather than damned Garrucho, whom he portrayed as a kind and energetic missionary presiding at Guevavi over "a scattered mob of haughty thieves." Not only does this account provide many valuable details of beleaguered Sonora between 1750 and 1760, but also it shows the Pima Uprising to have been a decade-long affair. Though this important document is unsigned, its author's admission that he was Father Utrera's secretary during the 1754 visitation and that he was missionary at Cucurpe establishes it as the work of Father Peña. "Convite Evangelico á compasion, y Socorro de la Viña del Señor, destrozada, y conculcada con el Alzamiento de la Pimeria Alta, desde el dia 21 de Noviembre del Año de 1751, y sus lastimosos progressos en la siguiente Decada, hasta el año de 1760." Labeled "An account of the uprising against the Jesuit missions in *California* [italics mine], from 1751–1766," apparently at the University of California at Los Angeles; microfilm 71, UAL.

[48] Ruiz de Ael to Ortiz Parrilla, Terrenate, December 17, 1751; Ortiz Parrilla testimonies, 2.

[49] Fontes, "Diario de la marcha q.e hizieron los Alferezes D.n Jph de Fonttes, y D.n Antt.o Olguin con la tropa de su Cargo," *ibid.* Fontes reported in addition that the rebels had burned "the Church and Father's house" in Tubac. Fontes to Ortiz Parrilla, *ca.* December 17, 1751.

the convento, survived to serve another day.[50] But for the time being, the apostate Luis held sway — and he defied any Minister of Doctrine for His Majesty to return.

At the invitation of Father Stiger the mission of San Ignacio became an armed camp. At seven in the evening of November 30, Governor Ortiz Parrilla and his party arrived there. Soldiers and refugees milled about in the plaza awaiting the Governor's orders. Some of them would be dismayed, for Ortiz Parrilla seemed resolved to wage a strikingly un-Spanish campaign against the rebels, one of delay and appeasement, reminiscent of Huidobro's disgraceful performance a decade earlier.

Not only was Don Diego stalling until reinforcements arrived; apparently he was also seeking a way out of a personal dilemma involving his relationship with the rebel leader. In the past he had heaped praise and honors upon Luis Oacpicagigua for his part in the Seri campaigns. Had his trust in Luis been so plainly misplaced, or was this basically good and loyal vassal of the Spanish king fighting a just war against his Jesuit oppressors? The Governor's actions clearly spoke his answer. He sent out peace missions to Luis, he limited offensive action to reconnaissance, and he began taking anti-Jesuit testimony. When the uninformed Captain Menocal executed Pedro and advocated striking the rebels before they had a chance to consolidate, Ortiz Parrilla court-martialed him.

In the early dawn of January 5, 1752, near Guevavi's deserted visita of Arivaca, Luis abruptly lost his advantage. At the head of a bungling horde, reportedly two thousand strong and including neophytes from Guevavi, he fell upon eighty-six Spaniards and was beaten. After that he was more willing to talk peace. There were, however, conditions. Father Keller must be removed from the Pimería, and Father Garrucho now serving loyal Ópatas at Oposura 150 miles southeast of Guevavi,

---

[50] It is possible that the new church was not in use by the time the revolt broke, and that these references are to the old one. Señor Cásares, the master builder, was still in residence on November 21, 1751. He testified later that he had been in Guevavi supervising the building of a church for the preceding three months; he spoke of Garrucho's fair treatment of the workers on "la principiada Yglecia"; but he did not say how far along the project was. Cásares, September 20, 1754. Because it survived the rebellion, while other churches did not, and because there is no mention of Garrucho's successor having to carry on the work, it would appear, however, that the references are to the new one, which served until the early 1770s, even after the Jesuits were expelled.

must return the Pima houseboys he had taken with him when he fled the revolt.

After parleys in the Santa Catalina Mountains north of Tucson and a belated ultimatum from Governor Ortiz Parrilla, Luis Oacpicagigua gave up. On March 18, 1752, just as the sun dropped behind the craggy Tumacácoris, he came alone to Tubac where the Governor's representative, Captain Joseph Díaz del Carpio, and his men were encamped. Falling at the Captain's feet, "with great humility and respect," this Indian, "who does not know his age but from his appearance must be forty-six years old, more or less," accepted the Governor's offer of amnesty.

Forty of the ex-rebels, disenchanted and probably hungry, soon reappeared in the Tubac area and began the return to normalcy. Meanwhile, more than a hundred repentant natives had come down out of the Santa Ritas to Sonoita and there had sworn obedience anew to God and king. It was almost as if the clock had been turned back to the days of Kino. "They came out to meet me," wrote Captain Díaz del Carpio, "and they lined up in a demonstration of submission. As a sign of peace, they carried high two wooden crosses." By mid-April governor Juanico Cipriano and sixty-five others were back at Guevavi.[51] For more than a year, however, they would resist a missionary's return. They had come home, but they had not given up.

Why, royal officials demanded to know, had the revolt of Luis and his malcontents occurred in the first place? In an attempt to find a suitable answer, three separate sets of testimony were compiled, two by governors of Sonora and one by the Jesuits.

In the mind of Governor Ortiz Parrilla there was never any doubt that the Black Robes were to blame. For support, the Governor relied upon his vehement, Jesuit-educated secretary, Don Martín Cayetano Fernández de Peralta, whom at least one Jesuit referred to as that "Judas" Peralta.[52] To substantiate their charges, Ortiz Parrilla and Fer-

---

[51] Díaz del Carpio, Diario [March 5–24, 1752], and "Padron de los Pueblos citados al norte de esta Pimería alta . . . [April–May, 1752]"; Ortiz Parrilla testimonies, 5. The adults of Guevavi were listed by their Christian names only. Native family names were included in the Tubac census.

[52] Peña, "Convite Evangelico," 7. At one stage during the Yaqui troubles, Fernández de Peralta had referred to himself as "un hijo amantísimo de la Compañía de Jesús." Navarro García, *Sublevación Yaqui,* p. 35.

nández de Peralta summoned several dozen gente de razón and mis-treated Indians to testify. All dutifully damned the Jesuits. That the declarations were scandalously fraudulent, extracted in some cases under the most extreme duress — including the threat of banishment to the dungeons of San Juan de Ulúa — was later charged.[53]

The Governor, the Jesuits concluded, was a man of little character, a man who owed his high office not to merit but to an uncle at the Court of Madrid. He had been sent to Sonora in the first place only because the Viceroy wished to get him out of Mexico City. Don Diego, clearly a vain and insolent troublemaker, harbored a deep dislike for the Jesuits, they alleged, even before he left the capital.[54]

When Ortiz Parrilla's successor arrived in Sonora in 1753, he carried explicit orders from the Viceroy to reestablish harmonious rela-tions with the Jesuits. This move, the Padres were convinced, was based not upon the Viceroy's favorable disposition toward them, but instead upon political expediency. Nonetheless, the declarations Don Pablo de Arce y Arroyo solicited from thirty gente de razón, some of whom had also testified before Ortiz Parrilla, all but exonerated the Padres. Once Ortiz Parrilla had resigned and left Sonora, those who testified did not hesitate to attribute to him a major share of the blame. Most frequently they denounced the former governor for showering excessive praise on Luis after the Indian leader had fought well against the Seris. As a result, they claimed, Luis grew so vain and proud that he began to consider himself the rightful owner of the Pimería and everything in it. Only then did he begin to plot against the Spaniards.

Finally, the Jesuits sent Father Visitor General Joseph de Utrera to the frontier "to carry out the most rigorous investigation and to remove those Fathers who might have failed to observe in some way the gentle religious conduct of Jesuit missionaries."[55] During the course of this investigation the Pimas' "natural inconstancy," their accustomed infi-delity, and their innate desire to be free and to live like savages began

---

[53] Ignacio Romero, Oposura, January 25, 1754, *et al.*; Arce y Arroyo testimonies. Garru-cho to Utrera, December 6, 1754.

[54] Burrus, *Misiones Norteñas,* pp. 56–57.

[55] Peña, "Convite Evangelico," 5. "Ynstruccion de como ba de proceder el P. Vicitador en la causa criminal que se le comete, sobre el levantamiento de los Indios Pimas, y averigua-cion de si los PP. Missioneros fueron la causa de el, ó en el tubieron alguna culpa y de el porte de dhos PP. con los Indios sus sujetos, trato con los Ministros y Justicias R.ˢ"; WBS, 89.

to emerge as basic causes of the debacle. In October of 1754 the Visitor General arrived at Santa María Soamca, where he spent twelve days asking questions.

Captain Francisco Elías González of Terrenate, first to answer, had not actually taken part in suppressing the revolt. The Captain, a Spaniard by birth and subsequently the founder of a large and illustrious Sonora family, had come to the northern frontier at an early age. According to Father Utrera's secretary, Don Francisco had married a daughter of Captain Díaz del Carpio, and recently had succeeded his father-in-law as commander at Terrenate.[56]

A second Captain responded to Father Utrera's summons. He was Don Juan Thomás Belderrain, formerly of the presidial company of Sinaloa and now in command of the new presidio at Tubac. Four of the Romeros — Don Nicholás, Don Joseph, Don Ignacio, and Don Gregorio Antonio — joined the gathering. All gave essentially pro-Jesuit accounts, as was expected of them.

Seven Indians now testified, among them the governors of Guevavi, Sonoita, Tumacácori, and Bac. The spontaneous answers of these uneducated natives caused the Father Visitor General a few anxious moments, during which he was forced to resort to some rather jesuitical cross-examination. At the same time, several incidents involving Father Garrucho were brought to light.

Ignacio, who had replaced Juanico Cipriano as governor of Guevavi, was asked if Father Garrucho punished his neophytes unduly. Ignacio answered that the Padre did slap them and order the justicias to whip them, though he did not know for what offenses. Furthermore, Father Joseph had beaten Ignacio's father with a stick and the latter had died.

This would never do. How had such a thing happened? Were there wounds? Were the blows the cause of death? questioned Utrera. Ignacio's father, a village official, had neglected his duty, it seemed. For this reason Garrucho hit him a few times with a stick, which left no visible wounds. Afterward, the disgraced Indian went out to work in the fields for three or four days. He then fell ill and for two months

[56] Peña, "Convite Evangelico," 12. Almada says that Elías González married "his cousin María Agueda Campoy" on February 15, 1729. *Diccionario,* p. 239.

suffered recurring fevers from which he ultimately died. And "the witness was convinced that he had died from the blows!"

The remainder of Ignacio's answers were more acceptable. Father Garrucho did indeed give his neophytes time to plant and to cultivate their fields. He lent them oxen, plows, and seed. He provided them with plenty to eat, and he permitted them to go on campaigns. Now, added Ignacio, Guevavi had better justicias and all was well.[57]

Juanico of Sonoita had only one complaint against Garrucho: the Padre had taken a choice piece of land below the *ciénega* which Juanico and six others had farmed for two or three years. Had Juanico and his fellows reported the incident to the missionary's superior? No, because they really did not mind giving up the land when the foreman told them it was for their Padre. What were the names of the seven Indians, Utrera asked incidentally. Juanico named himself and six others. A short time later Utrera repeated the question. Juanico substituted Phelipe for Marcos. The final time he was asked, he included both Phelipe and Marcos and ended up with eight, not seven. Obviously this Indian did not know what he was talking about.[58]

An incident Juanico might have mentioned but did not, one that Luis Oacpicagigua and several other Indians were supposed to have related to Governor Ortiz Parrilla, concerned a former native governor of Sonoita whose son Garrucho allegedly sent off to see the world with a muleteer. The lad's parents never heard of him again.[59]

Phelipe of Tumacácori had fled to the hills in the direction of Tres Alamos because everyone else was doing it, not because Father Garrucho had mistreated him. On the contrary, their Padre "gave food to those who did not have it, confessed them, and married them, and did not harm them at all."[60]

Christóbal of Bac related how he had warned Pauer and thus saved the Padre's life. He had taken no part, he said, in the burning of the "church or ramada where Mass was said," nor had he joined in mistreat-

[57] Ignacio, Soamca, October 15, 1754; Utrera testimonies.

[58] Juanico, Soamca, October 15, 1754; *ibid.*

[59] Luis Oacpicagigua, San Ignacio, March 24, 1752. Antonio Sayastiot, Pasqual Quiquitubac, and Joseph Qubacus, San Ignacio, March 16, 1752; Ortiz Parrilla testimonies, 8.

[60] Phelipe, Soamca, October 15, 1754; Utrera testimonies.

ing the cattle and horses and killing the sheep their missionary had given them. All that was the doing of bad Indians. One of the infamous hechiceros of Bac who had incited the natives was now locked up in jail at Tubac. As for Father Pauer, Garrucho's successor at Guevavi and San Xavier, "he was good and they liked him, and he had done them no harm whatsoever." [61]

With that, the Father Visitor General concluded his fact-finding mission at Soamca. Early in the morning of October 21, he and his party mounted up and headed south. On the trail that day, they halted for a meal at Cocóspera, where Utrera noted that both church and house had been burned by Apaches six years earlier. At Ímuris they ate again, and finally, after some fifty miles in the saddle, arrived to spend the night at San Ignacio. In his diary Father Utrera explained why he had chosen not to visit either Guevavi or Bac.

> I did not go to Guevavi because I found Father Pauer [by then assigned to Guevavi] suffering from chills at Soamca, and because at Guevavi there is still no way to maintain or lodge those persons who must accompany and escort one. Neither did I go to San Xavier del Bac, because there is no Padre there, and because that mission is without provisions, or church, or anything. There is no property nor account book; neither is there an account book at Guevavi yet.[62]

A dramatic climax to Father Utrera's investigation occurred at San Miguel de Horcasitas, residence of the governors of Sonora. There he came face-to-face with Luis Oacpicagigua, taken prisoner by Ortiz Parrilla's successor. Father Salvador Ignacio de la Peña, the Father Visitor's articulate secretary, described the scene:

> Luis of Sáric... on both knees, bowed in veneration before Father Visitor Utrera, cried out that he be pardoned for all of his crimes and his barbarous ingratitude toward his beloved Father Ministers.... The Indian declared almost sobbing that he did not resent the Fathers, nor had the Fathers been at all to blame. The Devil had deceived him and he alone, blinded by this deception, had acted rashly. "Tell me then," the Father Visitor asked the Indian through an interpreter,

---

[61] Christóbal, Soamca, October 19, 1754; *ibid*.

[62] Utrera, "Derrotero, y Jornadas, q voi haciendo desde el dia 17 de Enero de 1754 q salí de Mexico á visitar las Missiones"; WBS, 67.

"why did you make such a strenuous point of not giving yourself up until first Fathers Jacobo Sedelmayr, Ignacio Keller, and Joseph Garrucho left the Pimería? Are we to believe then that these Fathers molested you in some way?" "In no way," answered the Indian contritely. "I confess that I asked for their removal not because they had bothered me, indeed they were once my Fathers and they loved me and were good to me, but instead because they understood my native language well and I imagined that if I were placed in their presence, daily my own ingratitude would be thrown in my face." [63]

Garrucho was perfectly capable of defending himself, though he probably would not have deigned to do so had not the Father Visitor General ordered it. His long letter, begun on the feast of the Presentation of the Blessed Virgin Mary, November 21, and concluded on December 6, 1754, to no one's surprise was a strongly worded indictment of Governor Ortiz Parrilla.

The Governor, Garrucho claimed, hated the Jesuits. Why, he asked pointedly, if indeed the conduct of the Padres and their treatment of the natives had been so egregious, had not the Governor taken steps to remedy the situation? Certainly from the reports of the various military men he sent out periodically to inspect the state of the missions and to speak with the neophytes, he should have known of any such abuses. [64]

As for the specific charges made by the Governor against him, Garrucho took a number of them one at a time and told his side of the story. He had not ordered governor Joseph of Tubac beaten because he went on a campaign with the soldiers, but instead because of his disorderly conduct upon his return. In defending himself, Garrucho hinted at the petty intrigues that were apparently a part of any missionary's life. He told of how the natives of Tubac, not long after his arrival, had complained to the Father Visitor that he was not ministering to them properly. Upon investigation it was learned that Garrucho was hardly to blame — during the time his accusers claimed they were being neglected, he was still in Europe.

In retrospect Garrucho could cite numerous signs of the gathering revolt. The Governor had been forewarned by Father Sedelmayr and

---

[63] Peña, "Convite Evangelico," 12.

[64] Father Provincial Balthasar had used the same line of reasoning in a letter to the viceroy, dated in México, January 18, 1752. Ortiz Parrilla testimonies, 11.

others, but he had chosen to do nothing. From the time Luis Oacpica-gigua got back from his successful campaign against the Seris of Tiburón Island, one year before the revolt, his course was set, a fact later confirmed by his own second-in-command. The authority, the honors, and the prospect of commanding a one-hundred-man native presidio on the Gila — all conferred upon him by Ortiz Parrilla — made Luis vain, proud, haughty, and an instrument of the Devil. Soon he began ordering the natives of all the villages to do his bidding. In Tubac he told the people to build a house and plant a field for him so that when he or Pedro Chihuahua passed that way they would be well provided for. Furthermore, he began to counsel the village governors and justicias not to punish their people and not to correct their abuses, telling them that Governor Ortiz Parrilla had ordered it.

When an incorrigible native of Tubac ran off with another man's wife, Garrucho naturally ordered the village governor to apprehend and punish him. But when the transgressor returned, not a hand was laid upon him. Noting that the native governor had not obeyed his Padre's orders, foreman Juan de Figueroa asked for an explanation. Just as he suspected. Luis was back of it.

On another occasion the high and mighty captain general of all the Pimas went so far as to "unmarry" two natives of Guevavi married by the Church; and even worse, he gave their wives to other men. And that was not all. Toward the end of July of 1751, not four months before the revolt, a delegation of Indians from Caborca arrived in Tubac. Why, they asked foreman Figueroa, had he gone to the trouble of planting beans? Did he not know that within the year the world was coming to an end? When Figueroa told Garrucho of the incident the Padre put little stock in it, just another absurd superstition of the Indians. Several days later, however, the people of his visita of San Francisco de Borja de Sonoita [65] wanted to know if it were true. Was the world really going to end that year? That, Garrucho told them, was something only God knew.

Perhaps the most ominous sign of all, Luis had changed his name. No longer was he content with Oacpicagigua. Instead, he now chose

---

[65] Father Kino called the village Los Santos Reyes de Sonoita. Its patron sometime later became San Ignacio. To confuse the issue further, an early nineteenth-century land grant nearby was known as the San José de Sonoita.

to call himself Bacquioppa, which according to Garrucho "meant in their language, 'Enemy of Adobe Houses.'"

Because Luis had committed himself to his dastardly course and had begun agitating for revolt a full year before the thing actually came to pass, it was obvious, the Padre pointed out, that neither the Romero-horsethieves affair nor the Pedro-baton affair, nor any other of the alleged incidents, had brought on the debacle. Garrucho, in his own mind, had had nothing to do with it.[66]

Father Visitor Carlos de Roxas, addressing himself to Ortiz Parrilla's successor, was no less direct. He, too, held the former governor accountable — first, for precipitating the revolt by his indiscretion, and second, for trying to cover up by blaming the Jesuits. Ortiz Parrilla waged war not with the sword, alleged Roxas, "he only fenced with and bloodied the pen, letting off the carnivorous Pima wolves and sacrificing the innocent missionary lambs." At the very first news of trouble had he not spontaneously begun to shout accusations at the Padres? "Yet how was this possible?" the Jesuit continued.

> Either Señor Parrilla is a prophet, or he knew of the uprising before-hand. No, he neither knew of the uprising, nor is he a prophet, but rather, imagining without proof that the Father missionaries were to blame, he sought to avoid reproach by putting the blame squarely on these same missionaries. He hoped that in the controversy it would be impossible to extract the truth and that he could through judicial proceedings and litigation hide the real cause. It seems that he did not fool me.[67]

Luis's revolt, in which two Padres and at least a hundred gente de razón and peaceful Indians were slain, in which churches were burned and holy objects profaned, in which "Enemy of Adobe Houses" and his followers poured forth their resentment, was a revolt against the whole colonial system, a system in which the Governor of Sonora, Garrucho of Guevavi, and all the settlers between — partisan or not — had their places. Initial contact accompanied by material benefits for the natives, increasing Spanish demands and controls, violent native reaction, Spanish retaliation, and final sullen acceptance of domination — the

---

[66] Garrucho to Utrera, December 6, 1754.
[67] Roxas to Arce y Arroyo, January 18, 1754.

cycles of Spanish conquest had run their familiar course in the Pimería.[68]
And rebellion was part of it. When, after eight years and thousands of
pages of inconclusive testimony, the Queen Mother, Elizabeth Farnese,
acting for her son Charles III, decreed that the matter be relegated to
"perpetual silence," she was merely admitting this fact.[69]

Christopher Columbus was really to blame.

As Father Visitor of Sonora in the early 1760s, and for a brief
period as Father Visitor General,[70] Garrucho might have returned to
Guevavi once more had not "his attacks" made riding so painful. From
Oposura in 1763 he did send orders to have the ailing Father Pfefferkorn
removed from that baneful mission, dispatching in his place the last
Jesuit to live and labor at Guevavi, a twenty-nine-year-old Spaniard
named Custodio Ximeno,[71] who, like Father Pauer, also had a very
large nose.

At Oposura Father Garrucho served fifteen years, until the day of
the Jesuits' rude expulsion. Though his neophytes were initially inclined
to be unruly, he apparently soon straightened them out.[72] The mission
church he inherited at Oposura was reputedly "one of the best in this
province." To enhance it, Father Joseph acquired additional rich furnishings, and with oval paintings he arranged a small chapel to the Holy
Virgin of Loreto.[73] Though Garrucho had difficulty learning another
Indian language, by 1765 Father Nentuig could report that "even Father
Garrucho, who had thought it would be utterly impossible for him, now
preaches in Ópata."[74] Evidently Garrucho could be overbearing, how-

---

[68] Spicer, *Cycles of Conquest*, p. 16, *et passim*.

[69] On June 28, 1759, the royal fiscal had recommended that the case of the Pima rebellion
be closed. Ewing, "The Pima Uprising, 1751–1752: A Study in Spain's Indian Policy," p.
336. The text of the royal cédula, signed on September 27, 1759, by the Queen Mother at
Buen Retiro, is printed in Burrus, *Misiones Norteñas*, pp. 104–105.

[70] When Father Visitor General Ignacio Lizassoain was stricken Father Visitor Garrucho
apparently functioned for him. Pradeau, *Expulsión*, p. 151.

[71] Garrucho to Father Provincial Pedro Reales, Oposura, July 13, 1763; AHH,
Temp., 17.

[72] Nentuig to Father Provincial Francisco Zevallos, Opotu, July 18, 1764; *ibid*.

[73] Aguirre to Zevallos, Bacadéguachi, February 18, 1764; *ibid*. This document includes
the Father Visitor's one-paragraph description of Oposura under Garrucho.

[74] Nentuig to Zevallos, Guásavas, February 22, 1765; BL.

ever. In recognition of this tendency, Governor Pineda took delight in referring to the Jesuit sarcastically as "the Lord Bishop of Oposura."[75]

Father Joseph's neighbor downriver at Batuc was none other than the disputatious Father Alexandro Rapicani. Both men had begun their missionary careers at Guevavi, and there, apparently, what they had in common ended. In 1766 Rapicani heard that Garrucho had been named Father Rector, "although to me His Reverence has said nothing about it." In matters of food and drink, Rapicani continued grudgingly, Father Joseph had gained "a splendid reputation with himself and with his guests." Pursuing the point, he added: "I hear he is getting bloated."[76]

His first experience as a missionary, Joseph Garrucho had gained at Guevavi. He endured there longer than any other Jesuit, either before or after him. Under his watchful eye and firm hand, the mission was transformed from a marginal, wilderness operation into a relatively prosperous frontier community. When he left, however, he fled. Fortunately for Jesuit Guevavi, his successor proved more than equal to the difficult task of reconstruction.

---

[75] Donohue, "Jesuit Missions," p. 318.

[76] Rapicani to Father Joseph Hidalgo, Batuc, September 19, 1766; BNMex, 45/723. Garrucho had been Father Rector earlier and in 1758 had investigated certain of the charges leveled periodically at the controversial Rapicani. WBS, 66, ff. 367–78, 383–88, and 1745, ff. 473–74. For other details of Garrucho's administration at Oposura, see Roca, *Paths of the Padres,* pp. 193–94, and Pradeau, *Expulsión,* pp. 151–52. The biographical sketches of the expelled Jesuits included in Dr. Pradeau's *Expulsión* supplement those of the other Padres found in Pradeau and Burrus, "Los Jesuitas."

"This mission suffered greatly with regard to its properties, but neither house nor church was burned, and the vestments were saved. Only at Sonoita did they burn the Father's house, which served as a church."
Father Visitor Carlos de Roxas, 1754

"Today the following [seventy-eight] adults of the ranchería of Doacuquita were congregated at Calabazas. . . . The justicias and people of this village of Guevavi were their godparents. As soon as the baptisms were over, they were married in facie ecclesiae *before the same justicias and people."*
Father Francisco Xavier Pauer, 1756

5.

Reconstruction
The Administration of Francisco Xavier Pauer, 1753-1759

THEY WERE BRINGING HIM IN. The crowd in the plaza at San Ignacio waited impatiently — curious militiamen who had never seen him, Pimas who refused to follow him, and settlers vengeful in mourning for the relatives he had killed. They were bringing in Luis Oacpicagigua, scourge of the Pimería. The Governor of Sonora waited too.

But there would be no execution at San Ignacio that day in March, 1752. The head of Luis would not be severed, hoisted up, and displayed as a warning to others. Luis would not feel the lash; they would not even shave his head. The Governor had another plan, a plan whereby, he was convinced, he could regain the loyalty of this Pima who had served him well in the past. He would forgive and forget.

When he had received the rebel leader at San Ignacio "as if he were some famous Captain of the ancient Romans," when he had dressed him in "Moorish slippers, red stockings, and other clothing," and subsequently released him, Governor Ortiz Parrilla departed for Horcasitas persuaded that he had successfully pacified the Pimería.[1] The

---
[1] Gregorio Antonio Romero, Soamca, October 16, 1754; Utrera testimonies. Christóbal de Osef, Todos Santos, September 16, 1754; *ibid.*

natives, he informed Father Visitor Segesser, had repented; they would now willingly accept Padres.

Though he must have viewed the Governor's patronizing assertion warily, the astute Father Visitor knew that the sooner he reestablished the Pima missions, the better the Jesuits' case would look. His problem was personnel. Fathers Sedelmayr, Keller, and Garrucho had been removed from the Pimería as one of the conditions of peace insisted on by Luis. To replace the first of them, Segesser now assigned to Tubutama the Spaniard Luis Vivas, a new man. Juan Nentuig, formerly of Sáric, he designated for duty at Soamca, knowing that it would not be easy for anyone to follow Keller there. Guevavi, Garrucho's former domain, he gave to Francisco Xavier Pauer, the refugee from San Xavier. Then, during his visitation, evidently in January of 1753, he tried to install them.

At Tubutama the Pimas passively accepted Luis Vivas. At Soamca, however, the Indians wanted no part of any Padre but Keller. They had objected, perhaps at his prompting, when their missionary for twenty years was taken from them, and now they objected to the substitution of a different Padre. Nentuig, nonetheless, was left among them, ill at ease.[2] The proximity of the presidio of San Phelipe should have been of some consolation to him. The soldiers were, after all, only five leagues away.

At Guevavi, the mission whose "baneful influence" had nearly killed him two decades earlier, Father Visitor Segesser met with a cold reception. Since he had come, the natives grudgingly permitted him to say Mass, but then, they informed him, he and the minister he wished to install were to be on their way. Indicative of the people's mood, they still wore "the caps they are accustomed to wear during campaigns and uprisings."[3] Prudently, Father Pauer withdrew to Soamca. From there, however, he could do little to bring Guevavi's wayward children back to the fold. His plight reminded Father Visitor Carlos de Roxas, Segesser's successor, of a fable, a variation on Aesop's "The Mother and the Wolf."

An old woman, it seemed, had told her fretful child that if he did not stop crying she would feed him to the lions. Just by chance, a lion passing by overheard this good news and waited patiently outside the

---

[2] Between January 21, on which date he baptized seven at the presidio of Terrenate, and May 9, 1753, Father Nentuig seemed to stick it out in the area of Soamca. Soamca, Bautismos de los Pueblos de Visita.

[3] Juan Ygnacio Rodríguez Soto, Horcasitas, November 15, 1753; Arce y Arroyo testimonies.

cottage. When the woman discovered that there really was a lion nearby, she quickly changed her tune, threatening to kill the beast to protect the child. All of which caused the lion to walk away muttering in Latin, *"In hoc tugurio aliud dicunt et aliud faciunt.* [In this cottage they say one thing and do another.]" The Pimas of Guevavi "say with their mouths that they want Padres, but by their actions they say quite the contrary."[4]

Seemingly thwarted, Father Pauer, Guevavi's Padre-in-name-only, rejoined Father Segesser in Ures, 160 miles south, there to await a more propitious occasion to return. For the time being at least, the natives of Guevavi had their way, and no Padre.

Keller, whom Governor Ortiz Parrilla had characterized as a blacker villain than even Garrucho, had been obliged to leave Soamca and answer the charges leveled against him. In Mexico City he had submitted to the Viceroy an impassioned account of the troubles and their causes as he saw them.[5] Then, after a brief stay at the Jesuit college in Guadalajara, "it was deemed necessary by the Father Provincial to remove him from there and send him back to his mission again (and this is a point worthy of note) because its Indians were determined to have 'their Father Keller' (as they would say) and not to accept any other."[6]

His reentry into Soamca in the spring of 1753 was triumphal. They received him with a touching display of loyalty and rejoicing.[7] "Their" Padre was back. So strongly did he still feel about Diego Ortiz Parrilla that when writing in the book of baptisms for Soamca's visitas a note explaining his absence, Keller could not resist denouncing his archenemy again. But already Don Diego had resigned.

If they met on the Camino Real, ex-Governor Ortiz Parrilla on his way to Mexico City and Father Keller returning to the frontier, it is not likely they spoke. The Jesuits believed that Ortiz Parrilla deserved censure and punishment for his actions, before, during, and after the Pima uprising.

---

[4] Father Visitor Carlos de Roxas to Governor Pablo de Arce y Arroyo, Arizpe, November 27, 1753; *ibid.*

[5] Keller to the viceroy, México, August 25, 1752; AGN, Historia, 17.

[6] Father Miguel Quijano to the viceroy, México; quoted in Ortiz Parrilla testimonies, 9.

[7] Gabriel Antonio de Vildósola, Cuquiárachi, September 9, 1754; Utrera testimonies. Father Provincial Ignacio Calderón to the king, México, March 15, 1755; letter transmitting the Utrera testimonies, *ibid.*

They were disappointed several years later to learn that the first Conde de Revillagigedo, Viceroy of New Spain, had not reprimanded Don Diego but instead had recommended him highly to the succeeding Viceroy, the Marqués de las Amarillas. When the Padres heard that the Marqués had granted Ortiz Parrilla's request to command the military arm of the San Sabá project in Texas, which they referred to as "a profitable captaincy among the Franciscan Fathers," they could do little but swallow their consternation and hope that the Sons of Saint Francis "do not experience the same fate as the Society of Jesus suffered on his account. . . ."[8]

The San Sabá venture proved a costly fiasco, although not really because of Ortiz Parrilla. He, nonetheless, found himself involved once again in a heated controversy with missionaries, this time Franciscans instead of Jesuits. Writing to the viceroy from Texas, the perplexed commander lamented the conflicts that seemed to follow most unjustly upon his best efforts to do his duty and the royal will. "I, like many others," Ortiz Parrilla continued,

> have not forgotten certain events in the Province of Sonora, where . . . [the Jesuit Fathers] circulated rumors and destructive and stupid criticisms of my actions, which spread even as far as that city [México]. The two governors who have succeeded me in that command have also availed themselves of the opportunity [to criticize], unaware that approbation and esteem are earned by correcting mistakes rather than by proclaiming them.
>
> But, Most Excellent Sir, there were no such mistakes! These persons are merely endeavoring to conceal their own shortcomings at the expense of one who is absent. They had no recourse but to connive deliberately for the favor of those [Missionary Fathers] who in the end will repay them as they did me when I took a firm stand for the general welfare, and who will do the same again when the governors are far away or fail to favor them as much as they desire.[9]

---

[8] Burrus, *Misiones Norteñas,* p. 63.

[9] Ortiz Parrilla to the Marqués de las Amarillas, San Luis de las Amarillas, April 8, 1758; quoted in Paul D. Nathan, trans., and Lesley Byrd Simpson, ed., *The San Sabá Papers: A Documentary Account of the Founding and Destruction of San Sabá Mission* (San Francisco: John Howell, 1959), pp. 134–35. Characterizing Ortiz Parrilla, Robert S. Weddle writes, "He was clearly a man of action, as shown later by his campaign from San Sabá against the northern tribes — and an egotist, as shown by his boastfulness and his efforts to excuse himself for all his mistakes." *San Sabá Mission,* p. 38.

Both the Jesuits and Ortiz Parrilla feared the effects the other would have on subsequent events. When, for whatever reasons, missionaries and civil-military authorities clashed, the very existence of a frontier province could be imperiled — and often it was.

One positive result of Luis' bloody rebellion, a result that tended to soften the refusal of Guevavi's natives to accept Father Pauer, was the creation of a second garrison in the Pimería. Activated on April 1, 1752, during the administration of Ortiz Parrilla, this company of fifty men, commanded by Captain Juan Thomás Belderrain, took up temporary quarters in Santa Ana, a largely Spanish settlement south of San Ignacio.[10] There they lived and from there they went forth to keep the peace while the Governor sought from persons both "knowledgeable and experienced" opinions concerning a permanent location for a new presidio. Among the sites suggested by these frontier notables, who despite Ortiz Parrilla's alleged hatred of the Jesuits included Fathers Sedelmayr, Segesser, and Stiger, were Aguacaliente, Arivaca, Arizonac, Ocuca, Santa Catalina, Sáric, Tubac, Tucsón, and El Tupo.

While the Governor was making up his mind, the soldiers, argued Father Stiger, should be stationed temporarily between Guevavi and Tubac. Someone had to put a stop to the stealing of cattle and horses from the unattended mission and from the residents of the San Luis Valley. Stiger knew who the culprits were — Pápagos and Pimas "who live in certain rancherías in the area of Baboquívari."

By early June of 1752 Ortiz Parrilla, it seems, had reached a decision. To Tubac, the site of Luis' surrender, he would dispatch Captain Belderrain and his fifty men. Twenty of them, rotating monthly, would serve at Ocuca, south of Tubutama.[11] Yet not for another six months was the Governor willing to act. By then he had the viceroy's concurrence.

On January 23, 1753, in conference with Captains Belderrain and Díaz del Carpio, the Governor explained his and the viceroy's plans for

---

[10]A listing of the men who made up the original company is in "Extracto de rebista de la nueva comp.a," March 26, 1752; Ortiz Parrilla testimonies, 5.

[11]*Ibid.*, 11. The opinions of Sedelmayr and Segesser, in the form of written statements, are included in Dobyns, *Pioneering Christians among the Perishing Indians of Tucson* (Lima, Peru: Editorial Estudios Andinos, 1962), pp. 8–10.

Tubac.[12] When construction of the presidio actually began, not even the Marqués de Rubí could find out. Not a single document in the presidial archive in the year 1766 provided the answer. From the evidence he was able to gather during his inspection, however, the Marqués inferred that the garrison had moved to Tubac in March of 1753.[13] Rubí seemed to know that the company had been activated on April 1, 1752, for several of the men he interviewed reckoned the length of their service from that date.[14]

Whatever day it was that the soldiers of His Majesty formally took possession of Guevavi's visita of Tubac, it marked a turning point. Henceforth, there, on a rise overlooking the river, near water and pasture and irrigable fields, adobe walls and armed men would cast their shadows. Surely from that time on, the Indians of Guevavi would be more receptive to a Padre and to the word of God. Father Pauer, for one, fervently hoped so.

Not long after Father Keller had returned to Soamca, an astonishing report reached the authorities in Sonora. A native of considerable influence was haranguing the people of Guevavi. He urged them not to take up arms, but rather to obey and to accept the ministration of Father Keller, "a good man." It was the chameleon — Luis Oacpicagigua.[15]

When Keller did ride over from Soamca in October, 1753, he was met in the vicinity of Guevavi, still without a Padre of its own, by a patrol from the new garrison. Presumably by this time the soldiers had made themselves at home at Tubac. Keller asked several of them to act as godfathers to Indian children.

When Phelipe, native captain of Tumacácori and soon to become village governor, brought a daughter to the Padre, it was only fitting that an officer accept the obligations of *padrino*. Ensign Juan Ramírez volunteered. Thus he and captain Phelipe, already neighbors, became com-

---

[12] Ortiz Parrilla testimonies, 5. The garrison was evidently still residing at Santa Ana on January 31, 1753, when its Lieutenant, Simón de Roxas y Taboada wrote to the Governor from that place. *Ibid*. Once Belderrain's men did move to Tubac, a contingent of soldiers from the presidio of Sinaloa commanded by Captain Bernardo de Urrea took their place at Santa Ana.

[13] "Exttractto de la Rebistta de Ynspeccion, executtada de Orden del Rey, por mi el Mariscal de Campo de sus Exttos, Marqs de Rubí, á la Expresada Compañia," Tubac, December 21, 1766, signed at the Presidio of San Miguel, February 21, 1767; AGI, Guad., 511.

[14] Declarations, Tubac, December 22–27, 1766; AGI, Guad., 274.

[15] Belderrain, Soamca, October 11, 1754; Utrera testimonies.

padres.[16] Hopefully this additional bond between them would insure continued friendship, on Spanish terms of course.

Eighteen months earlier, in the spring of 1752, when censuses were being compiled to record the return of repentant natives to their villages after the great uprising, captain Phelipe and his family had been counted at Tubac. Now they lived at Tumacácori, perhaps not entirely to their liking. When presidial soldiers and their dependents had begun preempting the good land at Tubac, apparently in March of 1753, the displaced natives were congregated at this site called Tumacácori, one league south of Tubac on the same side of the river, the *west* bank.

In Father Kino's day, and perhaps as late as the village's probable destruction in the uprising a half century after, Tumacácori had been located on the river's east bank, and it had been known as San Cayetano. On or about March 19, the feast day of San Joseph, in 1753, Captain Belderrain with fitting flourish may have designated the new west bank village San Joseph de Tumacácori,[17] a name and patron that stuck. Two of Guevavi's former visitas — San Cayetano and Tubac — thus became one. To the Spaniards this arrangement seemed ideal. But to the many families now living at Tumacácori, who knew that the irrigable fields of the new composite village could not yield enough maize to sustain them, it meant hunger.[18]

For the Padre who eventually came to live at Guevavi, the royal presidio of San Ignacio de Tubac would mean added security. It would also mean added responsibility, for he would be expected to serve as "interim" chaplain to the men and their families. Whether he wished to or not, the missionary would become an important member of the presidial community.

Meanwhile, the itinerant Keller of Soamca filled in for him, during 1753 looking after three missions and two presidios. Early in December

---

[16] Soamca, Bautismos de los Pueblos de Visita.

[17] A similar situation occurred nine years later at Tucsón, when Captain Francisco Elías González recorded the settlement there of several hundred Sobaípuris. Because it was Saint Joseph's Day he, too, renamed a village in honor of that saint.

[18] "Breve Resumen de los desastres, Muertes, Robos, y asolamentos acaezidos en la Provincia de Sonora Obstilizada de Apaches, Seris, y Pimas alzados, y en particular desde el año de 1755 hasta el presente de 1760"; AHH, Temp., 17. This 117-paragraph report describes depredations in all of Sonora between 1755 and 1760. Nentuig, "Descripcion," IX, 2.

Father Ignacio answered a call from Tubac. There he had the pleasure of baptizing Joseph Antonio, newborn son of the Captain and his Señora, "Doña María Theresa Butrón Prudhom y Muxica de Belderrain," evidently the daughter of Baron Prudhom, formerly of Arizonac.

If not by blood, most of Sonora's frontier elite were related in compadrazgo, and, like the rest of the Spanish world, polarized in groups representing regions of the mother country. Captain Belderrain, of Basque descent, named Don Gabriel Antonio de Vildósola and Doña Gregoria de Anza as little Joseph Antonio's godparents, thereby not only providing for his son's future but further tying himself and his family to Sonora's Basque community.[19]

By late fall, life at the presidio of Tubac was settling into the routine of a frontier post. Soon it would be safe for Father Pauer to return.

Ortiz Parrilla's interim replacement, Don Pablo de Arce y Arroyo, wasted no time implementing the viceroy's orders "to preserve the maximum degree of harmony and best relations with the Very Reverend Fathers . . . as the best means of advancing the service of God and of king."[20] Ironically, the individual who appeared before him in November, 1753, to plead for the return of a Padre to Guevavi was none other than the reformed scourge himself, Luis Oacpicagigua. The natives of Caborca and Guevavi had truly repented, Luis told the somewhat chary Governor. San Xavier del Bac, the Indian continued, was still unfit to receive a Padre — there was no church, no house, no harvest — "but the one who administers Guevavi could easily visit San Xavier from time to time."[21] That was an old story.

Perhaps there were no Padres available, had Luis thought of that? Perhaps they did not want to return to the ungrateful Pimas. In any case, the Governor assured the Indian, he would write to Father Visitor Roxas, which he did that very day.[22] Then, even before he heard from

---

[19] Doña Gregoria de Anza, wife of Don Gabriel Antonio de Vildósola, was apparently the sister of both Don Juan Bautista de Anza the younger and Don Francisco de Anza. Vildósola was thus the brother-in-law of the Anza boys.

[20] Arce y Arroyo to Calderón, Horcasitas, June 26, 1754; AHH, Temp., 17. Arce had been a city councilman of Mexico City when he accepted the Sonora post. Almada, *Diccionario,* p. 77.

[21] Arce y Arroyo, Horcasitas, November 18, 1753; Arce y Arroyo testimonies.

[22] Arce y Arroyo to Roxas, Horcasitas, November 18, 1753; *ibid.*

the Jesuit superior, he alerted Captain Belderrain to the possibility that Father Pauer might soon be sent back to Guevavi. He instructed the Tubac commander to do everything he could to see the Padre duly installed. He further ordered Belderrain to provide a military guard for the missionary, to get along well with him, and to keep the natives in line.[23]

When the Father Visitor answered with eloquent restraint that missionaries stood ready, despite the manifold dangers, to renew their labors among the Pimas,[24] the people of Guevavi had all but lost their bid for life without a Padre.

Again Keller prepared the way. At Guevavi on the feast day of the Immaculate Conception, December 8, he preached of a return to active Christianity. So convincing or so intent was he, that they brought to him then and there twenty-nine children to baptize. By December 14 Pauer had arrived at Soamca.[25] Because Guevavi's book of baptisms was

Fr̄s Fran.ᵒ Pauer. m·ɗ·ρ·l·m.

still in safekeeping, Father Francisco borrowed the book Keller used when on the trail.[26] Not much neater as a penman than Keller, at least Pauer wrote larger. His first entry, dated December 21, recorded the baptism of a Yaqui Indian child, though where he administered this sacrament Father Francisco did not say. If he were not yet in Guevavi, he soon would be.

With new resolve, and Keller at his side, Pauer reentered Guevavi and was surrounded by the villagers who had rejected him not long before. They would accept him now. Captain Belderrain of Tubac was there to see that they did. He had commanded that the natives of the

---

[23] Arce y Arroyo to Belderrain, Horcasitas, November 23, 1753; *ibid.*

[24] Roxas to Arce y Arroyo, Arizpe, November 27, 1753, *ibid.*

[25] Soamca, Bautismos.

[26] From December 21, 1753, through August 26, 1755 (the last date in the remaining portion of the book) Father Pauer used the book of baptisms for Soamca's visitas in place of Guevavi's book. When finally he did get the original Guevavi records back, he noted briefly the uprising below Garrucho's last entry (November 21, 1751) and then proceeded to transcribe all of the entries from the Soamca book into the Guevavi book. Thus there are two records of the baptisms he performed during this period. Soamca, Bautismos de los Pueblos de Visita. Guevavi, "Tubaca y Otros."

surrounding rancherías be there too. Looking over this large convocation of seemingly peaceful Pimas, Keller may have recalled a similar gathering he attended at Guevavi twenty-one years before. He hoped they would not dispose of his present companion as they had allegedly disposed of Grazhoffer.

Like the elder Anza before him, Captain Belderrain "through a skillful interpreter" delivered an admonitory speech "about the fidelity with which they should love God and the king, our lord (whom God guard), about the love and reverence with which they are obliged to treat their Father Minister, about attending the teaching of doctrine and the service of Mass, and about keeping clean and venerating their churches." They had heard it all before, and they were reported, as usual, "agreeable, giving signs of pleasure and fidelity." [27] As a Jesuit who later served at Guevavi put it, there was nothing like a bit of pageantry "to awaken interest, deference, and fervor among the Indians." [28]

Francisco Xavier Pauer, a Moravian baptized Franz Bauer, was born on January 6, 1721, in the town of Brno. When a lad of sixteen he entered the Jesuit novitiate. After nearly a dozen years of study he set out on February 1, 1749, from the college at nearby Olomouc, Keller's hometown, evidently made good connections, and reached the hospice overlooking the Bay of Cádiz on May 12. By Spanish authorities Father Francisco was described as "not well proportioned (de mal cuerpo), having clear swarthy skin, a thick nose, and brown hair." [29]

In the fleet of twenty-one ships that sailed on June 16, 1750, Father Pauer had passage either aboard the Corazón de Jesús commanded by Don Antonio Vicuña or the Condé, a French trading ship flying the Spanish flag and rammed accidentally by the Loreto while setting sail. On the other side of the formidable ocean, Pauer and his companions disembarked at Vera Cruz on the twenty-third day of the steaming month of August and after a hasty Te Deum of thanksgiving in the Jesuit church made directly for Mexico City. En route they were delighted at Puebla by fireworks and a display of lively Mexican dancing.

That fall ten of them, including Father Francisco, set out from the

---

[27] Belderrain to Arce y Arroyo, Tubac, January 6, 1754; Arce y Arroyo testimonies.

[28] Pfefferkorn, Sonora, p. 269.

[29] AGI, Contratación, 5550. Zelis, Catálogo, pp. 32–33. Pauer's name was variously spelled in New Spain — Pauer, Paver, Paber, Pauver, etc.

capital for the far Northwest. They followed not the central route through Durango and north, but instead the west-coast corridor, traveling the entire length of their order's northwest missionary empire. From Guadalajara they rode mules over roads that one of Pauer's companions believed were in general "still as they were in the year One after the creation of the world." [30]

By late May, 1751, Father Francisco had reached San Ignacio. After a briefing by Stiger he rode still farther north to San Xavier del Bac. When he had been missionary at "that unfortunate mission" no more than a few months, his neophytes caught the fever of the great rebellion and Father Francisco had to run for his life. Since then he had been spurned by the natives of Guevavi. Yet, late in 1753, for some reason he wanted another chance with these Pimas. The Padre's tenacity more than made up for his *mal cuerpo*.

Eagerly Father Pauer began his delayed ministry. On New Year's Day, 1754, he embarked on a brief but productive visitation of his diocese-size territory, first baptizing thirty-four Pima children at Tubac, twenty-nine of whom had been brought by their parents from San Xavier. Such a show of fealty by his former charges deserved his personal attention. Riding beside Captain Belderrain at the head of a column of Tubac soldiers, Father Francsico returned to Bac almost as a conqueror. The people from whom he had fled two years before, now swore obedience and brought forth twenty-three of their children for the ceremonial of the water.

He christened another twenty-eight at Tucsón, where the Captain told the natives that their best course was "to live as Christians in peace and tranquility. Likewise in these places all of them demonstrated a true and loyal intention." [31] Back in Tubac on January 6, the Padre added four more young ones to the fold, and the next day another ten

---

[30] Johann Jakob Baegert, s.j., *Observations in Lower California,* ed. and trans. M. M. Brandenburg and Carl L. Bauman (Berkeley: University of California Press, 1952), pp. xiii-xv. For an excellent description of their journey from Spain to Mexico City and from there to the frontier, see Dunne and Burrus, "Four Unpublished Letters of Anton Maria Benz, Eighteenth Century Missionary to Mexico," *Archivum Historicum Societatis Jesu,* Vol. XXIV (1955), pp. 338–39, 342–69 (introduction and most of the notes in English, text of the letters in German). For a particularly damning description of the road from Guadalajara to Sinaloa, written during Kino's time by a government official, see Navarro García, *Sonora y Sinaloa,* pp. 40–41.

[31] Belderrain to Arce y Arroyo, January 6, 1754.

at Guevavi. In one week he had baptized ninety-nine heathens, two less than had Garrucho in his first three years. Father Francisco then rode south to Arizpe on business.

In a letter to Governor Arce y Arroyo, dated at Tubac on January 6, 1754, Captain Belderrain described his part in the successful renewal of missionary activity in the northern Pimería. As for a military guard to protect the missionary, several soldiers to live at Guevavi, he had not yet committed himself. Father Pauer at the time was on his way to Arizpe to reclaim certain of the Guevavi church furnishings that had been stored there during the troubles. As soon as the Padre returned, Belderrain assured the Governor, he would be provided with as many men as were needed for his safety.[32]

In mid-February, 1754, when Father Francisco again approached his mission, presumably bringing back the santos and vestments on pack mules, the story of poor Christóbal Salazar was being told all along the valley. At the rancho of Buenavista, no more than three leagues south of the mission, Salazar had been murdered by the barbarous and audacious heathen Apaches. To Father Francisco fell the task of laying the body to rest in the church at Guevavi. "The Lord giveth and the Lord taketh away."

Except for the patching and renovating made necessary by the revolt, his first months at Guevavi seem to have been routine, his neophytes seem to have resigned themselves to his presence. He baptized a daughter of native governor Juanico Cipriano and a son of Don Nicholás Romero. He buried in the church the wife of one of Don Antonio de Rivera's servants and in the cemetery the wife of Marcos the cook.

Then one day in the middle of the spring he got an urgent call to report to San Ignacio. The native revolt in Pimería Alta was far from dead. Rumor had it that Luis was fanning the flames again. Bands of Pimas wearing Apache war caps were making a mockery out of Ortiz Parrilla's peace. They were stealing stock, even murdering vecinos. The situation called for immediate action.

Governor Arce y Arroyo and Father Visitor Roxas hastened north to assess the threat, arriving at San Ignacio on April 25 and 26 respectively. To that mission, used before as a headquarters by Ortiz Parrilla, they summoned all the Padres of the Pimería — Pauer from Guevavi,

---

[32]*Ibid.*

Keller from Soamca, Vivas from Tubutama. Also present at the council were Father Rector Stiger, missionary of San Ignacio, and a new man on his way to Caborca, Father Alonso Espinosa, a thirty-four-year-old Canary Islander with an uncanny affinity for hard luck.[33]

The frontier captains of Sonora — Belderrain of Tubac, Elías of Terrenate, Vildósola of Fronteras — left their lieutenants in command and joined the Governor and the Padres at the San Ignacio conference. Only Captain Bernardo de Urrea of the presidio of Sinaloa, serving temporarily as Belderrain's replacement at nearby Santa Ana,[34] was absent, chasing some of the malicious Indians.

Earlier, two prime suspects, Luis Oacpicagigua of Sáric and one of his alleged principal henchmen, Luis of Pitic, had been brought to San Ignacio for questioning. On May 15 they removed Oacpicagigua from "the public jail of this village" to the *"casas de comunidad"* where a board of inquisitors — the three Captains present — awaited him. Ever since the general amnesty granted by Ortiz Parrilla he had been, he maintained, a good Indian. The continuing depredations in the Altar Valley and Caborca areas were none of his doing. They heard the last of his testimony the following day. The witness did not know his age but looked to be somewhat older than forty.

Luis of Pitic, about fifty, was called next. The original revolt had been Oacpicagigua's fault, he told the Captains, he had merely followed orders out of fear. Since that time though, Luis of Pitic also claimed that he had been a good Indian, helping to rebuild burned churches, returning stolen furnishings, and reporting thieves to the Spaniards. When the sun had set on May 16 the Captains suspended the interrogation until the following day.

Only moments later, however, Ensign Juan Ramírez rushed to report to the Governor a bizarre happening. After the Captains had finished with Luis of Pitic, Ramírez, as ordered, had taken care to separate him and Oacpicagigua. Once the Indian was secured in irons (*prisiones*), Ramírez went on about his business. Suddenly the soldiers

---

[33] Roxas to Calderón, Arizpe, July 3, 1754; AHH, Temp., 17.

[34] The following year, 1755, Captain Urrea and his men would also leave their temporary quarters in Santa Ana to found a permanent presidio, the Pimería's third, at Altar to the west, a move that Father Sedelmayr had been advocating since the revolt of 1751. Sedelmayr, Guásavas, December, 1753; WBS, 1708.

standing guard heard the sounds of a commotion coming from Luis of Pitic's cell. Throwing open the door, they found Luis, unconscious, his cotton sash pulled tight around his throat and his tongue hanging out. Quickly they cut the sash and soon the prisoner began to regain consciousness. Luis of Pitic had tried to hang himself, and almost succeeded. The rest of the night the guards kept him under constant surveillance.

In the morning the Captains asked Luis of Pitic why he had attempted to take his own life. The Indian broke down. His crimes were so bad that in his heart he knew he deserved death. He had listened to the Devil, who told him to end it all by hanging himself. Now he knew that God had not willed his death just then, that He had given him the chance to tell the truth and to ask for mercy.

Luis of Pitic now admitted that he, too, bore some of the blame for the revolt of '51. After all, he knew that what Oacpicagigua ordered was wrong — nonetheless, he had gone with his relatives to Caborca and they had killed the Padre. Why, the Captains asked, did Oacpicagigua call for the death of Padres? In answer, Luis of Pitic recalled a seemingly harmless conversation with Oacpicagigua, one that in retrospect took on ominous significance.

The two were on their way home from the Seri campaign on Tiburón Island. They had stopped to rest at a place called El Tupo. There Oacpicagigua asked Luis of Pitic if he knew how their relatives had killed the Padre of Caborca many years ago. The latter replied that he did not, but Oacpicagigua kept on asking leading questions. Luis of Pitic now realized that these questions were indicative of the Pima captain general's malice toward the missionaries. From that time on, Luis Oacpicagigua was plotting revolt and the murder of Padres.[35]

"Remember El Tupo!" That indiscriminate slaughter of Pimas at the place called El Tupo in 1695, a half century before, had not been

---

[35] Proceedings at San Ignacio, May 15–17, 1754, including the testimonies of Luis Oacpicagigua, May 15–16, and Luis of Pitic, May 16–17, certified copies prepared for Father Visitor General Utrera, Horcasitas, November 22, 1754; BNMex, 40/718. Relating the story of the suicide attempt six years after it took place, Father Peña claimed that both Luises were actively involved. By tying themselves together with the cotton sash and then pulling mightily they had nearly succeeded in committing double suicide. Both of their lives were spared, Oacpicagigua's so that later that same year he might personally confess his perfidy and ask for mercy before the Father Visitor General. Peña, "Convite Evangelico," 12.

forgotten. In the mind of Luis Oacpicagigua it was directly related to the burning alive of gente de razón at Sáric in 1751.[36]

Continuing his testimony, Luis of Pitic told of events following the great uprising. Contrary to previous reports, Oacpicagigua had not been content with amnesty. About a year after accepting Ortiz Parrilla's terms, he had sent a message to the native *capitán de guerra* of Tumacácori. If the latter wished to revolt again, he could count on the assistance of Oacpicagigua. If not, he must keep quiet.

How did he find out about this, the Captains asked Luis of Pitic? A native of the ranchería of Comaqui named Xabon had told him. The governor of Toacuquita was apparently also involved. When Xabon was caught stealing mares and Luis Oacpicagigua sent him as a prisoner to Horcasitas, Xabon was happy for the chance to tell the Governor of Sonora that the Pimas' *capitán grande* was scheming again. Xabon had also told Luis of Pitic that Oacpicagigua was not going to include him in the new revolt, because the former was getting too friendly with Captain Belderrain and the vecinos of Santa Ana. Concluding his testimony, Luis of Pitic knew now that even if they killed him for what he had done he would go to God and not to the Devil, for he had told the truth.

Obviously the safest place for both Luises, the Governor concluded, was the jail at Horcasitas.

Despite indications of continued native unrest, the consensus at San Ignacio was optimistic. The Padres were willing to return to their missions. Governor Arce y Arroyo assured them that he would do everything in his power to protect them. He had, in fact, requisitioned from the Sonora presidios fifty soldiers, some of whom he intended to assign to guard duty in the missions. Pauer and Keller were the first to return to their flocks.

Then, on May 20, 1754, the Governor and Father Visitor Roxas, accompanied by the fifty soldiers, set out to assess the state of Pimería Alta for themselves. They rode first west to Caborca, where the natives seemed to be perpetually restless. Father Espinosa, assigned to that mission, sampled the Indians' mood and returned to San Ignacio to await

---

[36] Bolton described the martydom of Father Francisco Xavier Saeta at Caborca in 1695 and the resultant slaying of Pimas at El Tupo in *Rim of Christendom*, pp. 288–318. See also Burrus, *Vida del P. Francisco J. Saeta*.

a more favorable time. Governor and Father Visitor rode on, side by side, admonishing, exhorting, and demonstrating to the natives that a new unity prevailed between the representatives of king and God. Both wanted peace.

Traveling up the Altar Valley they passed by charred ruins that attested to the Pimas' inconstancy. North to Guevavi's abandoned visita of Arivaca and east through the ranchería of Sopori, whose people "went to live at Guevavi," they proceeded, until on June 4 they arrived at the "new presidio" of Tubac — what there was of it.

Captain and Señora Belderrain did their best to make the distinguished pair and their parties comfortable. It must have been hot. Meanwhile, Father Pauer had passed the word up the line to San Xavier and Tucsón, and the justicias of those villages had come to Tubac to swear allegiance and to ask for a Padre. The Governor entrusted them with new sacred vessels and vestments for the mission of San Xavier "where all was lost," and he told them that their Padre was on his way, although that, the Father Visitor later admitted, was somewhat doubtful.

On June 7 and 8, 1754, "with the same solemnity and ceremony as in the other places," the Governor and the Visitor conducted their inspections of Guevavi. "This mission," wrote Father Roxas, "suffered greatly with regard to its properties, but neither house nor church was burned, and the vestments were saved. Only at Sonoita did they burn the Father's house, which served as a church."

During the course of the inspection Governor Arce y Arroyo discovered evidence of a native craft of which he heartily disapproved. Guevavi's neophytes were actually brewing a tub of mescal liquor. Did they hope for early summer rains or merely a bacchanalian escape from life in the mission? Unwilling to overlook what he considered a punishable transgression, the Governor ordered the liquor dumped out and the native or natives responsible brought before him for a whipping. No less excited than their white contemporaries by the prospect of public punishment, the natives "all cooperated in this." The lashes, the Governor believed, were justified "because of the excesses brought on by drunkenness, in which the Upper Pimas distinguish themselves to a great extent from the other tribes in these parts." But the Padres objected.

"It hardly seems right," reasoned Father Roxas, "that here in the north they are punished for the least of their sins — and one common to the whole tribe — while the people of the west are forgiven far greater sacrileges and misdeeds. After all, the people of the north do have the virtue of never having killed Fathers."[37] Had he forgotten about poor Grazhoffer?

In August, during the rainy season when the arroyos were apt to be awash with torrents of dirty water, and the humid afternoon air alive with insects, Father Francisco traveled again to San Xavier and Tucsón to preach and to baptize. Forty-three more children felt a trickle of holy water on their heads. Then in his book he wrote the names of each of them. In October Guevavi's overworked Padre fell ill and was taken to Soamca, where Father Visitor General Utrera, come to hear the revolt of '51 relived, found him suffering from chills.

Because of the difficulties involved in getting to either Guevavi or Bac, and because of their rudeness and poverty, the Visitor General willingly accepted secondhand what Father Pauer told him about those two unhappy missions. Guevavi at least possessed a house and a church "but without doors or windows or furniture." The mission owed no debts, nor could it claim any accounts receivable. A hundred cattle, four hundred sheep, forty horses, and two mares grazed its lands. In the village of Guevavi there now lived no more than twenty families. As visitas "without houses or churches" Utrera listedTumacácori with only ten families, which seems too few; Sonoita with twenty-two families; and Arivaca, which others considered abandoned, with twenty-seven families. In the wake of the revolt some of them still roamed about at will.

As for San Xavier del Bac, Father Pauer "told me," wrote Utrera, "that the house, the church, the vestments, and all manner of livestock perished in the uprising. The mission has nothing and owes nothing. He did not even know how many families there might be, because they have not even been gathered up or brought together and therefore he was unable to get an idea."[38]

Leaving Pauer at Soamca with the chills, Father Utrera pushed south again. At San Ignacio he found more sick Padres. Luis Vivas of Tubutama, recovering from severe fevers and chills, told the Visitor General of his mission's woes. Alonso Espinosa, also convalescing at

---

[37] Roxas to Calderón, July 3, 1754. Arce y Arroyo to Calderón, June 26, 1754.

[38] Utrera, "Derrotero, y Jornadas, q voi haciendo desde el dia 17 de Enero de 1754 q salí de Mexico á visitar las Missiones"; WBS, 67.

San Ignacio, had not yet ventured back to Caborca, a village "still very restless." "Partly because of his little health and partly because of his big fear that they might kill him," Utrera reported, Espinosa had the idea that perhaps if there were several Padres in a mission "they would be less likely to excite these unruly and fickle natives."[39] At least they would not send him back to Caborca. Instead, Utrera assigned Espinosa to San Xavier del Bac, "which is not so restless." While the natives of Bac built him a small house, he was to operate from Guevavi, where the recovered Francisco Pauer had once again taken up residence.

The fact that he was less than well proportioned did not seem to hamper Father Francisco in the least. Early in 1755 he journeyed again to Arizpe, a hundred miles south. This was a special occasion. On the second day of February, the important feast of the Purification of the Blessed Virgin, he professed his final solemn vows before Father Visitor Roxas.[40] While temporarily beyond the call of his own demanding neophytes, he probably took the opportunity to fulfill his annual obligations, the eight-day retreat and the reading of recent edicts from the Holy Office. He then jogged back to Guevavi.

After a rest of no more than a few days, he was off again, this time north sixty miles to "his other mission" of San Xavier del Bac. As he baptized more of their children he may have told them yet another time that a permanent Padre of their own was coming. Then back to Guevavi.

At 6:00 o'clock in the morning on Saint Joseph's day, March 19, Señora Belderrain gave birth to another son. The same day Father Francisco observed the patronal feast at Tumacácori only a league from Tubac. The Padre, evidently by now a close friend of the Belderrains, may have kept the previous night's vigil with the family, or he may have called on them during the day to extend his congratulations. The christening of the commander's new son was set for April 6, the Sunday after Easter.

On the appointed day Father Francisco reined up outside the Captain's house, for as yet the royal presidio of Tubac had no church. Father Keller was present too, presumably on his best behavior with the guests. Keller, in fact, not Pauer, would baptize the child, who would

[39] Utrera to Calderón, San Ignacio, October 24, 1754; AHH, Temp., 17.
[40] Roxas to Calderón, Arizpe, May 14, 1755; *ibid.*

be called Joseph Antonio. A wee brother of the same name, baptized by the same Father sixteen months earlier, must have died.

This time the Belderrains had asked Father Francisco to be the boy's godfather. It was an honor. It made him a compadre of the Captain and Doña María Theresa. Later he would be named godfather of other Belderrain children — María Josepha Antonia in 1758 and María Ignacia Francisca Xaviera in 1759.[41] This was more on Captain Belderrain's part than mere compliance with the Governor's orders to get along with the Jesuit. The Captain obviously had great respect for the game, thick-nosed missionary of Guevavi.

For nearly twenty years — broken only by Pauer's own brief stay in 1751 and the revolt — the more populous mission of San Xavier del Bac had been administered for all practical purposes as a distant visita of Guevavi. Now, late in 1755, it stood a good chance of getting a resident Padre. A new governor had taken over the headaches of Sonora that summer. He was Colonel Don Juan Antonio de Mendoza, formerly of the Prince's Regiment in Spain, an energetic and valiant Castilian who planned to rout the Seris, Apaches, and rebel Pimas and at the same time to push northward the rim of Christendom.[42]

Like his interim predecessor, Colonel Mendoza toured the Pimería. He, too, had a missionary to install, the same one in fact. Alonso Espinosa, once again sound of body and spirit, was going to San Xavier. Evidently Mendoza and his baggage, his soldiers, and Father Espinosa passed through Guevavi on the trail to Bac. At the invitation of Father Pauer, Espinosa baptized a native boy and signed the mission book on the last day of 1755.[43]

If he was able, Father Francisco doubtless joined the Governor's caravan and took part in the installation of the long-promised Padre at San Xavier. Not only did Espinosa's presence there relieve Pauer of a great burden, but more important, it provided hundreds of heathens

---

[41] Guevavi, "Tubaca y Otros."

[42] Almada, *Diccionario,* pp. 463–64.

[43] Mendoza did tour the Pimería in January of 1756. Donohue, "Jesuit Missions," p. 281. Whether he saw to Father Espinosa's installation personally at San Xavier is not certain. Later that spring, Father Roxas reported that Espinosa was indeed serving there. Roxas to Calderón, Arizpe, May 30, 1756; AHH, Temp., 17.

and marginal Christians, whether they liked it or not, with a chance for salvation. Such reasoning the Governor understood. He was a religious man, and pro-Jesuit, a good example for the province.

Don Juan Antonio, furthermore, was a man of action. A Jesuit eulogy later would rank him with Cortés and Pizarro.[44] Colonel Mendoza recognized what needed doing. The neglected natives of Tucsón, "gateway to the Gila," and the brave Sobaípuris who formed a buffer along the San Pedro against the Apaches, they, too, deserved salvation — and Don Juan Antonio vowed that they would receive it.

Jabanimó, or Crow's Head, the old chief of the Gila Pimas, wanted no part of salvation and did his best to convince the people of Bac and Tucsón that they did not either. Early in 1756 it was rumored that Jabanimó also intended to incite the Pápagos, native people of the vast desert west of Guevavi and San Xavier. To maintain the population of his mission, Pauer, like those who served at Guevavi before him, had been actively recruiting Pápagos. As the Pimas proper who lived along the rivers died from the white man's diseases the Padres endeavored to replace them with the closely related desert Pápagos. When the latter came, as they had done for centuries, to trade or to work for food among the Pimas, the missionaries, and on occasion the soldiers, persuaded them to stay.

Personally, Father Francisco did not believe that Jabanimó was stirring up the Pápagos, but his superiors wanted him to find out. To a parley called by the Padre, Jabanimó "did not come because of his age." He sent his son instead. What they said about his father and his people was false, the Indian assured Pauer. The Pápagos of Atí, he continued, had indeed requested Jabanimó's aid in resisting conversion, but Jabanimó had refused.[45] If Father Pauer trusted the Gileño chief, he was soon to rue that trust.

By his very presence at San Xavier, Espinosa may have brought the frightful attack down upon himself. That it occurred in the early fall, at about the time of the natives' traditional harvest festival, may or

---

[44] Peña, "Convite Evangelico," 14.

[45] Roxas to Calderón, May 30, 1756. The Atí referred to by the native was evidently the desert ranchería west of Tucsón known to Kino as San Francisco de Adid, not the Pima village of Atí on the Altar.

may not indicate that he tried to suppress their habitual "immorality" and drunkenness.[46]

Whatever the provocation, in a savage show of strength Jabanimó and his willing warriors — including Pápagos and some of the mission's own neophytes, it was reported — fell with full fury upon San Xavier, sacking and pillaging, and intent upon killing Espinosa.[47]

Somehow the Padre escaped, and word of the attack was carried to the presidio of Tubac. With only fifteen soldiers, Ensign Juan María de Oliva rode to the rescue, met the lingering enemy in battle, and put them to flight, killing fifteen in the process. Three of the soldiers were slightly wounded.[48] While Bac smoldered, Espinosa took refuge at Tubac.

Colonel Mendoza was not the sort of governor to overlook such an outrage. He would see Jabanimó punished. Quickly he organized a punitive expedition of soldiers from the various presidios and recruited a large contingent of native auxiliaries. At their head, the Governor and his

[46] Dobyns, *Pioneering Christians,* p. 11. Dobyns maintains that this was indeed the cause, apparently following Pradeau, *Expulsión,* pp. 139–40, 178. Both of these authors suggest that Father Bernardo Middendorff shared the blame for provoking this attack. According to them, Middendorff founded a mission at Santa Catalina near Bac in September, 1756. Actually, the innocent Middendorff did not set foot in the San Xavier-Santa Catalina-Tucsón area until after the attack. He had only just arrived in the Pimería when he was named chaplain of the punitive expedition of November, 1756. In December he apparently returned to San Ignacio where he waited with several companions for a permanent assignment. Sedelmayr to Balthasar, Mátape, December 6, 1756; quoted in Arthur D. Gardiner, "Letter of Father Middendorff, S.J., dated from Tucson, 3 March 1757," *The Kiva,* Vol. XXII (1957), p. 1. At the base of this confusion seems to be a statement by Father Joseph Och: "Father Middendorff established a new mission among the Pápagos in Santa Catalina, but the Indians were soon tired of it because they were barred from their vices, nightly dances and carousing. . . ." Treutlein, *Travel Reports of Joseph Och,* pp. 43–44. It was not until early in January of 1757 that Middendorff went among the Indians of the Santa Catalina-Tucsón area to found his ill-fated mission.

[47] Dobyns and Pradeau credit Luis Oacpicagigua with an active part in Jabanimó's attack. At this time Luis, a prisoner of the Governors of Sonora since mid-1754, was either languishing in jail or already dead. He died, according to Father Peña, "at the beginning" of Mendoza's administration. "Convite Evangelico," 12. Mendoza assumed control in July, 1755.

[48] "Breve Resumen de los desastres." This coup by Ensign Oliva quite naturally went down on his record. Nearly twenty years later, however, when Colonel Oconor cited the incident, Oliva's adversaries were said to have been 200 *Apaches.* The number of them he was credited with killing remained at fifteen. "Extracto de Revista de Ynspeccion pasada por el Coronel de Ynfanteria dn Hugo Oconor . . . al expresado de Sn Ygnacio de Tubác," 1775, Quaderno 1; AGI, Guad. 515.

second-in-command, Captain Elías of Terrenate, rode north during November through San Ignacio, where they acquired the services of a chaplain, the Westphalian cartographer, Bernardo Middendorff, one of five newly arrived German Jesuits.

Pushing on, presumably again through Guevavi, the expedition picked up Espinosa en route and reinstated him at San Xavier.[49] From there "by march both irksome and of many days' duration," they followed the enemy's fresh tracks to the banks of the Gila. Along the river they engaged the foe in a disappointing running battle, which Father Middendorff described blow by blow.[50] They then turned back. Having failed on this occasion to distinguish himself by destroying his enemy, Colonel Mendoza did "with great edification" lay the first stone for the new church Father Espinosa intended to build at San Xavier del Bac.[51]

At this very time, the late fall of 1756, another formidable Indian-hunting force — 110 regulars from five presidios, 140 Ópata archers, 60 Tarahumara archers, and a band of armed vecinos — led by Captains Bernardo Bustamante and Gabriel Antonio de Vildósola, was combing previously unexplored territory to the east along the upper Gila in search of Apaches. Riding with this expedition as chaplain was the missionary Bartholomé Sáenz, who seven years earlier "full of apprehensions" had sought temporary asylum with Garrucho at Guevavi.[52] While the soldiers of His Most Catholic Majesty and their native auxiliaries may not have been killing many hostiles, they were proving their own courage, and that was important.

Luis Oacpicagigua died in jail at the beginning of Governor Mendoza's administration, but "his sons" refused to let the rebellion die

---

[49] Sedelmayr to Balthasar, Mátape, December 6, 1756.

[50] Middendorff to Balthasar, San Augustín de Tucsón, March 3, 1757; in Gardiner, "Letter of Middendorff," *Kiva,* XXII, pp. 3–8. From Middendorff's letter one might easily be led to believe that Mendoza's force had fought Ensign Oliva's San Xavier battle in which fifteen of Jabanimó's braves were killed, when actually the governor's punitive expedition did not arrive until several weeks afterward, and failed to kill anyone. Both Donohue, "Jesuit Missions," pp. 281–82, and Dobyns, *Pioneering Christians,* p. 11, seem confused on this point.

[51] Burrus, *Misiones Norteñas,* p. 70. For the next five years Espinosa worked on the new church at Bac.

[52] Sáenz to Balthasar, Cuchuta, March 6, 1757; BNMex, 197/875, translated by Kessell as *Spaniard and Apache on the Upper Gila, 1756: An Account of the Bustamante-Vildósola Expedition by Father Bartholomé Sáenz, S.J.* (Santa Fe: Stagecoach Press, in press).

with him. As the fifties wore on, these die-hard Pimas, far more than the Apaches, gave Father Francisco of Guevavi and his neighbors nearly constant cause for alarm. Time and time again they struck, driving off livestock from the mission and from the embarrassed garrison at Tubac, until the losses ran to hundreds of head.

Once, near the presidio, the rebels killed a Spaniard and carried away alive five natives whom they surprised in the maize fields. They became so bold that they dared to raid the horse corral inside the village of Guevavi. When they broke up the observance of Holy Week in 1758, the mission's neophytes rallied, gave chase, and, to their Padre's delight, recovered the stolen animals. On another occasion Father Francisco's charges even managed to wound Ciprián, the rebel leader.

In June, 1759, the rebels encircled Sonoita in such large numbers that the frightened villagers "were fortunate" to suffer only one death and the loss of all their gentle horses. The gente de razón of the ranches of Buenavista, San Luis, and Santa Bárbara, south of Guevavi, also suffered these raids. The apostate Pimas got off with Don Nicholás Romero's mules, while the Apaches, who were not entirely inactive during these years, stole Ignacio Romero's whole horse herd. In September of 1758, the hostiles caught Francisco Figueroa, a vecino of Tubac, and left him lying dead in their wake.[53] For nearly a decade after the major uprising of 1751, the settlers in the valley suffered its appalling aftermath, and the less resolute among them thought of leaving. For Father Francisco there was no such escape: he was resolved to stay.

In spite of the harassment, he made Guevavi grow. He continued to bring in and to baptize more heathens than his predecessors had — fifteen children of "Pápago immigrants" from the ranchería of Gahcat on November 23, 1755; fourteen *recién agregados* ranging up to twenty years of age from Mamturss on May 10, 1756; ten adults settled at Tumacácori, June 9, 1758.

Possibly the largest single contingent of natives ever reduced by a Guevavi Padre, seventy-eight in all, was moved from the oft-mentioned ranchería of Doacuquita, or Toacuquita, to a place called Las Calabazas just south of the confluence of Sonoita Creek and the river. The name and patronage of San Cayetano, formerly associated with the east-bank village of Tumacácori, soon was applied to Calabazas, as it was to the

---

[53] "Breve Resumen de los desastres. . . ."

large mountain just north of the village. Because the seventy-eight neophytes had received instruction beforehand, Father Francisco was able
to baptize and marry them all according to the precepts of the Holy
Council of Trent on the very day of their arrival, November 1, 1756.[54]

Henceforth, the visitas of Guevavi were San Cayetano de Calabazas, Sonoita, and Tumacácori. Tubac had become a presidio, and
Arivaca, consumed in the 1751 rebellion, never really recovered.

At two of his visitas Father Pauer apparently found the time and
the means to build churches. When the wife of Juanico, native governor
of Sonoita, died in that village early in 1756, the Padre noted that she
was buried "en Aquella Yglesia." Perhaps the house "which served as
a church," burned in 1751, had been renovated. Three years later, Pauer
buried Sonoita's foreman of oxherds in what he termed "la Nueva Iglesia," presumably there at Sonoita. But not even the village site, let alone
the ruins of the "new church," is known today.

Before July 7, 1757, there had been no mention of a church at
Tumacácori. On that day, however, Lorenzo, native alcalde of the
village, was interred beneath the earth floor of "Aquella Yglesia." It was
customary to bury native officials and exemplary neophytes, as well as
most of the children who died, inside the church. Gente de razón of note
rated the same terminal privilege. When a horrible, unexplained epidemic hit Tumacácori early in the spring of 1758, Father Francisco
wrote a single entry in the book of burials for thirty-six dead, twenty-one
of whom were buried in the village church.[55] During the early 1960s the
National Park Service outlined at Tumacacori National Monument
the foundations of what appears to be Pauer's adobe church. They
measure roughly 60' x 20' and lie within the convento and the shadow
of the later massive Franciscan church.

True to his vow, Governor Mendoza saw to it that missionaries were
sent to Tucsón and to the San Pedro Valley, but the natives they were
intended to serve refused to cooperate. During the first days of 1757,
two of the five German Padres who had arrived on the frontier late in

---

[54] Though Pauer had mentioned Calabazas earlier that year (in a baptismal entry, April
20), the village seems to have been considered a visita of Guevavi from the day the seventy-
eight natives of Doacuquita were moved there.

[55] Guevavi, "Tubaca y Otros."

*Foundations of
Father Pauer's church
at Tumacácori (above),
and artist Cal Peters'
re-creation of the church*

1756 made ready to begin their missionary careers.[56] Fathers Francisco Hlava and Miguel Gerstner, in the company of the unyielding twenty-four-year-veteran Keller, rode forth from Soamca with a military escort down the valley of the San Pedro to the north. At long last, the loyal Sobaípuris were to have their reward.

But instead of the welcome the young Jesuits expected to receive from these heathens, instead of the usual show of compliant obedience, this time the Sobaípuris wore menacing looks. They wanted nothing to do with the two new men. Keller, Padre of Soamca, was their Padre, they asserted, and his church was their church. What more did they need?

The natives of the San Pedro, it seemed, had grown used to Christianity at a distance, Christianity on their terms. While they were willing to remain allies of the Spaniards and to go on their campaigns, the Sobaípuris said they would kill any other missionary sent to live with them. Whether intentionally, as some of his brethren alleged, or otherwise, Father Keller had become lord and master to the Indians of his baronial jurisdiction. While he lived, they would accept no other. "In a word, they want to be baptized, but to live as they wish, to be Christians only in name."

There was no alternative but retreat. The two disappointed would-be missionaries went back to Soamca. Just in case these obstinate natives, who were known to change their minds "in a matter of hours," did relent, the rejected Padres stayed close by. Hlava looked after Cocóspera, while Gerstner joined Pauer at Guevavi.[57] But the Sobaípuris did not relent, and the Jesuit superiors were loath to force the issue. For Father Francisco at Guevavi the luxury of a Jesuit companion lasted no more then a few weeks. At least that mission's neophytes had the chance to meet Father Gerstner. Later they would see more of him.

In August, after seven trying months *entre infieles,* another rejected missionary stopped over for several weeks' rest at Guevavi. The previous January 5, the day before Epiphany in 1757, Father Bernardo Middendorff, with ten soldiers for his protection, had gone out to Tucsón to found a mission. With gifts of dried meat he soon attracted some seventy

---

[56] The five were Francisco Hlava, Miguel Gerstner, Ignacio Pfefferkorn, Bernardo Middendorff, and Joseph Och. For a delightful and perceptive description of their travels from Germany to the Pimería, see Treutlein, *Travel Reports of Joseph Och,* pp. 1–45.

[57] Roxas to Calderón, Arizpe, March 15, 1757; AHH, Temp., 17.

families. "I had neither house nor church," he recalled, "and in the first days had to sleep under the open sky until I was able to erect a brush and willow hut for a lodging. . . . I celebrated Mass under a matting or cover of rushes and reeds which had been raised on four poles in the field." Then on a May night his beginnings were viciously and suddenly destroyed, as "about five hundred savage heathen" swept down and ravaged the village. The Padre and his ten soldiers fled before the onslaught and made it to San Xavier by daybreak.[58]

In describing Middendorff's unhappy ministry in the Tucsón area, one of his brethren wrote that "the Indians were soon tired of it because they were barred from their vices, nightly dances and carousing, and plagued the good father in every conceivable way, and stole from him all victuals sent to him. Absence of nourishment and of shelter — he had to endure heat, cold, and wet under the open sky — so reduced this robust man that he would have died of an inflammatory fever had he not been removed from there, half dead. With a bit of refreshment and a deep sleep of two days and two nights his strength was somewhat restored."[59]

When Middendorff reached Guevavi on his way to another unfortunate experience at Sáric, Tucsón once again had reverted to the status of a visita of San Xavier del Bac.[60] That year, 1757, saw the Jesuits' strongest bid since 1732 to expand the vineyard of the Lord in the northern Pimería. That bid failed completely — and there were to be no more.

The loss of two of his close associates marred Pauer's last months at Guevavi. The seemingly indestructible Keller of Soamca, after enduring the hardships of service on New Spain's farthest frontier for nearly three decades, died some time after mid-August, 1759.[61] Ailing, he had hastened nonetheless a great distance to the side of a Pima of the north, "a poor neophyte" who was in danger of dying without confession.[62] In so doing, the zealous Padre, evidently aware that he was himself near death, forsook the comfort of spending his last moments in the company

---

[58] Treutlein, "Father Gottfried Bernhardt Middendorff, s.j., Pioneer of Tucson," *NMHR*, Vol. XXXII (1957), pp. 316–17.

[59] Treutlein, *Travel Reports of Joseph Och*, pp. 43–44.

[60] Father Middendorff stayed with Pauer at Guevavi for at least two weeks. He baptized eight children there between August 6 and 21. Guevavi, "Tubaca y Otros."

[61] Keller signed his last baptismal entry in the Soamca book on August 19, 1759.

[62] Peña, "Convite Evangelico," 15.

of Europeans. Instead, by this final act, Keller demonstrated one of the noblest justifications for spending one's life as a missionary: "It is more blessed to give than to receive."

On September 7, 1759, the first captain of the royal presidio of Tubac, Don Juan Thomás Belderrain, died at Guevavi, just five weeks after a daughter had been born to him. As his life ebbed away, the comandante had been brought to the mission: Father Francisco was probably more skilled in the limited science of frontier medicine than anyone within several days' ride.[63] If the struggle to save his life proved hopeless, at least there was time for the last rites of the Church — viaticum, penance, extreme unction. Then the Captain's Jesuit friend and compadre laid the body to rest in a place of honor beneath the altar steps in the church at Guevavi.[64]

The support of these two fallen comrades, priest and soldier, had contributed much to the success of Father Francisco's ministry. Yet there was little doubt that he could carry on without them. His own tenacity and surprising energy had sustained him at Guevavi through six years. These qualities had not gone unnoticed.

Named by his superiors as Father Rector of Pimería Alta, Pauer was reassigned to San Ignacio, "gateway to the missions." Father Stiger, missionary at San Ignacio since 1736 and Pauer's predecessor as Rector of the Pimería, had been rendered almost helpless by his various maladies. Because "his ills and swollen feet" made it impossible for him to ride a horse, Stiger during the late fifties had leaned on a compañero, Father Och.[65] Now, in mid-January, 1760, Pauer took over. Stiger had earned his rest; two years later he was dead.

Before he left Guevavi, Father Pauer turned over to Father Miguel Gerstner, his replacement, a complete inventory of the mission's properties, its debts, and its credits. Pauer had arrived at Guevavi in the wake of the worst revolt in the history of Pimería Alta. For six years he had labored at reconstruction. He had managed to endure among

---

[63] See Treutlein, "The Jesuit Missionary in the Role of Physician," *MA,* Vol. XXII (1940), pp. 120–41, which is based largely on the writings of Father Pfefferkorn, one of Pauer's successors at Guevavi.

[64] Guevavi, "Tubaca y Otros."

[65] Roxas to Calderón, March 15, 1757.

Indians who, at least initially, did not want him, and he had baptized more of them than any other Jesuit. He had built churches at Tumacácori and at Sonoita. Despite rebel Pimas and thieving Apaches, he left Guevavi more prosperous than he found it. Only Joseph Garrucho, who guided Guevavi out of the wilderness, had served the mission longer. Which man contributed more is debatable.

After them, the Jesuits merely hung on.

"I have known that Father Custodio wanted to abandon Guevavi because it is afflicted so by the Apaches, but His Reverence has not written me about it, nor will I permit it. . . ."

Father Visitor Manuel Aguirre, 1764

6.

Hanging On
From Gerstner to Ximeno, 1760-1767

MIGUEL GERSTNER, rejected by the Sobaípuris at the outset of his missionary career, was "continually ill from the time he entered the Pimería."[1] A native of the place called Evenshausen in the southwestern German duchy of Franconia, he was not quite thirty-seven when he moved into the Padre's house at Guevavi.[2] For several days Father Gerstner, the newcomer, sickly and lean — "I am not fat," he noted on an order for clothes[3] — and Father Rector Pauer, his unprepossessing superior, discussed the trials and the rewards of serving at Guevavi.

Before he took leave of the village, Pauer reintroduced governor Antonio and the other justicias and helpers to their new Padre, and

---

[1] Father Visitor Manuel Aguirre to Father Provincial Francisco Zevallos, Bacadéguachi, February 18, 1764; AHH, Temp., 17; and quoted in Pradeau, *Expulsión,* p. 156.

[2] Gerstner, Puerto de Santa María, July 17, 1768; Archivo Histórico Nacional, Madrid, Spain, Jesuitas, 453. Franconia, the province of Father Gerstner's birth, was misread by the printer of the Zelis *Catálogo* and rendered incorrectly as *Francia,* or France. A German, not a Frenchman, Gerstner was born on March 17, 1723, and admitted to the Society of Jesus on July 12, 1744. When he volunteered for the missions he was a member of the Jesuit province of the Upper Rhine, which included Franconia. Lázaro de Aspurz, O.F.M., cap., *La aportación extranjera a las misiones españolas del Patronato Regio* (Madrid: Publicaciones del Consejo de la Hispanidad, 1946), Apéndice I, pp. 278–319; and Pfefferkorn, *Sonora,* p. 260.

[3] Quoted in Pradeau, *Expulsión,* p. 157.

The view south, upriver from Guevavi

On the trail from Guevavi to Tumacácori

begged their continued cooperation. Perhaps over a cup of hot chocolate, he confided to his successor which of the natives and which of the local settlers could not be trusted. Gerstner surely had questions, about the crops and livestock which were the basis of any mission's prosperity, about native vices, about the officers and men at Tubac for whom he would be chaplain, and about the reports of raids by marauding Pimas and Apaches. Had they felt up to it, the two men could have sat before a fire and talked through several long chill January nights.[4]

On the day of Father Francisco's departure a settler's wife, whose children he had baptized, may have wept. Some of the Indians may have asked him not to go. He was especially sorry to leave the appealing, disheveled, black-eyed native children, for in their innocence he could see a better day for Guevavi. But after a final Mass in the church, the last blessings, and appropriate shouts, Guevavi's Padre for six years climbed onto his horse and started down the slope to the river's level. From above, those left behind watched the small black-robed figure and his escort riding south beneath the bare cottonwoods, the mission fields on their left. When the dust kicked up by the animals' hoofs had settled on the brown hills, Father Miguel was on his own.

Not ten days later, Eusebio of Tumacácori, husband of María, met his death at the hands of *Indios Cimarrones,* evidently the vengeful rebel Pimas.[5] Gerstner was not intimidated. He called for his horse and an escort and took the trail north. His closest visita, two leagues distant, perched on a bluff well above the river's east bank. This was San Cayetano de Calabazas. It possessed little to distinguish it from a heathen ranchería — no church, not even a cemetery.[6] Noting this visita's needs, the Padre rode on.

Skirting the base of the mountain known as San Cayetano, he kept to the river trail through fertile bottom lands. Four leagues beyond

---

[4] Father Gerstner's first entry in the mission books as Padre of Guevavi recorded a burial on January 12, 1760. Father Pauer's last, noting a baptism, was dated January 15. The new Father Rector seems to have begun making regular entries in the San Ignacio baptismal book on January 23. Three weeks earlier, however, he must have made a preliminary trip to that mission, during which he recorded a baptism on January 2.

[5] Guevavi, "Tubaca y Otros."

[6] For thirteen years the dead of Calabazas were carried five miles to Guevavi for burial. Not until March 4, 1773, when the Franciscans began burying the bodies of Calabazas natives in the newly roofed church at that village, was the long funeral march rendered unnecessary. *Ibid.* and Tumacácori, "De Calabasas Bautismos."

Calabazas, set back from the west bank of the river in front of some rugged-looking mountains, stood the church Father Pauer had built for Phelipe and the people of Tumacácori. Because the presidio at Tubac, one league farther north, still had no church, the troopers and members of their families often met the missionary at Tumacácori, and there were baptized, married, or buried.

When he spoke to the natives of Tumacácori that day, it was through an interpreter, for Miguel Gerstner had trouble learning the Piman tongue.[7] He nonetheless christened four children, married three couples, and promised to return. Then, instead of giving his horse its lead and heading directly back to Guevavi, he detoured east, almost certainly taking the trail through the saddle between the Santa Ritas and San Cayetano Mountain, passing by the site of the later Salero Mine, and dropping down into the delightful valley of Sonoita Creek near present-day Patagonia.

At the village of Sonoita, his most distant visita, in another church he inherited from Father Pauer, he baptized and recorded the Christian names of six more children, three of whose parents lived in the San Xavier-Tucsón area. The native governor, Gregorio, stood as godfather

for a little boy, while Lieutenant Joseph Romero of the Padre's escort vowed to accept similar responsibilities for a little slave girl, a Nixora he may have just bought, eight or nine years old.

His initial contacts made, Father Miguel now rode back along the creek to the river, past Calabazas, and home again. When finally he dismounted in Guevavi, saddle-weary and dusty, he must have gone directly to the church and thanked God for his good fortune — he had ridden the circuit safely.

Though the Pima rebels kept on raiding at will, as one Padre put it, "their scourge had to come." When early in 1760 it did come, "in the

---

[7]Aguirre to Zevallos, February 18, 1764.

form of the most accomplished, valiant, and noble command of the new Captain of Tubac, Don Juan Bautista de Anza," the Jesuits rejoiced. "Legitimate son of his father, the deceased Captain Juan Bautista de Anza, he inherited with the name and surname not only the memorable merits of his father, but also a solid disposition, valor, rapport with his soldiers, and the ability to place himself on their level and to excel them in bearing the hardships and the duties as well as the good fortune of their expeditions."

He was only twenty-four and still a bachelor, but already a veteran. The Apaches had ambushed his father when young Juan stood hardly a *vara* tall. He had grown up around presidios and had been a cadet since early adolescence. He came to Tubac after a five-year hitch as lieutenant at Fronteras, his birthplace. At the side of his brother-in-law, the Captain of Fronteras, Don Gabriel Antonio de Vildósola, "scourge of the Apaches, hero of the entire province, and shining ornament of Spanish arms," young Anza had "learned to fear no danger, to trample the barbarians, and to earn for himself the applause of Governor Mendoza, of the province, and of all the garrisons."[8]

For a thousand pesos, nearly double his annual salary, Anza bought the captain's house at Tubac from Belderrain's mourning widow,[9] and into it he moved his household, which included his elderly mother, Doña Rosa. As the garrison's new commander "this still youthful Mars" wasted little time getting down to the business at hand — hostiles.

Tracking the rebels at the head of a squadron of his men, young Anza came upon a grisly scene south of the depopulated visita of Arivaca "in the Sierra de la Horca." Miguel de la Cruz, a fellow soldier from Tubac, lay dead on the ground. Over him stood his killers, removing the scalp from their prey. Anza was upon them with a vengeance. In the melee that followed, nine of the malfactors were slain, including Ciprián, their leader. The Captain had been fortunate: a sharp-pointed arrow had pierced his clothing but failed to find its mark. How different might have been the history of northern New Spain if Anza had died in combat that day in 1760. But instead, Don Juan was again the toast of Sonora.[10]

---

[8] Peña, "Convite Evangelico," 15.

[9] Cavallero de Croix to Josef de Gálvez, Arizpe, December 23, 1780; AGI, Guad., 277.

[10] "Breve Resumen de los desastres." Peña, "Convite Evangelico," 15.

Henceforth, the Padres of Guevavi had little to fear from "the sons of Luis" — the 1760s belonged to the Apaches.

The sixteen months that Miguel Gerstner spent at Guevavi proved to be a period of comparative peace. At Sonoita he succeeded in finishing Father Pauer's "new church," and at poor Calabazas he had the natives build a house for the missionary and begin raising the walls of that visita's first church.[11] The vital statistics he recorded during his stay, surprisingly enough, added up to a commendable ratio — 101 baptisms to only 27 burials, almost four to one. In addition, he united in the eyes of the Church twenty-three couples. His entries in the mission books for services rendered both natives and gente de razón told of some notable events and hinted at trends.

On September 15, 1760, two weeks before the feast day of San Miguel — the only time, incidentally, that a Padre named Miguel presided over the festivities at Guevavi — a gala social affair took place up the San Luis Valley in Buenavista, probably at the rancho of the perennial Don Nicholás Romero. Don Miguel Antonio Cásares of Parral, Chihuahua, a bachelor, took María Florencia Lisonda, a local girl, as his bride in a ceremony performed by Father Miguel. The music of guitars, the joking, and the drinking tended for a brief while to take their minds off the realities of an uneasy frontier.

Two weeks after the feast day of San Miguel, Captain Anza's mother died. Sorrowfully, they bore the body of Doña María Rosa Bezerra Nieto, "viuda de Anza," along the valley eighteen miles from Tubac to Guevavi, and the mourners followed. A grave had been dug beneath the altar steps in the church, and there beside Captain Belderrain, comrade of her husband and of her son, she was buried.

Providing for the spiritual needs of settlers and soldiers hardly left the missionary of Guevavi time to care properly for his own flock and tend to the manifold details of mission administration. Captain Anza, for one, tried to help. He tried to recruit a secular priest as chaplain for his men, Joseph Manuel Díaz del Carpio by name. Though Don Joseph signed several entries in the Guevavi book of baptisms during the early

---

[11] Entrega, May 25, 1761; WBS, 1744, ff. 381–84; translated in Appendix II of the present study.

1760s, evidently he did not find life at Tubac, still a crude frontier post, to his liking. His visits were of short duration.

In this particular — the spiritual well-being of the garrison — dashing young Anza may not have been thinking only of his men. Don Joseph, it seems, had a sister. And Don Juan was courting her. No less successful in love than in war, he won her promise. In Arizpe on San Juan's Day, June 24, 1761, Father Carlos de Roxas, who had baptized Anza twenty-five years before, now married the youthful commander and Ana María Pérez Serrano. The potential chaplain, Don Joseph Manuel, stood at their side as witness.[12]

Sister or no sister, Díaz del Carpio still did not take up permanent residence at Tubac, and Guevavi's minister continued to serve garrison and vecinos. In fact, as the Indian population kept declining and the non-Indian population kept rising, Father Miguel became more and more a parish priest and less and less a missionary among heathens. Four out of every ten persons he baptized were the children or the Nixora and Apache servants of gente de razón. An extreme example of this trend, noticeable during the Jesuit years in Pimería Alta and culminating in the later Franciscan period, was recorded at San Ignacio in 1818. For every one Indian, the Padre ministered to three dozen *Españoles y Castas*.[13]

Of the natives Father Miguel baptized, nearly half lived at Tumacácori, indicating that it had become by 1760 the mission's largest and most active village, despite its initial shortage of irrigable land. Gerstner seems to have done no wholesale native recruiting; he baptized only three Indian adults. An occasional Sobaípuri came or was brought to settle

---

[12] The Bishop of Durango reported that Díaz del Carpio functioned as chaplain at Tubac "because the Captain's wife is his sister." Pedro Tamarón y Romeral, *Demostración del vastísmo obispado de la Nueva Vizcaya, 1765*, introducción bibliográfica y acotaciones por Vito Alessio Robles, *Biblioteca histórica mexicana de obras inéditas*, Vol. VII (México, D.F.: Antigua Librería Robredo, 1937), p. 305; manuscript copy, M-M 232, BL. Anza's will and various other documents confirm the date and the lady's name. Perhaps some intricacy of Spanish usage accounts for the dissimilarity of Don Joseph's and Doña Ana María's surnames, or perhaps she was his half sister. The details of Anza's baptism and marriage are provided and jumbled by J. N. Bowman and Robert F. Heizer in *Anza and the Northwest Frontier of New Spain* (Southwest Museum: Los Angeles, 1967), pp. 30, 90–92.

[13] "Estado Espiritual y Temporal de las Misiones de la Pimería Alta ... 1818," Fray José Pérez, Oquitoa, December 31, 1818, copy, Colegio de la Santa Cruz de Querétaro, March 8, 1819; AGN, Misiones, 3. Nearby Santa Ana probably accounted for many of the non-Indians.

in Sonoita, and some Pápagos were added to the other villages, but apparently the heathen reserve was dwindling. Even among his "Christian" Indians the death rate was high. Only two of every ten burials was not an Indian. Half the natives he married were widows and widowers.

If Father Miguel had sensed that the mission of Guevavi was entering upon a period of decline, he probably had the chance to discuss the situation with his successor. But for one reason or another, very possibly ill health, Gerstner himself was preparing to leave.

On May 25, 1761, Father Miguel signed the entrega releasing him from responsibility for Guevavi. He then rode over to Sáric, hardly a more desirable post for a sick man. To take his place at Guevavi, Ignacio Pfefferkorn had arrived from Atí seeking "purer air and more healthful water." [14] It was rather like musical chairs — there was always the chance that the next chair would offer a less pernicious atmosphere.

Pfefferkorn of Mannheim in the Archbishopric of Cologne, born on the feast day of Saint Ignatius, was thirty-five years old and, like Phelipe Segesser, an astute observer.[15] He and Miguel Gerstner were well acquainted. Together they had shared the uncertainties of the thousands of miles from Germany to the Pimería. They never would forget the reception staged for them by the old Guevavi veteran Segesser. As they and several other missionary recruits approached his mission of Ures, a screaming horde of fearsome savages swept down upon them. Thrown to the ground as their mules bolted, the newcomers fully expected instant martyrdom. Instead, their painted adversaries helped them up. It was Father Segesser's idea of an initiation, a "friendly simile of attack." [16] A missionary without a sense of humor, he may have been trying to tell them, was a missionary at a great disadvantage.

---

[14] Pfefferkorn, *Sonora,* p. 263. Father Gerstner last signed the Guevavi book of baptisms on May 26, 1761. Two days later Father Pfefferkorn began making entries. The entrega turning Guevavi over to Pfefferkorn is in WBS, 1744, ff. 381–84, and is translated in Appendix II below. Pfefferkorn had given up Atí on May 19, 1761. Entrega, *ibid.,* ff. 377–80. Gerstner took over Sáric on June 14, 1761. Entrega; *ibid.,* ff. 385–86.

[15] Pfefferkorn had been a Jesuit since October 21, 1742. Details of his trip to the New World with Gerstner, Middendorff, Och, and the rest are in his *Sonora,* pp. 2–9.

[16] Pradeau, *Expulsión,* pp. 197, 154. Pfefferkorn, *Sonora,* p. 7. Treutlein, *Travel Reports of Joseph Och,* p. 43. "We saw immediately," Och maintained, "that they were not enemies, yet we were nevertheless frightened and our mules were so confounded by the din that they took to the woods and we were nearly dismounted."

Word soon reached Father Pfefferkorn at Guevavi that Father Visitor General Ignacio Lizassoain had begun in April, 1761, his dual-purpose visitation. To the Visitor General's already considerable authority as superior of the whole northwest missionary empire had been added by special commission that of Dr. Pedro Tamarón y Romeral, Bishop of Durango. In the more distant Jesuit missions Lizassoain was to function as episcopal visitor as well. But because he chose not to travel during the rainy season, it was November before he reached Pimería Alta, and then he, like his predecessors, shunned Guevavi.

Coming by way of Cananea and Terrenate he did stop over at Soamca, where Keller's successor, Father Diego Barrera, sought to favorably impress the tall, slender native of Pamplona. From Soamca the Visitor General then traveled southwestward through Cocóspera and Ímuris to San Ignacio. There during the following week the other Padres of Pimería Alta came to him.

Pfefferkorn, after nearly six months at Guevavi, rode the sixty-five miles to render his report on the mission's progress and its potential. He presented for inspection the records of baptisms, marriages, and

burials. Beneath his most recent baptismal entry the secretary of the visitation, Father Manuel Aguirre, recorded the Father Visitor General's approval and his admonition that each and every entry be fully written out and signed separately.[17] Some of Father Ignacio's predecessors habitually made multiple entries, signing them only once.

As instructed, Father Pfefferkorn had compiled and brought with

----

[17] The record of Father Lizassoain's visitation in the Guevavi books was dated November 19 at San Ignacio, which led Father Victor R. Stoner to conclude incorrectly that during Jesuit times Tumacácori was "often referred to as 'San Ygnacio de Tumacácori' .... Even the Jesuit Visitor General Lizassaoin (November 19, 1761) called it San Ignacio." "The Spanish Missions of the Santa Cruz Valley," unpublished master's thesis, University of Arizona, Tucson, 1937, p. 37.

him to San Ignacio a census of the villages in his charge. Guevavi's native population, the Father Visitor General noted, was distributed as follows:

	Guevavi	Calabazas	Sonoita	Tumacácori
Families	31	36	34	72
Widowers	5	6	2	7
Widows	5	8	2	8
Adults of both sexes receiving instruction (*doctrineros*) and children	29	30	19	40

Of the eight mission cabeceras in Pimería Alta, Guevavi had the fewest neophytes. Taken with its three visitas, however, Father Ignacio's mission was not quite last.[18]

Death played an ominous role in the administration of Father Pfefferkorn. For two years he buried nearly twice as many persons as he baptized. Always superstitious, the natives grew restive. At Tumacácori alone, during one four-month period their Padre recorded at least twenty admitted deaths. There may have been others unknown to him, bodies carried off by villagers and buried in the heathen manner.

When Phelipe, popular native governor of Tumacácori, succumbed, that was too much for the Pápagos. They fled — back to their desert. Only the few surviving Pimas stayed on in that accursed village and in Calabazas. Dutifully, Father Ignacio reported this exodus to Father Visitor General Lizassoain. No longer was his census of Guevavi correct.

At San Xavier del Bac, Father Espinosa, "the Job of the missionaries," was suffering similar humiliation. Nearly all his neophytes had deserted him. Only the aged and the infirm remained. The natives of Tucsón had abandoned their village in favor of the dense brush. All of which caused Father Lizassoain to observe that "the peacefulness of

---

[18] "Noticia de la Visita General del P. Ignacio Lizasoain Visitador General de las Missiones de esta Provª de Nueva España, q comenzó dia quatro de Abril de 1761 añ y se concluyó á fines de Henero de 1763 con algunas notas y addiciones q. pueden servir pª el conocimiento de dhas Missiones, y Provincias de ellas"; WBS, 47. Tamarón y Romeral, *Demostración*, p. 391. The Bishop incorporated Father Lizassoain's census figures in his own report, but by adding widowers and widows as families he arrived at a total of 41 families for Guevavi, 50 for Calabazas, 38 for Sonoita, and 87 for Tumacácori. He also included the number of individuals at each of the four villages: 111, 116, 91, and 199. *Ibid.*, p. 304.

many Upper Pimas and Pápagos, when they do seem quiet and peaceful, is like a live flame covered with ashes; but, alas, when exposed to the slightest breeze, its true nature is seen."[19]

Whether their fear of Apaches and diseases was genuine or simply a pretext to justify their flight, was hardly the point. The shadow of death hung over Guevavi's villages and that was plainly an ill omen.

The northern Pimería was in trouble. To save Soamca, Guevavi, and Bac, something had to be done to bring in and to hold more Indians. The Father Visitor General had noted the situation during his visitation. At Horcasitas in early December, 1761, he discussed it with interim Governor Don Joseph Tienda de Cuervo. And there a decision was reached, a decision which later events would brand as a tragic error.[20]

The Sobaípuris, long a combative buffer against the Apaches, still lived on the San Pedro beyond the effective control of the missionary. Why not move them into Soamca, Guevavi, and Bac, thereby reinforcing those missions and consolidating frontier defenses? Father Keller, who for one reason or another would surely have opposed such strategy, had been dead two years. The gallant soldier Mendoza, who had advocated planting missions on the San Pedro, had died an agonizing death the year before, the victim of a poisoned Seri arrow in the throat. Thus Joseph Tienda de Cuervo wrote the order.

As Captain of the Vera Cruz dragoons, Tienda de Cuervo had been on hand five years before to greet Father Pfefferkorn and his fellow Jesuits as they disembarked from the ship *El Victorioso*.[21] Now, unintentionally, the same officer as Governor and Captain General of Sonora released the traditional "brake on the enemy" and brought the full fury of the Apaches down on Pfefferkorn's frontier mission.

Captain Elías of Terrenate carried out the Governor's order. At Tucsón on Saint Joseph's Day, March 19, 1762, he presided as a census

---

[19] "Relacion clara, y distinta del actual estado, y deplorable sistema, de la parte mas Considerable, y mas digna de atencion de esta America, en las Proas de Cinaloa, Sonora, Pimeria, Taraumara, y las demas que Componen las dos bastas Governaciones de Cinaloa, y Nueva Vizcaia"; selected documents relating to Pimería Alta, mainly 1767–1800, from the Fr. Marcellino de Civezza Collection, Pontificio Ateneo Antoniano, Roma (Civ. Col.), microfilm 305, UAL. Another copy is in AGN, Historia, 16. It was Father Garrucho who aptly termed Espinosa "the Job of the missionaries." Garrucho to Father Provincial Pedro Reales, Oposura, July 13, 1763; AHH, Temp., 17.

[20] Aguirre to Zevallos, Bacadéguachi, December 30, 1763; *ibid*.

[21] Pradeau, *Expulsión*, pp. 153, 196. Almada, *Diccionario*, p. 787.

of Sobaípuri immigrants was compiled. The total reached 250. According to what their justicias told Father Espinosa, many more were wandering about nearby. "Heaven only knows if there are the number of souls they say there are," wrote the Captain to the Governor.[22] Thirty Sobaípuri families had been settled at Soamca.[23] And at his easternmost visita of Sonoita, Father Pfefferkorn began to baptize the children of couples brought in from their rancherías on the San Pedro.

"The good news" of the Sobaípuri reduction traveled in a courier's saddlebag from Governor Tienda de Cuervo to the viceroy. The missions thus newly strengthened, he assured his superior, now would be better prepared to fend off Apache blows.[24] The result, unfortunately, was quite the opposite.

Certainly Father Pfefferkorn's most lasting contribution as a missionary has been his description of Sonora, published in Germany three decades after he left Guevavi.[25] But because the worldly-wise ex-Jesuit was so determined not to write autobiographically, he related directly very few of his personal experiences. Not a word did he include about his two years at Guevavi,[26] though his observations while there obviously provided some of the background material he ultimately drew upon. When, for example, he described the *toloache* plant, or sacred datura, whose juice was particularly potent, Father Ignacio was clearly recalling an incident at Guevavi.

> The Indians have the foolish notion that by means of this juice they are transported into an ecstacy, during which wonderful things and

[22] Elías González to Tienda de Cuervo, "Guebabi [almost certainly the *presidio* of San Phelipe de Guevavi, alias Terrenate, not the mission of Guevavi]," March 22, 1762, certified copy, México, June 16, 1762; AGI, Guad., 511. Translation in Dobyns, *Pioneering Christians*, pp. 12–13.

[23] Tienda de Cuervo to the Marqués de Crujillas, San Miguel, April 5, 1762, certified copy, México, June 16, 1762; AGI, Guad., 511.

[24] *Ibid.*

[25] *Beschreibung der Landschaft Sonora samt andern merkwürdigen Nachrichten von den inneren Theilen Neu-Spaniens und Reise aus Amerika bis in Deutschland*, 2 vols. (Köln am Rheine, 1794–95). Thanks to Dr. Treutlein, Father Pfefferkorn's *Sonora*, cited above numerous times, has been available to English readers since 1949.

[26] Pfefferkorn admitted that he served as resident Padre at three missions, but he named only two, Atí and Cucurpe. Thus, on the basis of his *Sonora* alone, the identity of the third mission — Guevavi — was something of a mystery, even to Dr. Treutlein. *Sonora*, pp. 19–20.

pleasant fancies occur to them. They also firmly believe that from it they receive the power to cure sicknesses and also the strength to defeat their enemies. Therefore, they drink this damnable juice with nonsensical eagerness and soon thereafter become so inebriated that they fall to earth like lifeless blocks and only recover their faculties again after some hours. . . . I myself learned of two who drank themselves to death with toloache. As soon as these unfortunates had taken a good draft of it, they were seized by a general palsy; immediately afterward they pitched speechless to the ground and manifested no further signs of life.[27]

It was during his second autumn at Guevavi that Father Ignacio got word that Augustín, an adventurous lad who lived in Calabazas, had fallen desperately ill. Calling for a horse the Padre climbed into the saddle and hastened north. On the way someone stopped him and told him he need not bother. Augustín was dead.

Questioning the Indians, Pfefferkorn learned the cause of death — toloache. In Guevavi's book of burials on November 5, 1762, he wrote: "Augustín, a youth and native of Calabazas, son of Domingo, died crazy in the hills from having tried toloache . . . he was buried in a barranca." Perhaps the other toloache victim the Padre alluded to was Ignacio, a boy who several months later "died crazy in the village of Calabazas."

As an appendix to his chapter on native languages, Father Ignacio included a glossary of Sonora place names. Guevavi he rendered from the Pima as "large river"; Tumacácori as "pepper bush, place where the little round pepper is found in abundance"; Sonoita as "spring"; and Tubac as "soap-berry tree, place where it grows in abundance."[28] A modern scholar translates Guevavi "big spring," Tumacácori "caliche bend," and Tubac simply "rotten."[29]

Both Father Pfefferkorn and Father Segesser were insatiably curious; both were discerning reporters. It is a pity that neither man's constitution permitted him a longer stay at unwholesome Guevavi.

The "purer air and more healthful water" Pfefferkorn sought, he

---

[27]*Ibid.*, pp. 63–64.

[28]*Ibid.*, pp. 237–38.

[29]Dobyns, "Indian Extinction in the Middle Santa Cruz Valley, Arizona," *NMHR*, Vol. XXXVIII (1963), pp. 168, 166; and "Tubac Through Four Centuries," p. 2.

did not find at Guevavi. No one knew more about the summer heat and the disease-breeding marshes along the river near that mission than the current Father Visitor and amateur physician Joseph Garrucho. In the spring of 1763 when Garrucho heard that Father Ignacio lay at Guevavi miserably ill, he ordered the ailing Padre "removed from that climate" and brought to his own mission of Oposura for rest and recuperation.[30]

The German missionary and author-to-be managed to marry Joseph and María on May 30, 1763, before the assembled justicias of the village; very soon after, Ignacio Pfefferkorn rode or was carried south, away from Guevavi.

At Oposura he recovered. Reassigned to Cucurpe, where he found both the climate and the natives less harsh, he continued to serve the Lord and amass material for his book. German Padres, noted Garrucho in a letter to the Father Provincial, did not prosper in *tierra caliente;* they were better sent to cooler regions. With that in mind, the Father Visitor dispatched to Guevavi in Pfefferkorn's place a tall, dark Spaniard from southern Aragón.[31]

On May 1, 1734, the day Custodio Ximeno was born in Valdelinares "in cold and mountainous terrain," a Swiss Jesuit named Segesser, recently recovered from a five-month illness, was sweating at a poor mission among heathen peoples no one in Valdelinares had likely ever heard of. On San Miguel's Day, September 29, 1752, Custodio Ximeno, then a young man of eighteen, entered the Society of Jesus. Across the sea the natives of San Miguel de Guevavi after the great revolt were content without a Padre.

Brother Custodio, while still a student of theology, had requested and was granted a transfer to the Jesuit Province of Mexico. Leaving behind the security of the college at Zaragoza, he journeyed diagonally across Spain nearly five hundred miles to the hospice at Puerto de Santa María on the Bay of Cádiz. From there, after an unusually short wait, he and nineteen other Black Robes sailed with the fleet late in June, 1760, aboard the *Nuestra Señora de Begoña,* alias *El Vencedor.*[32] That

---

[30] Garrucho to Reales, July 13, 1763.
[31] *Ibid.*
[32] AGI, Contratación, 5550. Zelis, *Catálogo,* pp. 46–47.

same summer, Father Gerstner was learning how hot it could get at Guevavi.

After more study and his ordination, Father Custodio with a particularly close friend, Father Francisco Xavier Villarroya, set out for the Northwest. It was mid-spring in 1763 when they passed through Guadalajara and Culiacán in the company of the new Governor of Sonora, Don Juan Claudio de Pineda, who, like certain of his predecessors, was being sent to the frontier for disciplinary reasons.[33]

Fathers Ximeno and Villarroya, it seems, had been companions since college days in Spain. They had begged the Father Provincial that they be permitted to serve at missions not far removed from each other. When Father Visitor Garrucho informed the Provincial that Ximeno had been sent to Guevavi because "God willed him for the Pimería," he also had the satisfaction of announcing Villarroya's assignment to Atí.[34] The two friends would not be far apart, no more than a couple of days' ride.

Gratified, they went to their missions in June, as the heat built up before the summer rains. Soon the people back home in Valdelinares would know the name of Father Custodio's mission. They would speak with pride and respect of their missionary crusader far across the world ocean in an exotic and heathen land.

The new Padre soon learned about the enemy. For over a year raiding Apaches had swept unchecked through the deserted valley of the Sobaípuris, "an open door" to the northern Pimería. The few soldiers at Tubac and their hard-riding commander simply could not cope with the Apache surge. As if that were not enough, the beleaguered Governor of Sonora kept requisitioning troops from all the presidios for campaigns against the continually defiant, poison-arrow-shooting Seris.

The Apaches kept coming. Along the valley from Soamca through Guevavi to San Xavier del Bac, no one was safe working in the fields or riding herd. On moonlit nights especially, vaqueros drove their stock into corrals. Mission Indians and settlers alike were terrorized. The first two persons whose souls Father Custodio was called upon to commit to

---

[33] Garrucho to Reales, July 13, 1763. Donohue, "Jesuit Missions," p. 286. Almada, *Diccionario,* pp. 592–93.
[34] Garrucho to Reales, July 13, 1763. Pradeau, *Expulsión,* p. 241.

their Creator were victims of an Apache band prowling near Buenavista. The hostiles had killed Catalina, "commonly called 'the shorn one,'" and they had left the wounded Ventura for dead. The latter confessed, then expired. It was a grim initiation for the young missionary.[35]

Not all of those who died in the following months were killed or mutilated by Apaches, but the likelihood of such a grisly death gnawed at the resolve of the gente de razón who survived. A delegation of them went to Captain Anza. They wanted permission to abandon their homes in the San Luis Valley. Whether or not it influenced his decision, in October, 1763, they carried the body of the Captain's sister-in-law, Doña Victoria Carrasco, wife of Don Francisco de Anza, from Buenavista to its place of burial in the church at Guevavi.[36] Though Father Ximeno

Fr. Custodio Ximeno M.P.S.M.

recorded none of the details of her death, he soon ceased to mention in the mission's books the names of the settlements upriver from Guevavi. The sympathetic Captain had approved their evacuation. Only then did he report to Governor Pineda the *fait accompli*.

The Governor was not pleased. This time, Anza had erred in judgment.[37] No matter, the damage had been done. Already the intimidated vecinos had left their lands and crowded around Terrenate and Tubac within the shadows cast by presidial walls.[38] For at least forty years, interrupted only by the revolt of 1751, the pleasant valley that

---

[35] This double burial took place on July 27, 1763. Father Custodio had married his first couple at Guevavi on June 22. Unfortunately, none of his baptismal entries have survived. Pfefferkorn's entry of February 12, 1763, concludes the incomplete baptismal section of Guevavi, "Tubaca y Otros."

[36] Mr. Francis S. Ainsa of El Paso, Texas, owner of the well-known oil portrait of Juan Bautista de Anza the younger traces his family's descent from Don Francisco de Anza. The Captain himself had no children.

[37] Aguirre to Zevallos, Bacadéguachi, March 23, 1764; AHH, Temp., 17.

[38] Three years later Captain Anza of Tubac and Captain Elías of Terrenate compiled censuses of the vecinos at their respective presidios. Many of these settlers were former residents of the San Luis Valley. At Tubac there were twenty-eight married men and six widowers (including the dean of the settlers Don Nicholás Romero), ninety-six children, twenty lads from fourteen to fifteen years of age, plus twenty-six servants, fifteen of whom were married, for a total of more than two hundred. Anza, Tubac, April 2, 1767, and Elías, Terrenate, April 6, 1767; BNMex, 55/733.

extended south from Guevavi and bent east with the river toward Soamca had been home to these settlers, "more than a hundred with a great number of all kinds of stock." [39] Now that the ranchos of Buenavista, San Luis, and Santa Bárbara were mute and abandoned, Guevavi lay all the more exposed.

On San Miguel's day, 1763, as Father Custodio presided over whatever patronal festivities he thought were appropriate at harassed Guevavi, the new Father Visitor of Sonora, Manuel Aguirre, began his inspection of the missions. As secretary to the Father Visitor General two years before, he had already been to most of them. Father Lizassoain, however, had visited only Soamca and San Ignacio in Pimería Alta. Father Aguirre was determined to see them all.

Pushing on from Soamca, where he had noted the open foundations upon which Father Barrera hoped to build a more fitting house of God, he arrived at Guevavi to find poor Ximeno weak and feverish. "This is the fruit," he wrote to the Provincial, "that we reap in the Pimería, and with which the missionaries are tested as soon as they enter it." [40] Whether German or Spaniard, he who would serve at Guevavi, concluded the Father Visitor, had to be "very robust and very patient." [41]

Father Aguirre summarized his impression of Ximeno's mission as follows:

> Guevavi (San Miguel is the patron) has a very good church, vestments, and other ecclesiastical ornaments; the sanctuary alone is shored up, but it can easily be repaired. The Apaches are continually depleting the mission with regard to its livestock. The mission harvests sufficient wheat and maize. It owes very few debts and has the wherewithal to pay them. Here the Indians pray in their own language, but because he is so new, Father Custodio Ximeno does not yet understand it. [42]

Proceeding north from Guevavi, Father Aguirre became one of the few Jesuit Visitors to reach the "last mission" of San Xavier del Bac.

[39] "Ynforme, y Razon con arreglo á orden Sup.or fha 14 de Febro de Exmo S.r Virrey Conde de Revilla Gigedo del estado en q.e se hallava la Pimería Alta, Provincia de Sonora, la de Hostimuri, Sinaloa, y Culiacan. . . .," undated, unsigned draft; BNMex, 13/691.
[40] Aguirre to Zevallos, Bacadéguachi, December 29, 1763; AHH, Temp., 17.
[41] Aguirre to Zevallos, December 30, 1763.
[42] Aguirre to Zevallos, February 18, 1764.

There, thanks to the good works of "a true apostle," the enduring Canary Islander, Alonso Espinosa, he was privileged to sleep in a livable house and to say Mass in a new church.[43] Then with his escort the Father Visitor rode south and west to Sáric where he found another new church, this one built by the sickly Guevavi alumnus Father Gerstner. On down the trail at Caborca he inspected "the large church in the shape of a seven [a Spanish seven: 7]," then to complete his visitation of the Pimería he swung east again toward San Ignacio. That mission's church impressed the Jesuit superior as "the best in the Pimería, not because of its size, but because of the adornment of its altars and its vessels and vestments."

If only a way could be found to check the rapacious Apaches, these missions of Pimería Alta might actually prosper. Aguirre pondered the problem as he listened to the Padres recount their losses. Most of the horses and mules had been stolen from Soamca and now the vaqueros were unable to herd the cattle that remained. From a few calves at Bac Father Espinosa had built up a herd of nearly a thousand head. Yet now where five had grazed only one remained, "because the Apaches . . . persist in coming and driving them off. From there the Apaches have extended their operations to Guevavi, Santa María Soamca, Sáric, and the rest of the Pimería. When the Sobaípuris were taken out of their rancherías, the door was left open. . . ."[44]

When he got back to his own mission of Bacadéguachi, the Father Visitor sat up nights wrestling with the Apache problem. The reports that reached him from the Pimería were discouraging. "I have known," he confided to the Father Provincial in February, 1764, "that Father Custodio wanted to abandon Guevavi because it is afflicted so by the Apaches, but his Reverence has not written me about it, nor will I permit it. . . ."[45]

Abandonment, Aguirre was convinced, was not the answer. He had another solution. Like Father Torres Perea two decades before, the Father Visitor now proposed that Guevavi be divided in two. A new

---

[43]*Ibid.* Espinosa's "annual lists of needs for 1763, 1764, and 1765 were crammed with requests for vestments, furnishings, and statues for his church." Donohue, "Jesuit Missions," p. 289; memorias cited in AHH, Temp., 323. See also Donohue, "The Unlucky Jesuit Mission of Bac, 1732–1767," *AW*, Vol. II (1960), p. 135.

[44]Aguirre to Zevallos, February 18, 1764.
[45]*Ibid.*

mission should be created with Tumacácori as its cabecera and Calabazas as a visita. From Tumacácori, moreover, the missionary could with greater efficacy minister to the neighboring garrison at Tubac "when there is no chaplain, as at present there is not." He had even figured out the finances. The annual stipend allotted originally to Kino's mission of Dolores, and since its abandonment designated for the Sobaípuris who hopefully would settle at Cocóspera, should be utilized to support a Padre at the new mission of Tumacácori.

Father Custodio at Guevavi, Aguirre reasoned, would still be responsible for the natives of that cabecera and for those of Sonoita. He would as well continue to provide for the spiritual needs of the gente de razón along the San Luis Valley. This division of Guevavi, the Father Visitor concluded, would prove not only more feasible but it would better fulfill the Jesuits' obligation "to God, to conscience, and to king."[46] Only then did Father Aguirre learn that the vecinos south of Guevavi had fled their homes.

To repopulate the San Luis Valley and plug this hole he had created in the defenses of the province, Captain Anza conceived a plan. Writing to Governor Pineda, this time before he decided the matter, Anza suggested that the dissatisfied Sobaípuris of Tucsón, who had neither fields nor water enough there, be moved south the more than twenty-five leagues onto the rich lands abandoned by the vecinos. In the Tucsón area these natives had proven haughty and intractable; they were continually wandering around in search of food. Father Espinosa still had not succeeded in getting them together for confession. If transplanted to the fertile San Luis Valley, the Captain maintained, the Sobaípuris of Tucsón would soon take root. And there Father Ximeno of Guevavi could easily make practicing Christians of them.

Before the Governor acted on Anza's latest proposal, he wanted to know what the Father Visitor thought of it. Aguirre, Pineda soon found out, was not favorably impressed. The Visitor, it seemed, still hoped to see Tucsón elevated to mission status, just as he hoped that Tumacácori would be. He had even gone so far as to request a Padre for distant Tucsón. That assignment called for a particularly zealous missionary, one "desirous of converting heathens and possessed of a brave heart."[47]

---

[46] Aguirre to Zevallos, December 30, 1763.
[47] Roxas to Zevallos, Arizpe, January 15, 1765; AHH, Temp., 17.

If the Sobaípuris were to be moved anywhere, Aguirre continued, would it not be wiser to move them back to their own valley to fight the Apaches? Better still, why not bring in the Pápagos, who were unmanageable out on their inhospitable wastelands? These natives could be made to people both valleys, the San Pedro and the San Luis.[48] In the latter place, however, formal titles to the land should be secured in the Indians' favor to prevent the vecinos from taking it back once the Apache crisis had passed. In accordance with the Laws of the Indies relating to native reductions, the Father Visitor hastened to add, the Pápagos should not be made to move against their will. But once they had moved, he further pointed out, the garrison at Tubac could readily prevent them from returning to their desert homes. "I well know, Your Lordship, the difficulty of keeping them in one place because of their natural inconstancy and their innate tendency to wander about in the manner of gypsies."[49] The final decision, of course, rested with Governor Pineda.

While proposal and counterproposal sped by courier between Tubac, Horcasitas, and Bacadéguachi, and little came of them, Ximeno hung on at Guevavi, the village he wanted to abandon. He was saddened by the news that his friend Villarroya, close by at Atí, was being transferred south to replace a Padre who had died. Father Custodio himself during the fall and winter of 1764 suffered painful *cuartanas,* debilitating malarial fevers that recurred every fourth day "and gave him no peace."[50] His surviving fragmentary entries in the mission books reveal that death visited his neophytes with disturbing frequency. He married many more

[48] Aguirre to Zevallos, March 23, 1764. Aguirre to Pineda, Bacadéguachi, March 20, 1764; BNMex, 38/867. Pradeau, *Expulsión,* p. 142, and Donohue, "Unlucky Mission," *AW,* II, p. 134, have apparently confused the valley of the Sobaípuris (the San Pedro) and the San Luis, or Buenavista, Valley (the Santa Cruz south of Guevavi) as well as the two evacuations. The Sobaípuris were removed from their valley in the spring of 1762. The vecinos of the San Luis Valley petitioned Captain Anza to leave their lands late in 1763 or early in 1764.

[49] Aguirre to Pineda, Bacadéguachi, May 4, 1764; BNMex, 38/867. Aguirre to Zevallos, Bacadéguachi, May 26, 1764; AHH, Temp., 17. If the San Pedro Valley were repopulated, Father Aguirre believed, the presidio of Terrenate should be moved north into that valley. A dozen years later, the garrison was in fact relocated there, with particularly disastrous results. See Kessell, "Puzzling Presidio," *NMHR,* XLI, p. 38.

[50] Aguirre to Zevallos, Bacadéguachi, January 8, 1765; AHH, Temp., 17.

natives from the visitas than from the village of Guevavi itself, indicating that his cabecera continued its steady decline.[51] But despite lurking Apaches, a high death rate, and his own annoying illnesses, Custodio Ximeno went about his ministry with stoic resolve.

Sometime in the spring of 1765 a distressing rumor filtered down from San Xavier del Bac. Espinosa lay paralyzed. It was true. When the news reached Father Visitor Aguirre, he sent help. Twenty-six-year-old Father Joseph Neve, a poet as well as a Padre, who had just arrived in Sonora and who expected to fill the vacancy at Atí, now hastened instead toward San Xavier. "It is essential," wrote the Father Visitor, "that this mission not be left without a Padre to administer it, or else the fruit of so many years' labor will be lost."[52] Aguirre meanwhile had instructed Father Pauer to have the ailing Espinosa carried the 130 miles to San Ignacio. If he recovered, he could go to Atí.[53]

North through Guevavi young Neve rode in June on his mission of mercy. From Tubac Captain Anza escorted him on to San Xavier and introduced him to the natives there "without particular incident." On June 16, 1765, he took formal possession, signing the required entrega along with a feeble Espinosa. Exactly one week later, a soldier galloped into Tubac with a message for Anza from Governor Pineda. Inside a letter addressed to Father Ximeno would be one for Neve — it was important that it be delivered to the new missionary at once. Whether missent or lost, Anza had to report, the urgent letter for Neve did not arrive.[54]

At San Xavier, Espinosa's youthful replacement found the suffering apostle in too much pain to be moved, "with one leg already dried up."[55] In time, however, Father Espinosa improved enough to make the journey south, and eventually to serve "somewhat ailing" at Atí and then at Caborca, which a decade earlier had terrified him.

Early in 1766 the word went out that the missionaries should once

---

[51]Ximeno's last extant marriage entry is dated June 14, 1767, and his last burial entry, September 20, 1766. Guevavi, "Tubaca y Otros."

[52]Aguirre to Zevallos, Mochopa, June 30, 1765; AHH, Temp., 17. Pradeau, *Expulsión*, pp. 187–88.

[53]Aguirre to Zevallos, Bacadéguachi, May 18, 1765; AHH, Temp., 17.

[54]Anza to Pineda, Tubac, June 24, 1765; BNMex, 38/855. Entrega; WBS, 1744, ff. 427–30, and translated in Appendix II below.

[55]Aguirre to Zevallos, June 30, 1765.

again count their charges.[56] At Los Santos Ángeles de Guevavi and its visitas Father Custodio compiled the following figures:[57]

	Guevavi	Calabazas	Sonoita	Tumacácori
Married	24	52	44	42
Widowed	8	6	17	13
Single	26	35	34	25
Those who confess (the rest receiving instruction)	40	64	66	60

Ximeno's cabecera, in which he lived reluctantly, still ranked as the least populous in Pimería Alta. Since Father Pfefferkorn's census four years earlier, an influx of Sobaípuris and an exodus of Pápagos had boosted Sonoita's population and lowered Tumacácori's. A particularly bad epidemic, whose devastating effect several of the Padres farther south noted on their censuses for 1766, may have hit Guevavi just after Father Custodio's count was in, for during the first months of that year there seemed to be in his villages an inordinate amount of dying.

By December the village of Guevavi had shrunk to fifty souls, reported an army engineer who was passing through. At Calabazas, which the same officer described as "a small village repeopled by Pápagos," a terrible sickness had annihilated its former Pima residents.[58] The news of so much dying beneath the mission bell cannot have made recruiting any easier among the heathens who still roamed free.

---

[56] A general census of the Jesuit missions, dated 1765 but based upon the earlier Lizassoain visitation, showed for Guevavi's villages the same number of families, widowers, and widows that Lizassoain had, but in addition gave the following total populations: Guevavi, 100; Calabazas, 97; Sonoita (which the author confused with the former mission of San Marcelo de Sonoita), 98; Tumacácori, 164. "Noticia de las Missiones, q̃ administran los P.P. de la Compã de Jesus en esta Nueva España. Ano de 1765"; WBS, 68. See also Donohue, "Unlucky Mission," *AW*, II, p. 135.

[57] "Padron de los SS. Angeles de Guevavi con sus Visitas," [*ca.* January, 1766]. The censuses of San Xavier and Tucsón, dated January 20, and February 24, 1766, and apparently compiled by Father Neve, are extremely complete, including the names of individuals arranged in family groups. AHH, Temp., 17.

[58] Nicolás de LaFora, *Relación del viaje que hizo á los presidios internos situados en la frontera de la América Septentrional perteneciente al rey de España,* liminar bibliográfico y acotaciones por Vito Alessio Robles (México, D.F.: Editorial Pedro Robredo, 1939), pp. 126–27. Translated by Lawrence Kinnaird as *The Frontiers of New Spain: Nicolás de LaFora's Description, 1766–1768* (Berkeley: Quivira Society, 1958), pp. 108–109.

Cruel death at the hands of the Apaches, while far less frequent than death from disease, was much more vivid and dreadful to contemplate. All along the valley those who remained, including Fathers Ximeno and Neve, learned to live with the Apache menace. Whenever Captain Anza could, he sought to punish the hostiles in their own haunts, but more often than not he found it a frustrating business.

During February and March in 1766, Anza led forth into the mountains and playas south of the Gila a column of regulars from Fronteras, Terrenate, and Tubac, supported by thirty Pima auxiliaries. While he chased their smoke signals, his crafty foe slipped in behind him and neatly rustled three hundred head of cattle from San Xavier. This time, however, a courageous corporal and the few men Anza kept stationed at Bac rode off in hot pursuit, and to the amazement and joy of Father Neve returned driving the herd before them.

When Anza led the Tubac detachment back into the presidio, he had by dint of his own cunning as an Indian fighter killed a few braves and scared a lot more. He presided as the soldiers cast lots for the meager spoils of the campaign. Then the next day the Captain dutifully wrote his report to Governor Pineda.[59] At Guevavi Father Custodio recorded the death *en campaña* of Felipe of Sonoita, husband of Catharina, whose service to God and king had proved fatal.

On December 19, 1766, front riders announced in the village of Guevavi the approach of a ranking Spanish nobleman and his entourage. At the mission they were expecting him — Don Cayetano María Pignatelli Rubí Corbera y San Climent, the Marqués de Rubí, at the time conducting an extraordinary inspection and evaluation tour of New Spain's northern defenses from the Gulf of Mexico to the Gulf of California. In his person the urgent reform efforts of Charles III reached out to the farthest frontier. If Father Custodio had a fatted calf to kill, he surely did so for the Marqués' meal that evening.

Afterward, in the Padre's quarters there may have been talk of the world situation. Spain in America now faced England alone. A showdown appeared imminent. At stake, King Charles believed, was Spain's very survival as an imperial power. In reform lay her only salvation.

---

[59]Anza to Pineda, Tubac, March 17, 1766; BNMex, 38/855; translated by Kessell as "Anza, Indian Fighter: The Spring Campaign, 1766," *JAH,* Vol. IX (1968), pp. 155–63.

Reform by all means, the Jesuits would have agreed, but Church-centered, moral reform. For several years they had looked on in alarm as "enlightened," secular-thinking ministers crowded around the king, ministers they knew to be hostile to the Society of Jesus and to all the traditional values for which it stood. But surely His Most Catholic Majesty would come to his senses and cast out the evil purveyors of French philosophy. Had he not entrusted the education of his own children to Jesuit tutors?

Next day as Rubí rode on down the valley toward his destination, the royal presidio of San Ignacio de Tubac, his Captain of Engineers, Nicolás de LaFora, described the scene. He was impressed with the number of giant cottonwoods along the banks of the meandering river, which led them northwest with some deviations to the north. "On the rest of the river plain are many mesquites and other bushes. The surrounding hills are rather bare. Between them on the right two ranges stand out, the Santa Rita, which has a very high peak, and the San Cayetano. These are notable because they serve as places of refuge for the enemy during their incursions." [60] For a fortnight Rubí and his staff scrutinized operations at Tubac, taking time out on this far rim of Christendom to observe the anniversary of the miraculous birth of Jesus Christ.

Like Diogenes, the Marqués de Rubí had been searching for an honest man among the frontier commanders. In Juan Bautista de Anza he found him. "Because of his energy, valor, zeal, experience, and notable disinterestedness" Anza was, in the opinion of the royal inspector, "a complete officer" worthy of the king's recognition. Yet because of the sudden death of the Viceroy who nearly seven years earlier had elevated him to the captaincy at Tubac, Anza still did not have a formal commission from the king. If anyone deserved it, he did. To him the king owed "the reduction of the Pápagos and the present peace of the Upper Pimas."

Tubac's second-in-command, Lieutenant Juan María de Oliva, who was also having trouble getting his commission, had been promoted from ensign after his successful dispersal of the rebels at San Xavier a decade earlier. He had served at Tubac from the beginning and had received in the king's service nine wounds. At the time, however, he,

---

[60] LaFora, *Relación,* pp. 126–27, *Frontiers,* pp. 108–109.

one corporal, and nine soldiers were absent on detached duty in the Seri campaigns to the south, thus reducing the effective Tubac garrison to forty men including officers.

The presidial arsenal, noted the Marqués, was well stocked with Catalan carbines of superior quality and with swords, lances, shields, and other gear appropriate to war on the frontier. The few, light, Mexican-made cannon which someone had taken the trouble to haul to Tubac were a greater menace to their users than to the enemy. When Anza's troopers had performed for him, Rubí concluded that they were better-than-average marksmen and superb mounted lancers.[61]

The testimonies of ten men and an audit of the presidio's books convinced the Marqués that Anza governed his garrison with a "generosity uncommon in these lands." Frontier captains, who exercised a monopoly of supplies at their isolated posts, were wont to charge their poor soldiers exorbitant prices at the "company store." Not Anza. He was actually selling supplies at Tubac for less than the prices set by army regulations. Rubí could scarcely believe it.

So impressed was the king's extraordinary inspector by Anza's fairness to his men that he attached to his inspection report a list of sixty-two items Anza sold at discount. The most expensive single article, the soldier's *cuera,* or protective leather jacket, the Captain of Tubac sold at 20 percent off, marking them down from fifty pesos to forty pesos. One of the least expensive items, a liturgical calendar printed on fine paper, he reduced from two and a half *reales* to two.[62] The excellent reputation he was building for himself at Tubac would prove of no small benefit to Captain Anza when several years hence he sought approval for a bold venture — the opening of an overland route to California.

While the Marqués listened to soldiers' routine gripes, Captain LaFora's promising young assistant, Lieutenant Joseph de Urrutia, was

---

[61] "Extractto de la Rebistta de Ynspeccion, executtada de Orden del Rey, por mi el Mariscal de Campo de sus Exttos, Marqs de Rubí, á la Expresada Compañía," Tubac, December 21, 1766, signed at the presidio of San Miguel, February 21, 1767; AGI, Guad., 511. For a description of the military frontier at about this time, see Sidney B. Brinckerhoff and Odie B. Faulk, *Lancers for the King: A Study of the Frontier Military System of Northern New Spain, with a Translation of the Royal Regulations of 1772* (Phoenix: Arizona Historical Foundation, 1965).

[62] "Prezios que conttiene el reglamentto de Presidios, con expresion de las rebajas echas por su Capitan Dn Juan Bapttistta de Anza"; *ibid.*

outside pacing off distances. It was his job to make maps of all the installations they visited.

Riding up from Tumacácori Urrutia had observed that the road followed along the river's west bank to a point somewhat less than half a mile south of the presidio. Here, where the river began a large graceful curve to the east in the form of an Indian bow, water was diverted into an irrigation ditch, which when diagrammed resembled the bowstring pulled back toward the west. Between bow and bowstring, Urrutia drew a neat patchwork of cultivated fields.

Continuing now along the west bank of the ditch, at a point about where the archer's fingers would grasp the bowstring, the road passed through a disorderly cluster of several dozen buildings, the homes of soldiers and refugee settlers. A few hundred feet north, on a rise, stood the presidio proper, dominated by a large U-shaped building which housed both the captain's quarters and the guard post. Just to the west, beside the road that led out to deserted Arivaca and then south to Altar, the Lieutenant outlined a cruciform building which Father Custodio no doubt had an interest in. It he labeled "church begun at the Captain's expense." Everything at Tubac, he added, was built of adobes.[63]

Young Urrutia, the mapmaker, may have been a favorite of the Marqués de Rubí, and he may have been very talented and very ambitious, but it is unlikely that even he, as he wiped the dust of Tubac from his boots, dreamed how far his military career would take him. Three decades later, he would pose for Goya at the Court of Madrid. His rank then — Captain General of all Spanish armies.[64]

Despite Anza's exemplary conduct, three complaints emerged from the soldiers' testimonies. One "common to the whole company" stemmed from the arbitrary duty assignments, the rigorous and unsystematic discipline, and various other indiscretions which they blamed partly on their sergeant but mostly on twenty-nine-year-old Ensign Joseph de

[63] The original of Lieutenant Urrutia's map of Tubac is in the British Museum, Additional Manuscripts, 17,662, no. 8.

[64] Urrutia as portrayed by Goya in 1798 appeared to be a rather harsh and peevish-looking officer standing, formally posed, with a spyglass in his right hand and his tricorn propped on a staff in his left. The painting hangs in the Prado. See Harry B. Wehle, *Art Treasures of the Prado* (New York: Harry N. Abrams, 1954), plate no. 62 and p. 238. Another Joseph de Urrutia served in Texas as Captain of the presidio of San Antonio de Béjar during the 1730s. Bolton, *Guide to Materials for the History of the United States in the Principal Archives of Mexico* (Washington: Carnegie Institution, 1913), p. 118; Weddle, *San Sabá Mission*, p. 15.

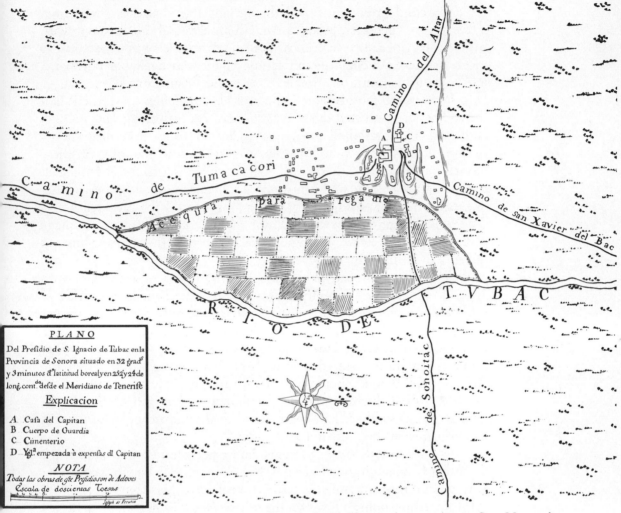

Lt. Urrutia's 1766 map of Tubac

Huandurraga. The Ensign, who was going to have to "improve his conduct greatly," had abused his authority while Anza was away. The
Captain, Rubí suggested, should take care to be more vigilant.

A second gripe concerned the rations they had been receiving.
Thus, before he left, Rubí standarized quantities and prices. Along with
his allotment of maize, wheat, or flour, each trooper was henceforth to
receive a quarter of beef every fifteen days, if it were available; otherwise,
a like quantity of mutton or salted meat could be substituted.

Perhaps the most serious complaint of Anza's men concerned their
duty. They had enlisted to serve as soldiers, they asserted, not common
vaqueros. They resented having to spend so much time and energy
herding horses and mules, particularly when the majority of these
animals, as many as a thousand head, belonged not to the presidio but
to the local settlers and to the missionaries. So many animals, they further
alleged, resulted in overgrazing, to the detriment of the presidial herds.
The Captain, in his own defense, was quick to point out the advantage
of having settlers near the presidio. By protecting their horses, he was
offering them incentive to stay.[65]

As for the presence of horses belonging to the missionaries, Anza
also had his reasons. To supply the garrison with beef, he relied of
necessity on the Padres. Ximeno of Guevavi, the only person for leagues
with cattle to sell, could not provide enough however — less than a
hundred head a year. Thus the Captain had contracted with Father
Pauer for monthly beef deliveries from San Ignacio. But when the
Apaches stole Pauer's horses, the Padre had no way to round up the
cattle and drive them to Tubac. Temporarily deprived of their meat
rations, Anza's soldiers had complained to the Governor, who in turn
had admonished the Tubac commander.[66]

As a last resort, Anza, it seems, had agreed to guard at Tubac the
horse herds belonging to Guevavi, San Xavier, and San Ignacio. Not
only was he insuring animals to drive beef to his garrison, but he was
at the same time doing a favor for the selfless Black Robes who ministered

[65] The declarations of the ten men, December 22–27, 1766, are in AGI, Guad., 274.
Rubí, "Puntos, que en vistta de las Confesiones juradas, que se han ttomado á los Soldados
de estta Compª de Tubac . . . ," Tubac, December 29, 1766; AGI, Guad., 511. Anza, "Sattisfazion . . . á los ttres Punttos," Tubac, December 30, 1766; *ibid*.

[66] Anza to Pineda, June 24, 1765.

to the presidial community without recompense. Now his soldiers were complaining about caring for all the horses.

After weighing the matter carefully, the Marqués de Rubí ruled that for the time being the settlers' horses, which were after all few in number, could stay, so long as each owner provided vaqueros in proportion to the size of his individual herd. Regarding the Padres' animals, it was the inspector's opinion that the benefits described by Anza were not sufficient to offset the resultant inconvenience to the Royal Service. The mission horses, therefore, must be separated immediately from the presidial herd and maintained totally at the expense of the Padres. Such expense, he reminded the Captain, was inherent in owning stock.[67] Anza had no alternative.

The Marqués de Rubí, Captain LaFora, Lieutenant Urrutia, their baggage, their servants, and their escort rode west out of Tubac on January 5, 1767, having subjected the garrison to the most thorough inspection in its history. Farther south in the missions at which the party stopped, the Jesuits outdid themselves trying to please the Marqués. One of them sent more than twenty leagues to have borrowed beef brought over. As a result, Father Visitor Nentuig reported, Rubí departed Sonora "much pleased with the good hospitality" and very favorably disposed toward the Jesuits.[68]

Less than two weeks after Rubí had left Tubac, Captain Anza dispatched a letter to him requesting that he rescind the order about meat rations. On the same day he also wrote to Governor Pineda asking for his support in the matter. Anza, it seems, had made a genuine effort to comply. He had approached the only man with cattle — and with the horses to get them to Tubac — namely, Father Custodio Ximeno of Guevavi. He had asked the Padre to supply thirteen head, enough for each soldier to have a quarter, every fifteen days. Father Custodio had declined.[69]

Realizing the Captain's predicament, Rubí evidently agreed to let him use his own judgment. A month later, Anza confided to the Gover-

---

[67] Rubí, "Rezoluziones, que en vistta del Sattisfazion dada por el Capittan Dⁿ Juan Bapttista de Anza, a los Puntos," Tubac, December 31, 1766; AGI, Guad., 511.

[68] Nentuig to Father Provincial Salvador de la Gándara, Ures, March 13, and Guásavas, April 13, 1767; BL.

[69] Anza to Pineda, Tubac, January 16, 1767; BNMex, 39/886.

nor: "I suspect that from now on I will be able to give the soldiers less meat than before. Because of the removal of the horses belonging to the two missionaries who were supplying it, the Padres do not wish to enter into any agreement, and I doubt if they ever will."

Almost before these lines had dried, bad news arrived from Father Ximeno: his mares, "the most valuable possession belonging to his mission," were gone. "His greatest worry now," added Anza, "is that the same thing will happen to his herd of riding horses, which by order of the Marqués he separated from ours. But in order to save it, as well as to prevent them from stealing the soldiers' herd from me along with it, I am of a mind to have him bring his herd back and put on a couple of Indians to look after it."[70]

On the Day of the Dead, November 2, 1766, Father Custodio was depressed. "May the Lord preserve my health," he wrote from Guevavi as he contemplated what lay ahead.[71] It was more than the danger of the roads, more than the fatigue involved. He felt a profound concern for the well-being of hundreds of Indian souls. As their Padre he owed them instruction and baptism and the promise of everlasting life. As if his efforts to hang on at Guevavi had not been enough, he had just been informed by his superiors that he must now shoulder the responsibilities of San Xavier del Bac as well.

The youthful poet Neve, who had gone north to relieve Espinosa, had suffered enough. The new Father Visitor of Sonora, Juan Nentuig, himself almost blind, dictated a letter to the Provincial explaining that he had transferred Father Neve to Cuquiárachi from Pimería Alta "because he had been ill ever since he arrived there, and now is already well."[72]

A Frenchman, Maximiliano LeRoy, who had served in Louisiana, had been named as a replacement for Neve, but Father Maximiliano, Ximeno knew, was having problems getting to the Pimería. Other Padres were coming, they told him. Already they were months overdue. Not

---

[70] Anza to Pineda, "Som̅s̅," February 17 and 20, 1767; *ibid*.

[71] Ximeno to the Father Treasurer, Guevavi, November 2, 1766; quoted in Donohue, "Unlucky Mission," *AW*, II, p. 136.

[72] Nentuig to Gándara, Guásavas, December 16, 1766; BL.

until mid-April, 1767, did Nentuig report that a new arrival, twenty-seven-year-old Father Antonio Castro, had been assigned to San Xavier.[73] But he probably never got there either.[74] Soon, it would be too late.

That very spring, as the warm breeze set a million fresh new leaves aflutter in the cottonwoods down by the river, an extraordinary royal decree was being conveyed to the New World in the strictest secrecy.

They might have expected it. Eight years earlier Pombal had implicated the Black Robes in a conspiracy to assassinate the king of Portugal, and as a result had brought about their banishment from all the Portuguese empire. Next the French king had cast them out. It remained only for their archenemy in Spain, the Conde de Aranda, an unregenerate heretic in their eyes, to make his move.

The ill-coordinated rising of Jesuit-taught, tradition-minded upper nobility and hungry rabble against Charles III in the spring of 1766 gave Aranda the opportunity he needed. Behind closed doors he presided as the king's ministers hammered out their case against the ambitious and dangerous Society of Jesus. The Jesuits, they convinced themselves, had incited the masses against the Crown. Recent riots gave them an outstanding if fictitious example of the Black Robes' perfidy to lay before the king. When His Majesty acted, "locking away in his royal breast the reasons for his decision," he did so in a most drastic manner. And through Aranda, the royal will was executed with relish and with consummate skill. The Jesuits had met their match.

As the guarded decree of expulsion and attendant orders were passed across the sea and down through the levels of the royal service, there was hardly a slip. Only because the special courier carrying the sealed packet of documents to Governor Pineda of Sonora fell ill was the schedule thrown off by a few days in that area. Instead of breaking the seal on July 8, the stipulated date, the portly Governor did so July 11. Working feverishly to make up the lost time, he wrote out detailed instructions for each of the Captains who, "because of his prudence, his readiness, and his devotion to the Royal Service," would be commis-

---

[73] Nentuig to Gándara, April 13, 1767.

[74] Donohue, "Unlucky Mission," *AW*, II, p. 137. Pradeau, *Expulsión,* p. 135.

sioned to oust the Padres of specified Jesuit rectorates. He trusted nothing to scribes. There must be no mistakes.[75]

Pineda might have dispatched the illustrious Anza of Tubac, long a friend of the Black Robes, to round up the missionaries of Pimería Alta. Instead he ordered Don Juan to Arizpe, seat of the Rectorate of San Francisco Xavier. There, the Governor believed, Anza's traditional good relations with the Jesuits might soften the blow. If his commission put the Captain of Tubac in a particularly difficult position personally, that could not be helped. Captain Anza, Pineda knew, would obey orders. On the appointed day he would begin the expulsion by notifying the elderly missionary of Arizpe, Father Visitor General Carlos de Roxas, his close friend, the very priest who had baptized him and who had married him to a local girl.

To expel the Jesuits from Pimería Alta, Pineda chose the veteran Captain Bernardo de Urrea of Altar. His orders, like those to the other Captains, arrived sealed. Across the packet appeared the admonition, "Do not open until July 23." From a letter of transmittal, Urrea learned that he had been commissioned, because of the Governor's special confidence in him, to execute the King's extremely urgent decree of the previous February 27. But presumably not until July 23 did the Captain learn His Majesty's shocking intent.[76]

Pineda left him no way out, no way to acknowledge but not comply. Upon his honor as an officer Urrea was bound to fulfill his commission "with the utmost readiness and secrecy." The Governor had designated the mission of Tubutama, residence of Father Rector Luis Vivas, as the logical place to concentrate the Padres, both because of its central location and "because the Indians of that village are not so volatile."

Taking fifteen men, "or as many as you deem necessary," the Captain began the task, a task he dreaded. On his way through Atí he asked the youthful missionary of that village, Father Pedro Rafael

---

[75] The complicated mechanics of expelling the Jesuits from Sonora are admirably explained in Pradeau, *Expulsión*, pp. 25–86. See also Dunne, "The Expulsion of the Jesuits from New Spain," *MA*, Vol. XIX (1937), pp. 3–30; and Burrus, ed., *Ducrue's Account of the Expulsion of the Jesuits from Lower California, 1767–1769* (Rome: Jesuit Historical Institute, 1967).

[76] Pineda's instructions, dated at San Miguel de Horcasitas on July 14, 1767, and his three letters to Captain Urrea dated the following day are printed in Pradeau, *Expulsión*, pp. 41–45.

Díez, to accompany him to Tubutama. There, on July 25, in private, Urrea told the Padres the painful purpose of his visit. He then requested the Father Rector to call in the other missionaries. None of the letters, he explained apologetically, must contain "the least indication" of what was really taking place. Henceforth, no missionary was to communicate with an outsider, either by letter or by word of mouth.

Despite the Father Rector's innocently worded summons, this, Ximeno must have known, was no routine matter.[77] Soldiers from Altar had been sent during the most miserable time of year to escort him from Guevavi. They did not even permit him to make arrangements for his absence. Instead, the Captain, without explanation, had ordered an inventory made of the mission's property.[78] Father Custodio was asked to surrender the mission records and his keys. The soldiers locked up everything they could, presumably entrusting one key to the native governor of Guevavi and another to the Captain's agent. They shut the church furnishings in the sacristy, with a warning that no one was to disturb them. If the Indians tried to interfere, the soldiers had orders to use force.

They told Ximeno he could take his personal belongings with him — his usual clothing, a change of linen, his snuffbox, tobacco, handkerchiefs, chocolate, and other such items. He was also free to take along

[77] Zelis erred in listing twenty-nine-year-old Pedro Rafael Díez as the Padre of Guevavi at the time of the expulsion. Ximeno he incorrectly placed at Caborca. *Catálogo,* pp. 134–35. Díez had reached the Pimería during the Jesuits' final spring. Father Visitor Nentuig assigned him not to Guevavi, but to Sáric to relieve the ailing Gerstner. Nentuig to Gándara, April 13, 1767. Father Díez seems to have been serving at Atí when Urrea began the expulsion. He was the last Jesuit to sign the Atí Libro de Casamientos on July 12, 1767, less than two weeks before the expulsion. In the surviving Caborca books of marriages and burials Father Alonso Espinosa, not Ximeno, made the final entries by a Jesuit. Parish Archive, Altar, Sonora; microfilm, Mission San Xavier del Bac, Tucson. Ximeno's fragmentary marriage entries in the Guevavi book carried through to June 14, 1767.

[78] One overall inventory of the Pimería Alta missions' wealth, drawn up in 1767, presumably at about the time of the expulsion, showed Guevavi to have been one of the least affluent, though by no means destitute. Its temporal resources consisted of: 21 pesos 6 reales under the heading "Reales," 2 pesos 3 reales of gold, 11 pesos 4 reales of silver, 700 cattle, 24 oxen, 240 ewes, 420 rams, 88 goats, 6 gentle mules, 18 gentle he-mules, 52 gentle horses, 24 colts, and 39 mares. Listed separately for Tumacácori were: 25 oxen, 23 rams, and 17 goats. San Xavier had no money, 387 cattle, 38 oxen, 330 ewes, 70 rams, 41 goats, 3 unbroken mules, 10 unbroken he-mules, 22 gentle horses, 24 colts, and 114 mares. Captain Anza owed Guevavi 200 pesos. "Apunte particular, de los bienes y efectos, que existen en cada Mission, y Pueblos de Visita de ellas"; BNMex, 54/732.

his breviary and the small prayer books he used in daily devotion. If for some reason he left without them, the Governor had ordered that they be sent to him later.

Leaving Guevavi involuntarily after four trying years was almost a relief. And yet as Ximeno looked around at the natives he had labored to save, they may not have appeared to him much closer to the kingdom of Heaven now than they had when he arrived. If he stopped to consider the amount of zealous energy that had been expended at this one mission since that day in January, 1691, when the almost-legendary Father Kino first spoke of the one supreme God to the parents and grandparents of these very neophytes, how sadly ironic it must have seemed. Surely God did not mean it to end here.

Behind him, as they escorted him away, he left a mission community he and his predecessors had built. It had cost the health of most of them, the life of one. For the last time Father Custodio had shut the door of the Padre's quarters in the convento, where he and others before him had lain burning with fever. The church, still visible from the trail below, would stand, perhaps until their return — the church Garrucho had begun to raise up before the revolt of Luis. But who now would distribute the harvest and see that the tools were returned to the storehouse? Who would make sure they came to pray? Who now would baptize the young?

From Tubutama Captain Urrea, by this time deeply depressed, led his prisoners south. Article 6 of the Governor's instructions provided that the Padres while on the road be made comfortable, "even more than usual, if possible." For each two missionaries the Governor ordered that a servant be hired to attend them and to saddle and load their horses. In the evening the Captain was to stop early enough and choose a decent site so that the Jesuits might get their accustomed hours of sleep.

On the road south of San Ignacio, Captain Urrea began to go to pieces. The strain of the past few days had been too much. One night after camp had been made, the Padres were roused by the Captain's voice "lugubrious and melancholy." "Woe is me," he moaned, "that I was ever born to see myself committed to this course of action. Very early in the morning all the soldiers must be ready and waiting with weapons and horses." He kept on. "Who would have wished to be born to see this."

"Those lamentations so unusual and of such terror," what did they mean? Who could blame the Padres for anticipating "some extraordinarily sorrowful happening." Full of apprehension, yet resigned to their fate and to the will of God, they awaited the first light of dawn.

Finally, when morning came, the soldiers went about breaking camp as usual. The Padres stared blankly at each other. "They all knew that the Captain had burst out with those exclamations because of his vehement regret and pain at having to carry out orders against those whom he loved and respected."

Sadly, Urrea returned to his home to rest, leaving his lieutenant to lead the Jesuits to whatever fate awaited them.[79]

In the impressive church at Mátape, sixty-five miles east of present-day Hermosillo, they were gathered together, about fifty of them, to hear the decisive decree read formally. Six of the ten Padres who had served over the years as resident missionary at Guevavi were present in that congregation. Ahead of them now lay months of confinement at the port of Guaymas in shacks not fit for animals, a frightening, disease-ridden voyage on the Gulf, and a pitiful death march across Mexico.

As they toiled up the road from Tepic to Guadalajara, more than a year after their rude journey began, weak and "sick unto death," at least twenty succumbed, among them Ximeno's friend Villarroya, Nentuig, Aguirre, and Bartholomé Sáenz. The outspoken son of Queen Christina's favorite, Alexandro Rapicani, fell at Ixtlán, two months before his sixty-sixth birthday.[80] He had begun his stormy career at Guevavi, more than three decades before.

---

[79] From a letter of Father Francisco Ita to Father Jaime Matheu, Puerto de Santa María, October 13, 1770, included in Matheu's "Destierro de los jesuitas misioneros de Sonora, Sinaloa y de la Tarahumara," and quoted by Pradeau, *Expulsión,* pp. 62–63; see also p. 64 for a discussion of the manuscript's authorship. The above account of what happened to poor Captain Urrea on the road to Mátape is of course a Jesuit interpretation. Captain Joseph Bergosa, who himself found the expulsion a trying business, confessed to the Governor, "I am glad that Urrea is better now; what a scare he put into your agents [i.e., the officers charged with carrying out the expulsion], at which Your Lordship will be amused." Bergosa to Pineda, Mátape, August 19, 1767; *ibid.,* p. 65.

[80] Rapicani expired on September 3, 1768. Matheu quoted by Pradeau, *ibid.,* pp. 99–100. A curious statement concerning the death of Rapicani, obviously an error, was attributed to Fathers Retz and Kloeber writing in 1749. Referring to a member of the Lower Rhine Province, they wrote: "The ungrateful California natives slew Father Rapicani through witchcraft." Burrus, *Ducrue's Account of the Expulsion,* 147–48. Perhaps the allusion, somehow jumbled, was to Grazhoffer's sad demise among the Pimas.

Among those who survived to be put aboard the Swedish storeship *Princess Ulrica* at Vera Cruz on November 10, 1768, were Fathers Garrucho, Pauer, and Ximeno. Gerstner and Pfefferkorn crossed later.[81] The beautiful hospice near Cádiz with its marble pillars, from which they had departed for the New World full of hope and zeal, now became their prison. There, on his forty-ninth birthday, Francisco Xavier Pauer returned his soul to God.[82] Father Francisco had braved the hostility at Guevavi after Luis' revolt and had built churches at Tumacácori and Sonoita.

Eventually those who refused to die were dispersed to monasteries throughout Spain. There they remained under house arrest while their friends attempted to get them released. Through the intercession of the Elector of Cologne, Father Pfefferkorn, who planned to write a book, emerged a free man late in 1777.[83] The Bishop of Würzburg secured a like release in 1780 for Miguel Gerstner who was "always ailing" in the Pimería and yet who had endured for a decade.[84] What became of the Spaniard Custodio Ximeno, Guevavi's final Black Robe, who was still a young man, apparently not even his ex-brethren found out.

A special reception awaited Joseph Garrucho, the Jesuit who spent more of his life at Guevavi than any other. When he disembarked at Cádiz he was not permitted to go with his fellow *expulsos* to the hospice at the Puerto de Santa María. Instead, he was placed under heavy guard and marched halfway across Spain to Madrid, there to be imprisoned.[85] An ex-missionary who had lived on New Spain's vulnerable northern frontier was, in the eyes of Spanish authorities, potentially dangerous. His knowledge in enemy hands could be used against the empire. Perhaps they considered Joseph Garrucho, the Sardinian, more suspect than the rest. Perhaps they were making an example of him.

In his cell, which he shared with a German lay brother, the congenial Father and his companion drew maps to pass away the time. Later,

[81] "Nota de los 20 Regulares de la Compª embarcados pª España en la Urca Sueca nombrada la Princesa Ulrrica," Vera Cruz, November 10, 1768; WBS, 1745, ff. 461–62. "PP. Jesuitas que se embarcaron para Cadiz en el Vergⁿ frances el Aventurero. Su Capⁿ d. Pedro Lavant, que salió en 9, de Abril de 1769"; *ibid.*, ff. 465–66.

[82] Zelis, *Catálogo,* p. 168.

[83] Pfefferkorn, *Sonora,* pp. 13–14.

[84] *Ibid.,* p. 14, n. 27.

[85] Matheu in Pradeau, *Expulsión,* p. 108.

while he was being held in a Hieronymite monastery, they told Garrucho he could go home. He refused. There in the sheltered atmosphere of the religious community he chose to set his soul in order. Where and when death finally closed the remarkable life and ministry of Joseph Garrucho, once of Guevavi, is still a mystery.[86]

At least ten priests of the Society of Jesus — any of whom might have had comfortable jobs teaching the sons of wealthy families — left the capital of New Spain and rode north hundreds of leagues to a primitive village of brush and adobe huts called Guevavi, there to live an uncertain, unhealthy life in rude surroundings, and there to minister to the childishly curious Pima Indians whose souls they thought worthy of salvation.

Ten years before they were banished, a superior in Mexico City, laying aside for the moment the rewards of serving one's God, graphically described what being a missionary entailed:

> It is possible to say of all the missionaries ... that their lives are filled with bitter disappointment and continual mortification. Aside from the headaches of mission administration and caring for souls; the ponderous studying of a barbarian tongue without the aid of teacher or books; the personal hardships which the mission's location and climate offer in the way of ruggedness and precipitousness, fording of swollen rivers without bridges or boats, oppressive and extreme heat, vermin and poisonous creatures, the rudeness and offensiveness of native character, the want of essentials and necessities; aside from all these, there are other circumstances which provide an abundant harvest of suffering. ... [87]

Yet they kept coming, the saintly and the selfish. Adventure; travel; an escape from the rigidity, the pettiness, or the unholy demands of society at large; the will to succeed at a strenuous and demanding task; and, in most cases, a genuine and idealistic desire to save souls in simple,

---

[86] Donohue, "Jesuit Missions," pp. 318–19. Zelis recorded the place and date of Father Garrucho's death as Lubianos, Spain, November 30, 1785, but as Father Donohue points out, the Jesuit who supplied this information later corrected himself: the Padre who had died was not Garrucho of Guevavi.

[87] Burrus, *Misiones Norteñas,* p. 81.

manly, dangerous emulation of Jesus Christ — such, it would seem, were their motives.

All the Jesuits of Guevavi were disciplined, intelligent, educated, devoted, and human. If Alexandro Rapicani flayed his opponents with particular relish, if Garrucho enjoyed toasting the guests at his table, if Keller displayed a fierce and jealous concern for his authority on the San Pedro, such actions only serve to make these mortals believable.

If the Black Robes of Guevavi seemed harsh in their insistence that the Indians give up the old ways, it was only because they believed so fervently that the new way was better. If they used food and force to facilitate conversion, they did so convinced that it was in the best interest of an inferior people who needed help and guidance.

And yet they nearly exterminated the natives of Guevavi, involuntarily. Time and time again they watched in horror as Old World diseases ravaged their apathetic neophytes. As a consolation they offered the one thing they could, the most potent medicine they possessed — holy baptism, a Christian chance for everlasting life. If all their toil, their good will, and their churches in the wilderness seemed only to speed the natives' demise, at least the Padres of Guevavi were concerned for the salvation of these poor souls.

The missionaries' purpose contrasted sharply with those of the secular exploiters on their own frontier, and, anachronistically, with those of the Anglo frontiersmen a century later who rushed across North America proclaiming the only good Indian a dead Indian.

At least the Jesuits of Guevavi were concerned.

Epilogue

ONCE THE JESUITS WERE GONE, their greedy neighbors all but devoured the missions. The royal overseers appointed to preserve the temporal goods which represented so much of the exiled missionaries' labor, instead consumed them.

Implementation of Governor Pineda's orders became a travesty. On paper these pronouncements looked commendable — all debts owed the missions were to be kept track of; secular priests would replace the exiled Jesuits immediately; henceforth, mission Indians were to enjoy the full protection of the Crown as brothers of the Spaniards; native governors were to see that the children were instructed, that everyone prayed and planted his crops, and that public sins and drinking were duly punished.[1]

But debts were forgotten, secular priests were too few, and natives were readily exploited by their Spanish brothers. The Jesuits' paternalistic rule had not prepared the mission wards to manage on their own.

No more than six weeks had elapsed when Captain Anza informed Pineda that the agent responsible for Guevavi and several other missions had done a stupid thing:

> Having told the Pimas that they were the absolute owners of the missions' goods and that as such they might dispose of them as they saw fit, he handed over to them the keys to the granaries. That was the end of the maize. In just a few days they must have consumed at

---

[1] Pradeau, *Expulsión,* pp. 59–62.

[189]

Tumacácori more than fifty *fanegas* without accounting for it. . . . The same thing was happening with the horses, cattle, etc. Everything would have been finished off within a few days. For this reason on my own initiative I have taken back the keys, leaving out enough provisions for their normal needs... until such time as the *comisario* appears, when I shall warn him not to proceed in such a disorganized manner.[2]

The first Franciscan came among them in the summer of 1768, and he, like Father Grazhoffer, called Guevavi "Los Santos Angeles San Gabriel y San Rafael." A compassionate forty-year-old Aragonese "with a clear, sonorous, and penetrating voice," Fray Juan Chrisóstomo Gil de Bernabé went about his ministry with a burning zeal that caused his interpreter to call him a saint.[3] Before they carried him south in the spring of 1771 a sick man, Fray Juan had learned for himself much the Jesuits could have told him about "the baneful influence of mission Guevavi."

Two years later, a troubled young Padre named Bartholomé Ximeno, who by then definitely resided at Tumacácori, reported on the state of the mission. It was a pitiful tale. Only nine families hung on at Guevavi, which he termed *la antigua cabecera*. He, like his black-robed predecessor of the same surname, urged the abandonment of that unfortunate village once and for all.[4] The Apaches saved him the trouble. When another Franciscan reported from Tumacácori in 1775, he listed only one visita. At Calabazas he counted among the 141 souls the survivors of abandoned Sonoita and Guevavi, finally beaten into submission "by the furious hostility of the Apaches."[5]

After eight decades, Christian Guevavi was dead.

But the scene had only shifted. Down the road at Tumacácori the

---

[2] Despite this act of gluttony, Anza assured the Governor that he could still provide the necessary pinole and meat for his infantry company in the upcoming offensive against the Seris. Anza to Pineda, "Soms.," September 7, 1767; BNMex, 39/886.

[3] Father Francisco Antonio Barbastro, "Compendio, de lo mas notable, qe han trabajado en Sonora los hijos del Colego de la Sª Cruz . . . desde el año de 1768 hasta el de 1783," Babiácora, September 10, 1788; Civ. Col.

[4] Kessell, "San José de Tumacácori — 1773: A Franciscan Reports from Arizona," *AW,* Vol. VI (1964), pp. 307–308.

[5] Kessell, "Father Eixarch and the Visitation at Tumacácori, May 12, 1775," *The Kiva,* Vol. XXX (1965), p. 79.

routine went on, actually little changed. The missionary now wore a grey robe instead of a black one, and he spoke Spanish without a foreign accent. But the troubles he knew were no different — Apache raids, epidemics, greedy settlers, a constant shortage of supplies, and apathy among those he hoped to save. The number of natives at Calabazas dwindled and eventually, like Guevavi and Sonoita, it too was given up, leaving only Tumacácori. At this last village the Franciscans rallied and put up a truly massive adobe church.

But that is another story — similar, sequential, and compelling, but nonetheless another story.

Archaeological excavations at Guevavi, 1965-66
— Photos, William J. Robinson

The Jesuits of Guevavi

Eusebio Francisco Kino of Dolores*	January, 1691 — March, 1711
Juan de San Martín	July, 1701 — fall, 1701 (1702?)
Agustín de Campos of San Ignacio* ⎫	
Luis Xavier Velarde of Dolores* ⎭	1711 — 1731
Juan Bautista Grazhoffer (d. Guevavi)	May, 1732 — spring, 1733
Phelipe Segesser (absent at least five months)	1733 — 1734
Gaspar Stiger of San Xavier*	1735 — spring, 1736
Ignacio Xavier Keller of Soamca*	spring, 1736 — May, 1737
Alexandro Rapicani	June, 1737 — fall, 1740
Joseph de Torres Perea	February, 1741 — spring, 1744
Ildefonso de la Peña**	spring, 1744
Ignacio Xavier Keller of Soamca*	summer, 1744 — May, 1745
Joseph Garrucho	May, 1745 — November, 1751
Francisco Xavier Pauer	December, 1753 — January, 1760
Miguel Gerstner	January, 1760 — May, 1761
Ignacio Pfefferkorn	May, 1761 — May, 1763
Custodio Ximeno	June, 1763 — July, 1767

* Nonresidents: Fathers Kino and Campos, and perhaps Father Velarde, passed through Guevavi occasionally preaching, baptizing, and encouraging its natives to visit them at their missions farther south. Fathers Stiger and Keller of neighboring San Xavier and Soamca looked in on the people of Guevavi when the mission was without a Padre of its own.

** Temporarily in residence, evidently as compañero to Father Torres Perea.

Appendix II

Entregas

When compared with other Jesuit missions, neither Guevavi nor San Xavier del Bac could ever have been considered rich. Yet each time a new Padre arrived to take charge he was required to sign a formal transfer of property, thereby accepting responsibility for whatever scant wealth there was. Four surviving examples of these entregas follow — two dated June 1, 1737, transferring Guevavi and Bac from Father Keller's absentee care to Father Rapicani; a May 25, 1761, document delivering Guevavi from Father Gerstner to Father Pfefferkorn; and the San Xavier entrega of June 16, 1765, executed by Father Neve when he replaced the moribund Father Espinosa.

Not only do these inventories portray the relative poverty of missions Guevavi and San Xavier, but they provide a useful checklist for the archaeologist. Similar items, or fragments of them, are known to have been excavated at the two sites, while others are still preserved at mission San Xavier. Today the original documents are part of the W. B. Stephens Collection, University of Texas Library, Austin. It is with the generous permission of the University of Texas that they are published here in translation.

[194]

Inventory of the Properties of the Church, House and Fields of Guevavi[1]

Furnishings of the House

4 charcoal-maker's axes, and 1 carpenter's axe, also a broken charcoal-maker's axe.
1 adze.   Also 1 pruning hook.
3 pickaxes.
some small pincers.
1 small hammer.
1 gouge.
1 small chisel.
1 small auger.
1 pair of nippers.
6 sawbucks (*tijeras de aria*).
2 hand saws, 2 whipsaws.
2 reaping hooks. Also a branding iron with its venting iron.
10 jugs (*botijas*).
8 pack saddles.
2 large kettles, 1 of medium size, 2 copper pots.
1 *comal*.
1 large skillet.
1 small kettle.
12 Mexican or Puebla plates. Also 12 china cups and saucers.
12 earthenware plates.
1 broken chocolate pot.
1 glass.
2 pewter plates.
1 large china cup.
1 tablecloth.
2 napkins.
1 chocolate cloth.
2 old silver spoons, 2 of pewter with their small forks.
1 Puebla saltcellar.
1 good chest with lock, also a number of old broken ones.
1 flask.
1 decanter.
2 old breviaries.
1 small inkwell with sandbox.
1 small table. Also 1 candlestick with brass snuffer.

[1] WBS, 1744, ff. 71–73.

Furnishings of the Church

5 new sets of damask vestments in the five colors.

2 copes, 1 black, the other white.

1 white processional canopy (*palio*) ruined by the water into which the chest fell on the road.

2 albs, 1 new, the other old, with their amices.

1 good cincture, another in ordinary condition.

1 Roman missal.

1 small portable altar.

1 tabernacle.

1 canvas depicting Saint John the Evangelist.

1 copper baptismal font.

1 copper holy-water pot.

1 altar cloth.

1 processional cross.

2 very small *palcas* [*palias?*] [2]

1 good corporal.

1 white damask cloth for carrying the Holy Sacrament.

1 oil cruet (*cornualtar*).

3 purificators.

1 silver chalice with its small spoon and paten.

1 silver ciborium.

some cruets and their small silver plate.

1 silver hand bell.

1 tall silver cross.

1 censer with its silver incense boat.

1 silver *rural*.

1 chrismal with its silver shell.

2 large or tower bells.

1 Roman Ritual, 1 Mexican.

6 brass candlesticks.

2 tin lanterns.

1 brass altar lamp with 6 small candle holders.

1 iron for baking wafers.

All of the items set forth were donated by the King (whom God guard) when this Mission was founded.[3]

also 1 old set of vestments of various colors which the Fathers of Sonora gave as alms.

also another set of vestments of all colors for services on the road.

---

[2] The word *palia* could mean several things here, among them tabernacle veil, altar cloth, or chalice cover.

[3] Refounded, in 1732.

2 embroidered silk *palcas* [chalice covers?]. Also another richer one.
1 tin waferbox.
also another iron for baking wafers.

Livestock

Cattle number of head	240.
Oxen	8.
Sheep	150.
Goats	50.
Gentle horses	12.
Mules and gentle he-mules	10.
Very small herds [of mares]	4.

I turned over that which is set forth in this inventory
on June 1, 1737, and I signed it.

Ygnacio Xavier Keller

I received it on the same day and in the same year.

Alexandro Rapicani

This transfer was made in my presence.

Gaspar Stiger

Inventory of the Properties of the Church, House,
and Fields of San Xavier del Bac[4]

Furnishings of the House

4 charcoal maker's axes, 1 carpenter's axe, also another very small pruning hook.
2 adzes with their straps.
1 small hammer.
1 pair of large tongs.
1 file.
8 chisels.
1 gouge.
1 small jack-plane.
some wooden carpentry tools.
1 auger, another very small one broken.
2 hand saws of which one is broken.
2 large plow points.
1 large copper kettle, another smaller one with holes.
1 large skillet in good condition.
1 decanter. Also a branding iron with its venting iron.
6 jugs.
some old chests.
5 earthenware plates.
3 Puebla or Mexican cups.
2 copper candlesticks with snuffers.

Furnishings of the Church

That which the King (whom God guard) has given for the establishment of this mission.
They are the same in number and kind as those of Guevavi, except for the altar lamp which was completely broken to pieces when the natives sacked the house.[5] Also of these vestments and other ecclesiastical ornaments the damaged processional canopy and censer are in the possession of Captain Anza[6] for repair. In addition, the green maniple is missing. All of these vestments have been rather

---

[4] WBS, 1744, ff. 67–68.

[5] In 1734.

[6] Anza the elder, in 1737 Captain of the presidio of Fronteras and justicia mayor of Sonora.

abused and the new altar cloths torn into pieces that could not be gathered up. Also one set of flowered vestments which Don Santos Fernández Ronderos, through the good offices of Don Santiago Ruiz de Ael,[7] presented as alms, though without frontal and linen.

Also a canvas depicting the seraphic Saint Francis.

Livestock

Cattle, number of head	240.
Sheep	150.
Goats	50.
Gentle horses	10.
Herds of a few mares	4.
Gentle mules	2.

I turned over that which is set forth in this inventory on June 1, 1737, and I signed it.

Ygnacio Xavier Keller

I received it on the same day in the same year.

Alexandro Rapicani

In my presence.

Gaspar Stiger

---

[7] Ruiz de Ael bore the imposing title of "Notary of the Holy Office of the Inquisition, Commissary General of the Royal Manufacture of Gunpowder, and member of the Royal Constabulary (*La Santa Hermandad*) for His Majesty in these realms and lesser provinces." Ruiz de Ael, Arizona, December 1, 1736; AGI, Guad., 185. During the period 1747–1751, Don Santiago served as Captain of the presidio of Terrenate, and later as Captain at Janos.

Transfer of the Mission of Guevavi in Pimería Alta which Father Miguel
Gerstner made to Father Ygnacio Pfefferkorn, May 25, 1761.[8]

There are 82 pesos in gold, 61 in silver.

Church

There remain the vestments and furnishings that I received, and as recorded
in the book and in the transfer of the past year. Added were 1 new alb with its
amice, 1 cincture of cloth and another of ribbon, 1 copper holy-water pot with
its aspergillum, 1 new stand for the missal, 4 pictures with gilt frames, 1 set of
clothing for an acolyte, and 2 silver-plated candlesticks (at Tumacácori).

House

All the furniture of the house remains as I received it; it has been moved or
improved as follows: There are 10 Puebla cups, 3 new napkins and 7 old ones,
a new pair of compasses, 4 plowshares though only 1 is good. I added 2 points,
also 2 axes, 3 spades, 2 hoes, and 1 large padlock for the maize storeroom (1 axe
is in the village of Calabazas).

In the bakehouse are 7½ loads *(cargas)*[9] of soda.

In the larders there are 6 bladders of lard, a little tallow, 8 strings of chile, 2 loads
of flour, and 8 *arrobas*[10] of boiled tallow for making soap.

Of maize there are about 15 *fanegas*.[11]

Among the gear for pack animals there are the 18 pack saddles newly repaired
and fitted with everything for their use, and 20 pack sacks.

In the storehouse I leave 6 candles of white wax, 3 crates of soap, 1½ loads of
salt, and 4 jugs of wine.

Luis Vivas Ihs [12]

Fields

There are about 815 head of cattle on the range *(vellotal)*. In the pasture there
were 55 head around the branding pens.

Sheep	723	Lambs not yet a year old	212
Year-old lambs	115	Ewe lambs not yet a year old	220

---

[8] WBS, 1744, ff. 381–84.

[9] Though the *carga* was both an arid measure and a measure of weight, which varied
greatly depending upon the commodity or the region, it apparently is used here to mean
simply load, perhaps the amount contained in one pack sack.

[10] As a dry measure the *arroba* was equivalent to about twenty-five pounds, as a liquid
measure to about four gallons.

[11] A *fanega* equaled up to 2.5 bushels, but also varied depending upon locality.

[12] Father Vivas of Tubutama signed as witness to the transfer at this point and again at
the end of the document.

Mules

The mission has: gentle mules 8

gentle he-mules 16

2 year-old he-mules, and 1 two-year-old 3

The ox herd consists of 10 yokes of oxen.

Horses

The mule-breeding mares (*manada del triste*) with their burro:

Brood mares including the lead mare 24

Two-year-old fillies 6

Year-old fillies 9

Year-old colts 10

Horses in the gentle herd 37

Colts already two and ready for breeding 9

Visitas

In Sonoita the new church is finished. There are 2 brass candlesticks there.
In the house are 3 plates, 3 Puebla cups, and 1 hand mill.
In the village, 2 axes and an adze.
3 yokes of oxen.
There is a new herd of 13 mares with its little burro. As for cattle, there are about
100 head there, probably minus 2 or 3.

Calabazas

This village has a new house with door and lock. The church I leave nearly half
built. In the house there is a holy-water pot, 1 hand bell, 1 table, 3 plates and 2
cups, an earthenware pitcher, and a hand mill.
In the village, 1 axe.

Tumacácori

Besides the 2 silver-plated candlesticks, the church has 1 old censer with its incense
boat, and a Santo Christo.
In the house 1 earthenware pitcher [chocolate pot?] or [and?] beater, 3 plates,
3 cups, a little chile and lard, and 2 table candlesticks with their snuffers. On the
doors a lock-plate and a large padlock. Also 1 saltcellar.
In the village there is an axe and an adze.
2 yokes of oxen.

Indebtedness

Indebtedness against the mission incurred during my time: there is none, no more than a few pesos owed the muleteer for his salary. The amount owed since before I arrived is very small; it is doubtful that it totals 15 pesos.

Indebtedness in favor of the mission

Captain Don Juan Bautista de Anza [13] owes 664 pesos, 1 real in goods; also 90 pesos in gold or silver, as is of record from the letter of payment he gave.

664.1.

90.

The company [of soldiers at Tubac] owes something, as do various settlers, in small amounts as recorded in the account book, the whole of which adds up in silver to

126.

Also on their word they owe the mission

30.4.

I turned it over. *Miguel Gerstner Ihs*

I received it. *Ihs Ygnacio Pfefferkorn*
Luis Vivas Ihs

---

[13] Anza the younger, in 1761 Captain of the presidio of Tubac.

San Xavier del Bac, June 16, 1765.[14]

On the said day this mission was transferred to Father Joseph Neve, Minister designate to this place. The transfer involved the following items:

Furnishings of the Church

1 statue of Saint Xavier with cassock of ribbed silk. Surplice of cambric and another of Brittany.

2 shirts of Brittany for the saint.

2 stoles for the saint, 1 of cloth and the other of embroidered ribbed silk.

1 set of black damask vestments, with its cope and frontal of ribbed silk.

1 set of white damask, with frontal now half worn-out.

1 set of white damask with raised flowers and gold galloon, with frontal.

1 set of rose-colored flowered silk and silk galloon, without frontal.

1 set of the same color damask, with frontal of satin and gold galloon.

1 set of rose-colored satin with flowers of gold and gold galloon, without frontal.

1 set of satin, of all colors, with frontal.

1 set of the same, violet-colored, with new frontal.

1 painted frontal with its frames.

1 cope of Persian silk with flowers of silver and gold.

6 altar clothes of Brittany with lace.

2 of the same without lace.

7 albs of Brittany and 4 amices.

6 chalice covers (*palias*).

8 corporals.

6 purificators.

4 cinctures, 2 of cloth and 2 of smooth ribbon.

1 surplice.

1 copper baptismal font.

1 tin box and three small crystal vessels with silver stoppers for the holy oils.

2 copper holy-water pots.

6 candlesticks of silver, I should say of silver-covered wood.

2 of the same, now old.

2 of the same of copper and 1 cross of the same metal.

4 old missals with two manuals.

4 chalices, 3 good and 1 broken.

1 small plate with cruets and hand bell, all of silver.

2 copper hand bells.

1 censer with its incense boat and spoon, all of silver.

7 *manutejos o Cornualtar*.

---

[14] WBS, 1744, ff. 427–30.

1 image of the Sorrowing Mother with her aureole and dagger of silver, her satin dress and blue taffeta mantle with silver galloon.

1 curtain of ribbed silk for the same lady.

1 gilded silver monstrance with its box.

1 silver-covered throne for the monstrance, with its cloth curtain.

1 gilded tabernacle with key.

2 pictures, 1 of the Holy Mother of Refuge and the other of Lord Saint Joseph.

1 of the same of Saint Xavier from the waist up.

1 cross sheath with new silver-covered wooden processional candleholders.

1 Puebla rug.

1 copper waferbox.

1 missal stand varnished with vermilion.

3 birettas (*bonetes*) of ribbed silk and cloth.

3 baptismal shells, 1 silver, 2 from the sea [Kino's abalone shells?], and 1 baptismal cap.

3 altar stones.

1 curtain of striped satin.

1 iron for baking wafers.

6 bouquets of paper flowers with their silver-plated *garras*.

6 metal wall candleholders.

1 kerchief of cambric with Flemish lace embroidered with gold, for the Holy Virgin of Sorrows.

2 strings of silver braid (*platilla*), 1 of false pearls and earrings of the same, 1 pair of bracelets of beads, and a Granada silk kerchief, all belonging to the Holy Virgin.

12 arrobas of northern wax.

Crops and Livestock

334 head of branded cattle.

125 of the same unbranded.

536 head of sheep.

14 yokes of gentle oxen.

24 horses saddle broken and halter broken.

14 colts.

100 brood mares with 4 studhorses and 2 stud burros.

17 branded fillies.

1 gentle mule.

3 of the same unbroken, and 7 unbroken he-mules, I should say gentle, also 8 unbroken. (Total mules, 19.)

Furnishings of the House

6 chisels of all sizes.

3 carpenter's planes.

 5 adzes.
 9 charcoal-maker's axes.
 3 of the same.
 1 whipsaw.
 7 sawbucks
 1 mason's trowel.
 3 worn-out spades.
 1 hoe.
 2 machetes.
 1 syringe.
 2 branding irons with their venting iron.
 5 augers.
 6 plates of English pewter.
 4 spoons with their forks.
 2 chocolate pots.
 4 table candlesticks with snuffers, I should say 1 pair.
 1 tablecloth with 6 Puebla napkins.
 2 towels.
14 cups and 2 saucers.
 3 poor tables.
 6 worse chairs.
 4 jugs of wine.
 1 empty jug.
11 old reaping hooks.
 2 small kettles.
 1 of the same without bottom.
 1 iron crowbar.
 5 pack saddles in poor condition.
10 hunks of salt.
 3 more metal forks, and 2 spoons.

In addition to what has been stated the mission has what is necessary, even to adequate crops of wheat and maize. Tallow, lard, candles, and soap in good supply, all kinds. There is also a field planted with wheat, another with maize, and another with various legumes, such as vetch, lentils, chickpeas, etc.

Ihs. Alonso Espinosa

I received everything set forth above, and in witness thereof I sign today, June 16, 1765.

Ihs. Joseph Neve

Ihs. Francisco Pauer [15]

---

[15] Father Pauer of San Ignacio witnessed the transfer.

Bibliography

MANUSCRIPTS: Principal Archives, Libraries, and Collections Cited

ALTAR, SONORA, PARISH ARCHIVE
ARCHIVES OF THE ROMAN CATHOLIC DIOCESE, TUCSON, ARIZONA
    Guevavi, "Tubaca y Otros"
    Tumacácori, "De Calabasas Bautismos"
ARCHIVO GENERAL DE INDIAS, Sevilla, Spain (AGI)
    Audiencia de Guadalajara (Guad.), legajos 135, 137, 185, 274, 277, 418, 419, 511, 515
    Contratación, legajo 5550
ARCHIVO GENERAL DE LA NACIÓN, México, D.F. (AGN)
    Historia, tomos 16, 17, 308, 393
    Misiones, tomos 3, 22, 27
ARCHIVO HISTÓRICO DE HACIENDA, México, D.F. (AHH)
    Temporalidades (Temp.), legajos 16, 17, 278, 393
ARCHIVO HISTÓRICO NACIONAL, Madrid, Spain
    Jesuítas, 453
ARIZONA PIONEERS' HISTORICAL SOCIETY, Tucson (APHS)
ARIZONA, UNIVERSITY OF, LIBRARY, Tucson (UAL)
    Civezza Collection (Civ. Col.)
BANCROFT LIBRARY, UNIVERSITY OF CALIFORNIA, Berkeley (BL)
    Bolton Research Papers (BRP)
    "Colección de Pimería Alta" (CPA)
    Mexican Manuscripts (M-M)
BIBLIOTECA NACIONAL, México, D.F. (BNMex)
BRITISH MUSEUM
    Additional Manuscripts
HUNTINGTON LIBRARY, San Marino, California
TEXAS, UNIVERSITY OF, LIBRARY, Austin
    W. B. Stephens Collection (WBS)

Manuscripts Frequently Cited

ARCE Y ARROYO. Testimonies. "Testimonio de los Autos formados en orden de Rl. Cedula de 4 de Octre. de 1752, sobre la averiguazn. del origen que tuvo el Alzamiento de los Pimas Altos, en la Provincia de Sonora," Governor Pablo de Arce y Arroyo, November, 1753–January, 1754; AGI, Guad., 418.

"Breve Resumen de los desastres." [Anon.] "Breve Resumen de los desastres, Muertes, Robos, y asolamentos acaezidos en la Provincia de Sonora Óbstilizada de Apaches, Seris, y Pimas alzados, y en particular desde el año de 1755 hasta el presente de 1760"; AHH, Temp., 17.

CANAS, *et al.*, to the Bishop, July 31, 1732. Christóbal de Cañas, s.j., *et al.*, to Bishop Benito Crespo, Pimería Alta, July 31, 1732, certified copy, Durango, November 19, 1733; AGI, Guad., 135.

GUEVAVI, "Tubaca y Otros." Mission Los Santos Ángeles de Guevavi, fragmentary baptismal, marriage, and burial records, 1739–1767; Archives of the Roman Catholic Diocese, Tucson.

KINO. "Favores Celestiales." Eusebio Francisco Kino, s.j., "Favores Celestiales de Jesus y de María SSᵐᵃ y del Gloriosissimo Apostol de las Indias S. Francisco Xavier Experimentados en las Nuevas Conquistas y Nuevas Conversiones...," 1699–1710; AGN, Misiones, 27.

NENTUIG. "Descripcion." Juan Nentuig, s.j., "Descripcion Geografica, natural, y curiosa de la Provᵃ de Sonora... 1764"; AGN, Historia, 393.

ORTIZ PARRILLA. Testimonies. The documents gathered by Governor Diego Ortiz Parrilla during and immediately after the Pima rebellion of 1751, November, 1751–March, 1753; AGI, Guad., 419.

PEÑA. "Convite Evangelico." Salvador Ignacio de la Peña, s.j., "Convite Evangelico á compasion, y Socorro de la Viña del Señor, destrozada, y conculcada con el Alzamiento de la Pimeria Alta, desde el dia 21 de Noviembre del Año de 1751, y sus lastimosos progressos en la siguiente Decada, hasta el año de 1760," [1760]; microfilm 71, UAL.

SAN IGNACIO, Bautismos. Mission San Ignacio, Libro de Bautismos, 1720–1762; CPA.

SAN IGNACIO, Entierros. Mission San Ignacio, Libro de Entierros, 1697–1787; CPA.

SOAMCA, Bautismos. Mission Santa María Soamca, Libro de Bautismos, 1732–1768; CPA.

SOAMCA, Bautismos de los Pueblos de Visita. Mission Santa María Soamca, Libro de Bautismos y Casamientos de los Pueblos de Visita, 1743–1755; CPA.

TORRES PEREA. Informe, March 16, 1744. Joseph de Torres Perea, s.j., "Informe de la Mission de los Angeles de Guebavi alias Guzutaqui de la Pimeria alta del Norte," Guevavi, March 16, 1744; "Cartas de las Misiones de la Compañía de Jesús en la Baja California y Norte de México," microfilm, UAL.

TUMACÁCORI, "De Calabasas Bautismos." Mission San José de Tumacácori, fragmentary baptismal, marriage, and burial records, 1768–1825; Archives of the Roman Catholic Diocese, Tucson.

UTRERA. Testimonies. Recorded by the Father Visitor General Joseph de Utrera, S.J., August–December, 1754, concerning the Pima rebellion of 1751; AGI, Guad., 419.

OTHER WORKS

ALEGRE, FRANCISCO JAVIER, S.J. *Historia de la Provincia de la Compañia de Jesús de Nueva España,* ed. Ernest J. Burrus, S.J., and Félix Zubillaga, S.J. 4 vols. Roma: Institutum Historicum Societatis Jesu, 1956–60.

ALMADA, FRANCISCO R. *Diccionario de Historia, Geografía y Biografía Sonorense.* Chihuahua: Ruiz Sandoval, 1952.

Apostólicos Afanes de la Compañia de Jesús. Barcelona: Pablo Nadal, 1754; México, D.F.: L. Alvarez y Alvarez de la Cadena, 1944.

ASPURZ, LAZARO DE, O.F.M., cap. *La aportación extranjera a las missiones españolas del Patronato Regio.* Madrid: Publicaciones del Consejo de la Hispanidad, 1946.

BAEGERT, JOHANN JAKOB, S.J. *Observations in Lower California,* ed. and trans. M. M. Brandenburg and Carl L. Baumann. Berkeley: University of California Press, 1952.

BANCROFT, HUBERT HOWE. *History of Arizona and New Mexico, 1530–1888* (Vol. XVII of his *Works*). San Francisco: The History Company, 1889; Albuquerque: Horn and Wallace, 1962.

———. *History of the North Mexican States and Texas,* Vol. I (Vol. XV of his *Works*). San Francisco: A. L. Bancroft, 1884.

BANNON, JOHN FRANCIS, S.J., ed. *Bolton and the Spanish Borderlands.* Norman: University of Oklahoma Press, 1964.

———. *The Mission Frontier in Sonora, 1620–1687.* New York: United States Catholic Historical Society, 1955.

BOLTON, HERBERT E. "The Black Robes of New Spain," *Catholic Historical Review,* XXI (October 1935), 257–82.

———. *Guide to Materials for the History of the United States in the Principal Archives of Mexico.* Washington, D.C.: Carnegie Institution, 1913; New York: Kraus Reprint, 1965.

———. "The Mission as a Frontier Institution in the Spanish-American Colonies," *American Historical Review,* XXIII (October 1917), 42–61.

———. *Rim of Christendom: A Biography of Eusebio Francisco Kino, Pacific Coast Pioneer.* New York: Macmillan, 1936; New York: Russell and Russell, 1960.

BOWMAN, J.N., and ROBERT F. HEIZER. *Anza and the Northwest Frontier of New Spain* (Southwest Museum Papers, XX). Los Angeles: Southwest Museum, 1967.

BRINCKERHOFF, SIDNEY B., and ODIE B. FAULK. *Lancers for the King: A Study of the Frontier Military System of Northern New Spain, With a Translation of the Royal Regulations of 1772.* Phoenix: Arizona Historical Foundation, 1965.

BURRUS, ERNEST J., S.J. *Kino and the Cartography of Northwestern New Spain.* Tucson: Arizona Pioneers' Historical Society, 1965.

Burrus, Ernest J., s.j. *La Obra Cartográfica de la Provincia Mexicana de la Compañia de Jesús (1567–1967).* Colección Chimalistac de Libros y Documentos acerca de la Nueva España, Serie José Porrúa Turanzas, 1–2. 2 vols. Madrid: Ediciones José Porrúa Turanzas, 1967.

―――, ed. *Correspondencia del P. Kino con los Generales de la Compañia de Jesús, 1682–1707.* México, D.F.: Editorial Jus, 1961.

✓   ―――, ed. *Ducrue's Account of the Expulsion of the Jesuits from Lower California (1767–1769).* Sources and Studies for the History of the Americas, II. Rome: Jesuit Historical Institute, 1967.

―――, ed. and trans. *Kino Reports to Headquarters: Correspondence of Eusebio F. Kino, S.J., from New Spain with Rome* (also *Supplement: Facsimiles of Documents and Kino's 1683 Map of Lower California*). Roma: Institutum Historicum Societatis Jesu, 1954.

―――, ed. and trans. *Kino Writes to the Duchess, Letters of Eusebio Francisco Kino, S.J. to the Duchess of Aveiro.* Rome: Jesuit Historical Institute, 1965.

―――, ed. and trans. "Kino's First Report on His First Permanent Mission: with German Text and English Translation," *Manuscripta,* V (October 1961), 164–69.

―――, ed. and trans. *Kino's Plan for the Development of Pimería Alta, Arizona and Upper California.* Tucson: Arizona Pioneers' Historical Society, 1961.

―――, ed. *Misiones norteñas mexicanas de la Compañia de Jesús, 1751–1757.* México, D.F.: Antigua Librería Robredo, 1963.

―――, ed. *Vida del P. Francisco J. Saeta, S.J.: Sangre Misionera en Sonora.* México, D.F.: Editorial Jus, 1961.

Castetter, Edward F., and Willis H. Bell. *Pima and Papago Indian Agriculture.* Albuquerque: University of New Mexico Press, 1942.

―――, and Ruth M. Underhill. *The Ethnobiology of the Papago Indians,* University of New Mexico Bulletin, Whole No. 275 (October 1935).

Chapman, Charles E. *Catalogue of Materials in the Archivo General de Indias for the History of the Pacific Coast and the American Southwest.* Berkeley: University of California Press, 1919.

―――. *Colonial Hispanic America: A History.* New York: Macmillan, 1933.

Chevalier, François. *Land and Society in Colonial Mexico: The Great Hacienda,* trans. Alvin Eustis, ed. Lesley Byrd Simpson. Berkeley: University of California Press, 1966.

Cuevas, Mariano, s.j. *Historia de la Iglesia en México.* 4 vols. I–III, Tlalpan, D.F.: Asilo "Patricio Sanz," 1921–24. IV, Santa Julia, D.F.: Colegio Salesiano, 1926.

Decorme, Gerard, s.j., *La obra de los Jesuítas mexicanos durante la época colonial, 1572–1767.* 2 vols. México, D.F.: Antigua Librería Robredo, 1941.

DiPeso, Charles C. *The Sobaipuri Indians of the Upper San Pedro River Valley, Southeastern Arizona.* Dragoon, Ariz.: Amerind Foundation, 1953.

―――. *The Upper Pima of San Cayetano del Tumacacori: An Archaeohistorical Reconstruction of the Ootam of Pimería Alta.* Dragoon, Ariz.: Amerind Foundation, 1956.

———, ed., and DANIEL S. MATSON, trans. "The Seri Indians in 1692 as Described by Adamo Gilg, s.J.," *Arizona and the West*, VII (Spring 1965), 33–56.

DOBYNS, HENRY F. "Indian Extinction in the Middle Santa Cruz Valley, Arizona," *New Mexico Historical Review*, XXXVIII (April 1963), 163–81.

———. *Pioneering Christians among the Perishing Indians of Tucson*. Lima, Peru: Editorial Estudios Andinos, 1962.

———. "Tubac Through Four Centuries: An Historical Resumé and Analysis." 3 binders. Unpublished report for the Arizona State Parks Board, 1959.

———, et al. "What Were Nixoras?" *Southwestern Journal of Anthropology*, XVI (Summer 1960), 230–58.

Documentos para la historia de Méjico. 21 vols. México: J. R. Navarro, 1853–57.

DONOHUE, JOHN A., s.J. "Jesuit Missions in Northwestern New Spain, 1711–1767." Unpublished Ph.D. dissertation, University of California, Berkeley, 1957.

———. "The Unlucky Jesuit Mission of Bac, 1732–1767," *Arizona and the West*, II (Summer 1960), 127–39.

DUNNE, PETER M., s.J. *Black Robes in Lower California*. Berkeley: University of California Press, 1952.

———. "Captain Anza and the Case of Father Campos," *Mid-America*, XXIII (January 1941), 45–60.

———. *Early Jesuit Missions in Tarahumara*. Berkeley: University of California Press, 1948.

———. "The Expulsion of the Jesuits from New Spain, 1767," *Mid-America*, XIX (January 1937), 3–30.

———. "Lower California an Island," *Mid-America*, XXXV (January 1953), 37–66.

———. *Pioneer Black Robes on the West Coast*. Berkeley: University of California Press, 1940.

———. *Pioneer Jesuits in Northern Mexico*. Berkeley: University of California Press, 1944.

———, ed. and trans. *Jacobo Sedelmayr: Missionary, Frontiersman, Explorer in Arizona and Sonora*. Tucson: Arizona Pioneers' Historical Society, 1955.

———, ed. and trans. *Juan Antonio Balthasar, Padre Visitador to the Sonora Frontier, 1744–1745*. Tucson: Arizona Pioneers' Historical Society, 1957.

———, and ERNEST J. BURRUS, s.J., ed. "Four Unpublished Letters of Anton Maria Benz, Eighteenth-Century Missionary to Mexico," *Archivum Historicum Societatis Jesu*, XXIV (1955), 336–78.

EWING, RUSSELL C. "Investigations into the Causes of the Pima Uprising of 1751," *Mid-America*, XXIII (April 1941), 138–51.

———. "The Pima Outbreak in November, 1751," *New Mexico Historical Review*, XIII (October 1938), 337–46.

———. "The Pima Uprising, 1751–1752: A Study in Spain's Indian Policy." Unpublished Ph.D. dissertation, University of California, Berkeley, 1934.

Ewing, Russell C. "The Pima Uprising of 1751," in *Greater America: Essays in Honor of Herbert Eugene Bolton*. Berkeley: University of California Press, 1945.

Gardiner, Arthur D., ed. and trans. "Letter of Father Middendorff, s.j., Dated from Tucson, 3 March 1757," *The Kiva*, XXII (June 1957), 1–10.

Hammond, George P., ed. and trans. "Pimería Alta after Kino's Time," *New Mexico Historical Review*, IV (July 1929), 220–38.

Hastings, James Rodney. "People of Reason and Others: The Colonization of Sonora to 1767," *Arizona and the West*, III (Winter 1961), 321–40.

Ives, Ronald L. "California no es Ysla," *Records of the American Catholic Historical Society of Philadelphia*, LXIV (December 1953), 189–98.

———. "Enrique Ruhen, s.j. — Borderland Martyr," *The Kiva*, XXIII (October 1957), 1–10.

———. "Mission San Marcelo del Sonoydag," *Records of the American Catholic Historical Society of Philadelphia*, LXVI (December 1955), 201–21.

———. "The Quest of the Blue Shells," *Arizoniana*, II (Spring 1961), 3–7.

———, ed. and trans. "The Report of the Bishop of Durango on Conditions in Northwestern Mexico in 1745," *Hispanic American Historical Review*, XIX (August 1939), 314–17.

———, ed. and trans. "The Sonoran Census of 1730," *Records of the American Catholic Historical Society of Philadelphia*, LIX (December 1948), 319–39.

Jacobsen, Jerome V., s.j. *Educational Foundations of the Jesuits in Sixteenth-Century New Spain*. Berkeley: University of California Press, 1938.

Kessell, John L., ed. and trans. "Anza, Indian Fighter: The Spring Campaign, 1766," *Journal of Arizona History*, IX (Fall 1968), 155–63.

———. "The Puzzling Presidio: San Phelipe de Guevavi, alias Terrenate," *New Mexico Historical Review*, XLI (January 1966), 21–46.

———, ed. and trans. *Spaniard and Apache on the Upper Gila, 1756: An Account of the Bustamante-Vildósola Expedition by Father Bartholomé Sáenz, S.J.* Santa Fe: Stagecoach Press, in press.

———, ed. and trans. "Father Eixarch and the Visitation at Tumacácori, May 12, 1775," *The Kiva*, XXX (February 1965), 77–81.

———, ed. and trans., "San José de Tumacácori — 1773: A Franciscan Reports from Arizona," *Arizona and the West*, VI (Winter 1964), 303–12.

Kino, Eusebio Francisco, s.j. *Kino's Historical Memoir of Pimería Alta*, ed. and trans. Herbert E. Bolton. 2 vols. Cleveland: Arthur Clark, 1919; Berkeley: University of California Press, 1948.

LaFora, Nicolás de. *The Frontiers of New Spain: Nicolás de LaFora's Description, 1766–1768*, trans. Lawrence Kinnaird. Berkeley: Quivira Society, 1958. Translation of the following entry.

———. *Relación del viaje que hizo á los presidios internos situados en la frontera de la América Septentrional perteneciente al rey de España*, liminar bibliográfico y acotaciones por Vito Alessio Robles. México, D.F.: Editorial P. Robredo, 1939.

Leonard, Irving A. *Baroque Times in Old Mexico: Seventeenth Century Persons, Places, and Practices*. Ann Arbor: University of Michigan Press, 1959.

LOCKWOOD, FRANK C. *With Padre Kino on the Trail.* (Social Science Bulletin No. 5.) Tucson: University of Arizona, 1934.

MANJE, JUAN MATHEO. *Unknown Arizona and Sonora, 1693–1721,* trans. Harry J. Karns and Associates. Tucson: Arizona Silhouettes, 1954.

MATTISON, RAY H. "Early Spanish and Mexican Settlements in Arizona," *New Mexico Historical Review,* XXI (October 1946), 273–327.

MILLS, HAZEL EMERY. "Father Jacobo Sedelmayr, S.J.: A Forgotten Chapter in Arizona Missionary History," *Arizona Historical Review,* VII (January 1936), 3–18.

————. "Jacobo Sedelmayr: A Jesuit in Pimería Alta, 1736–1767." Unpublished master's thesis, University of California, Berkeley, 1932.

MÖRNER, MAGNUS, ed. *The Expulsion of the Jesuits from Latin America.* New York: Alfred A. Knopf, 1965.

NATHAN, PAUL D., trans., and LESLEY BYRD SIMPSON, ed. *The San Sabá Papers: A Documentary Account of the Founding and Destruction of San Sabá Mission.* San Francisco: John Howell, 1959.

NAVARRO GARCÍA, LUIS. *Don José de Gálvez y la Comandancia General de las Provincias Internas del Norte de Nueva España.* Sevilla: Escuela de Estudios Hispano-Americanos, 1964.

————. *Sonora y Sinaloa en el siglo XVII.* Sevilla: Escuela de Estudios Hispano-Americanos, 1967.

————. *La Sublevación Yaqui de 1740.* Sevilla: Escuela de Estudios Hispano-Americanos, 1966.

[NENTUIG, JUAN, S.J.] *Rudo Ensayo, By an unknown Jesuit padre, 1763.* Tucson: Arizona Silhouettes, 1951.

OCARANZA, FERNANDO. *Parva crónica de la Sierra Madre y las Pimerías.* (Instituto panamericano de geografía e historia, Publicación num. 64). México, D.F.: Editorial Stylo, 1942.

OCH, JOSEPH, S.J.; *see* Treutlein.

PFEFFERKORN, IGNAZ, S.J. *Beschreibung der Landschaft Sonora samt andern merkwürdigen Nachrichten von den inneren Theilen Neu-Spaniens und Reise aus Amerika bis in Deutschland.* 2 vols. Köln am Rheine, 1794–95.

————. *Sonora, A Description of the Province.* Albuquerque: University of New Mexico Press, 1949. Translation of the above.

PRADEAU, ALBERTO FRANCISCO. *La expulsión de los Jesuitas de las Provincias de Sonora, Ostimuri y Sinaloa en 1767.* México, D.F.: Antigua Librería Robredo, 1959.

————. "Nentuig's 'Description of Sonora,'" *Mid-America,* XXXV (April 1953), 81–90.

————, and ERNEST J. BURRUS, S.J. "Los Jesuitas en Sonora." Unpublished manuscript, Los Angeles, 1965.

RICARD, ROBERT. *The Spiritual Conquest of Mexico: An Essay on the Apostolate and the Evangelizing Methods of the Mendicant Orders in New Spain: 1523–1572,* trans. Lesley Byrd Simpson. Berkeley: University of California Press, 1966.

Rivera, Brigadier Pedro de. *Diario y derrotero de lo caminado, visto y observado en la visita que hizo a los presidios de la Nueva España septentrional,* introducción y notas por Vito Alessio Robles (*Archivo histórico mexicano,* II). México, D.F.: Secretaría de la Defensa Nacional, 1946.

Roca, Paul M. *Paths of the Padres through Sonora: An Illustrated History and Guide to Its Spanish Churches.* Tucson: Arizona Pioneers' Historical Society, 1967.

Rowland, Donald, ed. and trans. "A Project for Exploration Presented by Juan Bautista de Anza," *Arizona Historical Review,* VII (April 1936), 10–18.

✓ ———, ed. and trans. "The Sonora Frontier of New Spain, 1735–1745," in *New Spain and the Anglo-American West.* 2 vols. Los Angeles: Privately printed, 1932.

Rudo Ensayo; see Nentuig.

Ruiz, Juanita. "Farewell, Batuc — A Lost Historic Site," *Journal of Arizona History,* VI (Autumn 1965), 152–54.

Segesser, Philipp, s.j.; *see* Treutlein.

Shiels, W. Eugene, s.j. "The Critical Period in Mission History," *Mid-America,* XXI (April 1939), 97–109.

———. *Gonzalo de Tapia (1561–1594), Founder of the First Permanent Jesuit Mission in North America.* New York: United States Catholic Historical Society, 1934.

Smith, Fay Jackson, John L. Kessell, and Francis J. Fox, s.j. *Father Kino in Arizona.* Phoenix: Arizona Historical Foundation, 1966.

✓ Spicer, Edward H. *Cycles of Conquest: The Impact of Spain, Mexico, and the United States on the Indians of the Southwest, 1533–1960.* Tucson: University of Arizona Press, 1962.

Stoner, Father Victor R. "Original Sites of the Spanish Missions of the Santa Cruz Valley," *The Kiva,* II (April–May 1937), 25–32.

———. "The Spanish Missions of the Santa Cruz Valley," *The Kiva,* I (May 1936), 1–4.

———. "The Spanish Missions of the Santa Cruz Valley." Unpublished master's thesis, University of Arizona, Tucson, 1937.

Tamarón y Romeral, Pedro. *Demostración del vastísimo obispado de la Nueva Vizcaya, 1765,* introducción bibliográfica y acotaciones por Vito Alessio Robles (*Biblioteca histórica mexicana de obras inéditas,* VII). México, D.F.: Antigua Librería Robredo, 1937.

Treutlein, Theodore E. "The Economic Regime of the Jesuit Missions in Eighteenth-Century Sonora," *Pacific Historical Review,* VIII (September 1939), 289–300.

———. "Father Gottfried Bernhardt Middendorff, s.j., Pioneer of Tucson," *New Mexico Historical Review,* XXXII (October 1957), 310–18.

———. "The Jesuit Missionary in the Role of Physician," *Mid-America,* XXII (April 1940), 120–41.

————. "Jesuit Travel to America (1678–1756) as Recorded in the Travel Diaries of German Jesuits." Unpublished Ph.D. dissertation, University of California, Berkeley, 1934.

————. "Jesuit Travel to New Spain (1678–1756)," *Mid-America*, XIX (April 1937), 104–23.

————, ed. and trans. *Missionary in Sonora: The Travel Reports of Joseph Och, S.J., 1755–1767*. San Francisco: California Historical Society, 1965.

————, ed. and trans. "The Relation of Philipp Segesser: The Pimas and Other Indians [1737]," *Mid-America*, XXVII (July 1945), 139–87 (October 1945), 257–60.

UNDERHILL, RUTH M. *The Autobiography of a Papago Woman*. American Anthropological Association, Memoir No. 46 (1936).

————. "A Papago Calendar Record," *University of New Mexico Bulletin*, Whole No. 322 (March 1938).

————. *The Papago Indians of Arizona and Their Relatives the Pima*. (A publication of the United States Department of Interior, Bureau of Indian Affairs.) Lawrence, Kansas: Haskell Institute, 1941.

————. *Social Organization of the Papago Indians*. (Columbia University Contributions to Anthropology, XXX). New York: Columbia University Press, 1939.

VELARDE, LUIS XAVIER, S.J.; *see* Wyllys.

VENEGAS, MIGUEL, S.J. *Noticia de la California, y de su conquista temporal y espiritual*, ed. Andrés Marcos Burriel, S.J. 3 vols. Madrid, 1757; México, D.F.: L. Alvarez y Alvarez de la Cadena, 1943–44.

WEDDLE, ROBERT S. *The San Sabá Mission, Spanish Pivot in Texas*. Austin: University of Texas Press, 1964.

WEHLE, HARRY B. *Art Treasures of the Prado*. New York: Harry N. Abrams, 1954.

WYLLYS, RUFUS K. *Pioneer Padre: The Life and Times of Eusebio Francisco Kino*. Dallas: Southwest Press, 1935.

————, ed. and trans. "Padre Luís Velarde's *Relación* of Pimería Alta, 1716," *New Mexico Historical Review*, VI (April 1931), 111–57.

ZELIS, RAFAEL DE, S.J. *Catálogo de los sugetos de la Compañía de Jesús que formaban la Provincia de México el día del arresto, 25 de junio de 1767*. México, 1871.

Index

his conditions for peace, 109, 122
pleads for reestablishment of mission at
  Guevavi, 128
returned to San Ignacio for questioning, 173
death in jail, 142
Och, José, s.j., assists Stiger at San Ignacio, 148
Oliva, Juan María de
  punishes Gila Pimas in battle at San Xavier
    (1756), 141
  serves at Tubac under Anza the younger, 174
Oposura, Kino at, 20; Garrucho at, 109,
  118–19, 164
Ortiz Parrilla, Diego, governor of Sonora, 103
  unfavorable criticism of Jesuits, 107, 109–11
  relations with Oacpicagigua, 103, 109–11,
    116–17, 121
  Garrucho's indictment of, 115–17; Keller's, 123
  establishes garrison at Tubac, 125
  leaves Sonora for Mexico and Texas, 124
  defends his policies, 124

Padilla, Francisco, 104
Pápago Indians, 13, 140–41, 170
  brought to missions as replacements for
    Pimas, 62, 140
Parrilla, *see* Ortiz Parrilla
Pauer, Francisco Xavier, s.j.,, 130, 171
  resident Padre at San Xavier del Bac,
    104, 106, 131
  at Guevavi, 114
  testimony concerning his activities during
    the Pima uprising, 113–14
  quoted, 121
  journey from Spain to the Pimería, 130–31
  begins delayed ministry at Guevavi and
    Bac, 129, 131
  attends San Ignacio conference (1754),
    132–35
  in Soamca during illness, 137
  professes at Arizpe (1755), 138
  builds churches at Tumacácori and Sonoita, 144
  named Father Rector of Pimería Alta and
    reassigned to San Ignacio, 148

assesses Guevavi for his successor Gerstner,
  151, 153
witnesses exchange of properties at San Xavier
  del Bac, 205
contracts to furnish beef to Anza at Tubac, 178
succumbs in Spanish prison after expulsion, 186
Paver, *see* Pauer
Peña, Ildefonso de la, s.j., to Guevavi (1744),
  82–84
Peña, Salvador Ignacio de la, s.j., 97, 114
Pfefferkorn, Ignacio, s.j.
  succeeds Gerstner at Guevavi, 158–64; signs
    inventory receipt for properties, 202
  removed from Guevavi by Garrucho
    (1763), 118
  reports to Lizassoain at San Ignacio, 159
  his published description of Sonora, 162
  reassigned to Cucurpe, 164
  freed in Germany after expulsion, 186
Pima Indians, 8, 12, 20, 23
  life style, 13–15
  Gila River Pimas, 13, 140–42
  slaughter of at Mototicachi, 23
  kill Saeta, 28
  slaughter of at El Tupo, 33
  ravaged by disease, 35, 37, 79, 91, 140, 172, 188
  ceremonial drunkenness, 54–55
  customs noted by Segesser, 55–56
  temporarily flee missions in the Pimería
    (1734), 57
  return to Guevavi after uprising, 110
  sack San Xavier del Bac, 140–41
  Pima rebels harass the Pimería, 142–43
  mission population declines, 157
Pima uprising 1751–1752, 102–10;
  investigation of, 111–18; causes, 117
Pimería Alta, 7, 10, 11
  physical characteristics, 11–13
  civil jurisdiction, 23
  Kino tours, 24–25, 32
  Salvatierra tours, 24–25
  under Keller, 59
  Pima uprising throughout, 102–10; continued
    harassment, 142–43
  Apache depredations, 76, 165, 168, 173

The Northern Pimería Alta
1691-1767

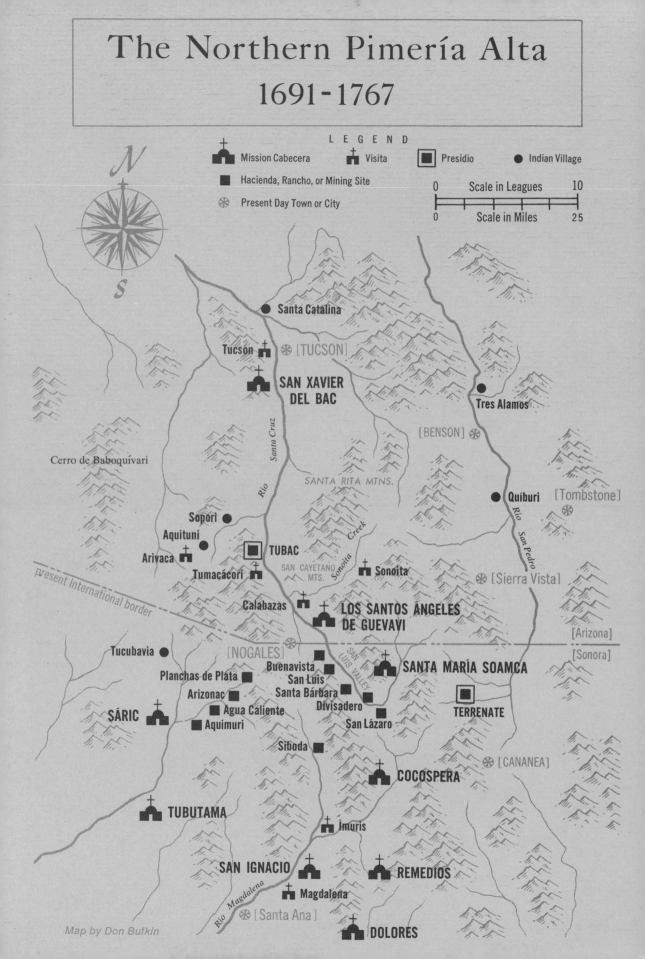

LEGEND

Mission Cabecera   Visita   Presidio   Indian Village

Hacienda, Rancho, or Mining Site

Present Day Town or City

0   Scale in Leagues   10

0   Scale in Miles   25

N
S

Santa Catalina

Tucsón   [TUCSON]

SAN XAVIER
DEL BAC

Tres Alamos

[BENSON]

Cerro de Baboquívari

Río Santa Cruz

SANTA RITA MTNS.

Quíburi   [Tombstone]

Río San Pedro

Sopori

Aquituni

Arivaca

Creek

Sonoita

Tumacácori

SAN CAYETANO
MTS.

TUBAC

Sonoita   [Sierra Vista]

present International border

Calabazas

LOS SANTOS ÁNGELES
DE GUEVAVI

[Arizona]

Tucubavia   [NOGALES]

[Sonora]

Buenavista

Planchas de Plata   San Luis

Santa Bárbara

SANTA MARÍA SOAMCA

SAN LUIS VALLEY

Arizonac

Agua Caliente   Divisadero

SÁRIC

Aquimuri

San Lázaro

TERRENATE

Siboda

[CANANEA]

COCOSPERA

TUBUTAMA

Imuris

SAN IGNACIO

REMEDIOS

Río Magdalena

Magdalena

[Santa Ana]

DOLORES

Map by Don Bufkin